AF581320

The Unseen Van Gogh

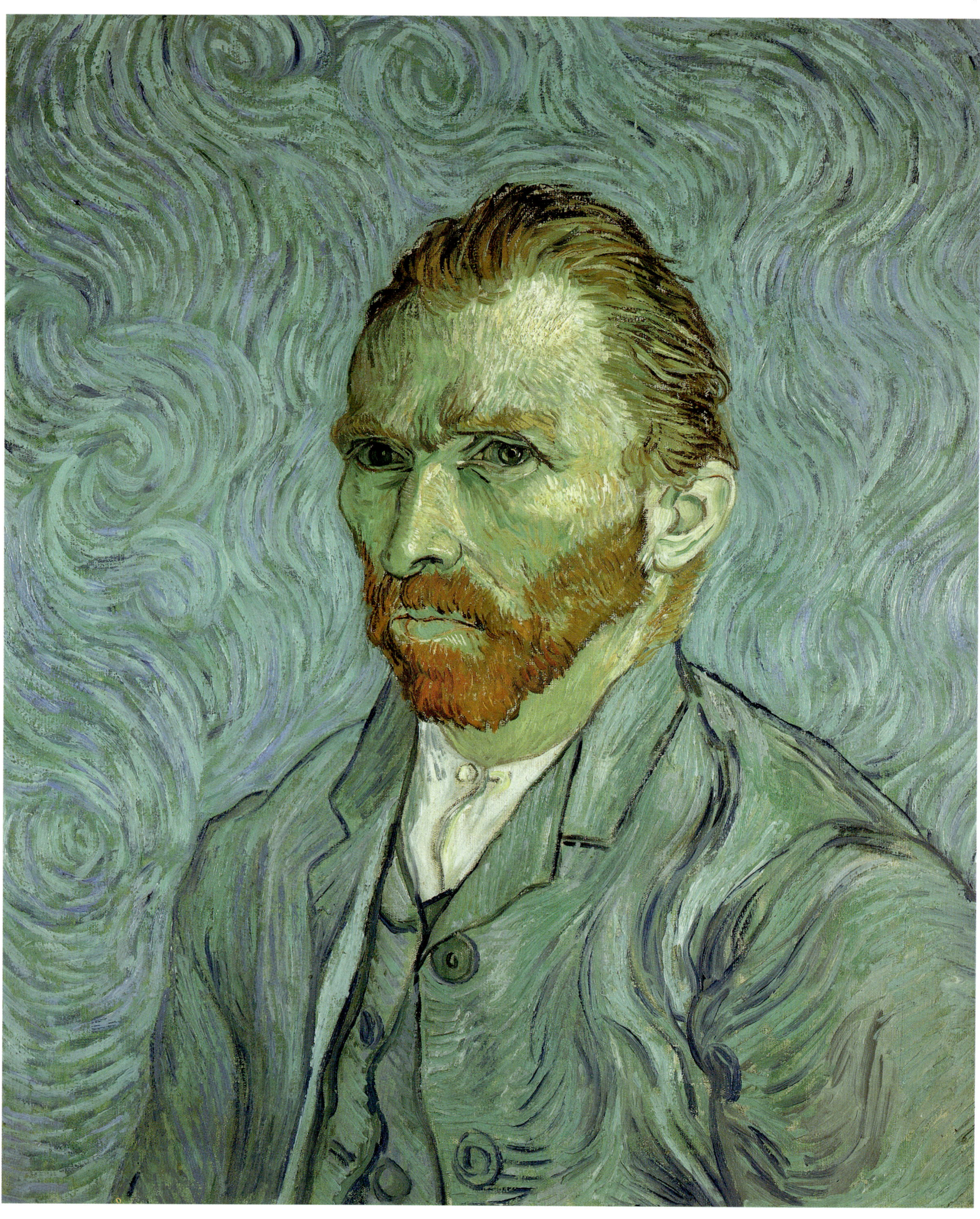

The Unseen Van Gogh

By Richard Mühlberger

Designed by Arnold Skolnick

FIRST GLANCE BOOKS, COBB, CALIFORNIA

Published in the United States of America
by First Glance Books

Distributed by First Glance Books
P.O. Box 960
Cobb, CA 95426
Phone: (707) 928-1994
Fax: (707) 928-1995

This edition was produced by
Chameleon Books, Inc.
31 Smith Road
Chesterfield, MA 01012

ISBN 1-885440-28-6

Printed in Hong Kong

President: Neil Panico
Vice President: Rodney Grisso
Designer, Picture Editor: Arnold Skolnick
Design Associate: KC Scott
Editorial Assistant: Laura J. MacKay
Copyeditor: Jamie Nan Thaman

(title page)

SELF-PORTRAIT, 1889
OIL ON CANVAS, 26 X 22 INCHES
MUSÉE D'ORSAY, PARIS/
ART RESOURCE, NEW YORK

Acknowledgments

Chameleon Books wishes to thank all the public institutions who supplied the wonderful images in this book. For their uncommon cooperation and courtesy, we especially thank Alison Jasonides and the rest of the staff at Art Resource; Mary Sluskonis, Museum of Fine Arts, Boston; Elizabeth Gombosi and Barbara Chabrowe, The National Gallery of Art; Liv Hensen, Cincinnati Art Museum; Mary Souzor and Emily Rosen, Cleveland Museum of Art; Jackie Burns, J. Paul Getty Museum; Ruth Roberts, Indianapolis Museum of Art; Avril Peck, Museum of Modern Art; Patricia Woods, Saint Louis Art Museum; Suzanne Warner, Yale University Art Gallery.

Special thanks to the Kröller-Müller and Van Gogh museums in the Netherlands—and to staffers Margaret Nab-van Wakeren and Josette van Gemert, respectively. As the principal custodians of Vincent Van Gogh's legacy, their collections account for a sizable portion of this book. Their cooperation was indispensable.

—Richard Mühlberger & Arnold Skolnick

CONTENTS

THE UNSEEN IS NOT INVISible—not in a work of art. An unseen element awaiting our discovery—a single color, the placement of a figure in a landscape, the shape of a cloud—may be the key to the composition of a painting. No, an artist wants every mark of his pencil or brush to be seen and appreciated. What we don't see, we have looked at too quickly.

The difference between looking and seeing is the difference between a glance or two at a painting in a museum or a reproduction in a book and what a connoisseur does when he encounters a work of art. He looks at it until he *perceives* it—until he experiences the "Ah-ha!" of realizing why the painting works, and how the artist achieved it. Now he has apprehended the painting; he has captured it in his mind's eye; he possesses it more truly than if he owned it. This book reveals the unseen; it is an invitation to look, then see, then savor.

The Unseen Van Gogh is about a great artist's quest for a "frank technique," a tool for expression that would be powerful in its simplicity. Vincent van Gogh began his career in art by describing things in words; by its end he had indeed found a forceful means of rendering his visions and expressing his feelings in paint. The tragedies in Vincent's life are well-known thanks to hundreds of biographies and psychological studies. They are ignored here in order to produce a book that does what the artist most wanted to do in life: to share his intense visual world with others through his paintings and drawings, so that they might *see.*

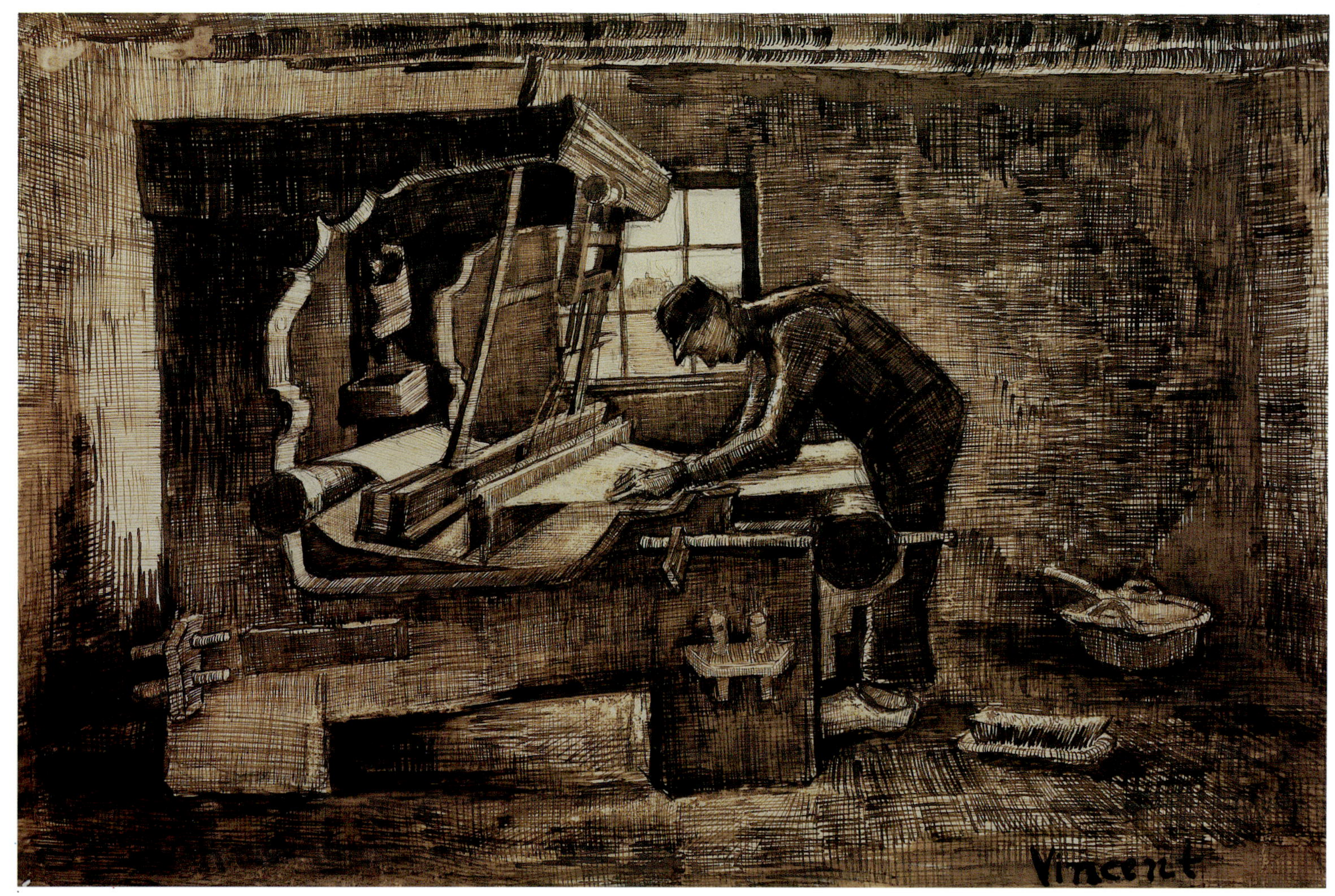

WEAVER, 1884
PEN, PENCIL, HEIGHTENED WITH WHITE ON THIN WOVE PAPER, 11 X 16 INCHES
KRÖLLER-MÜLLER MUSEUM, OTTERLO, THE NETHERLANDS

THE UNSEEN VAN GOGH
His Education in Art

Vincent van Gogh's exceptional gift for description provided the first inkling of a talent that would someday produce great art. Using words and ink, he described what he would later paint. His family was verbal: his father, an uncle, and a brother were preachers, and ancestors included three clergymen and a Bible teacher. Vincent himself was a lay preacher before he began to prepare for a life of art. Words came easily to him.

Vincent's vivid descriptions stay in the minds of many who read his famous letters. Close to eight hundred survive, about eighty of them to other artists and the rest to Theo, his younger brother by four years, and to other members of his family. The earliest—dated 1872, when Vincent was nineteen years of age—are little more than notes from The Hague, where he worked in his Uncle Vincent's gallery—part of a large Paris-based art publishing firm. The comfortable town did not inspire memorable descriptions, but when Vincent was transferred to the firm's London stockroom, he wanted to share what he saw. He wrote to Theo about his "quiet and intimate" neighborhood with its front gardens and "sort of gothic" houses and his new room, which he claimed he had "always longed for, without a slanting ceiling and without blue paper with a green border." His career as one of the most prolific and graphic correspondents of modern times had begun.

Over eighteen years of correspondence, Vincent's descriptions grew ever longer and more detailed. He often compared the places he saw to the paintings of contemporaries that he studied and loved. In the autumn of 1883, when he took a short trip to a village called Zweeloo in the northeast of Holland, he extolled the misty landscapes of Corot, a beloved painter who had died eight years earlier. Vincent declared that "all, all, all became exactly like the most beautiful Corots." He saw that the landscape around Zweeloo had "a quietness, a mystery, a peace," just as Corot had always painted it. He went on to describe "oak trees of a splendid bronze. In the moss are tones of gold green; in the green of the cornfields, tones of inexpressible purity; on the wet trunks, tones of black, contrasting with the golden rain of whirling, clustering autumn leaves—hanging in loose tufts, as if they had been blown there, and with the sky glimmering through them—from the poplars, the birches, the lime and apple trees."

Through such expressive passages, Vincent used his letters to share his intense visual experiences with others—for he never had traveling companions and day-to-day partners. These detailed descriptions also seem to be manifestations of the paintings he never painted. He wrote that when he died, he would look back with "love and tender regret, thinking: 'Oh, pictures I might have made!' " Once he committed a scene to canvas, he wasted few words recording how it looked. Most pictures went directly to Theo to try to sell. When he bartered a painting or sent one to another family member, Theo often received a drawing of it rather than a written description.

Long before Vincent began to study art, he had formulated a simple and direct philosophy to guide himself. Its tenets are scattered throughout several letters to Theo, written as Theo was beginning his career as an art dealer and needed advice. First, Vincent wrote, "Go to the museum as often as you can." Next, "Admire as much as you can; most people do not admire enough." Finally, "Try to take as many walks as you can and keep your love of nature, for that is the true way to learn to understand art more and more. Painters understand nature and love her and teach us to see her." Vincent's ideas were as humanistic as they were unacademic. Though he schooled himself with academic discipline, he never accepted the art school philosophy that placed higher value on copying plaster casts than on studying nature.

In 1883, Theo was struggling with the idea of becoming a painter himself. In a series of letters, Vincent laid out the tough road of discipline that his brother would have to follow to become an artist. He also advised, "If you ever decide to become a painter, do so with inner cheerfulness and all possible optimism," and counseled, "If you hear a voice within you saying, 'You are not a painter,' then by all means paint, boy, and that voice will be silenced, but only by working." Theo dropped the notion of a career change, but Vincent told his brother that he was an artist anyway, based on a description he had written in a recent letter. Theo's letters of this time are lost so we must trust Vincent's evaluation that the description was artistic.

Vincent's skill at description helped him to see more thoroughly, but he knew that the ability to draw and use color did not easily or naturally follow. The translation of verbal descriptions into painted ones was the difficult undertaking Vincent began in the summer of 1880 after attempts to be a schoolteacher and an evangelist left him in despair. "I will take up my pencil, which I have forsaken in my great discouragement, and I will go on with my drawing." He was homesick for "the land of pictures."

There was almost as much artistic talent in Vincent's family as there was verbal ability. An eighteenth-century sculptor was the first van Gogh to practice art. Three of Vincent's uncles were successful art dealers and their galleries introduced Vincent to the artists of the day and of the recent past. Anton Mauve, one of Holland's best painters, was the brother-in-law of Vincent's mother, and drawings of floral bouquets by Vincent's mother are proof of an artistic leaning in the household in which he grew up.

The earliest art known to be by Vincent van Gogh is a drawing of the heads of a dog, a cow, and three men—dated by some to the end of his eighth year but more likely done a few years later when he was a pupil in a private boarding school that offered drawing lessons. These and other childhood drawings seem to be copied from a model book—an aid to students of art in an age when copying was the primary exercise of learning. In fact, the practice of copying had been sanctioned by all of the art academies since the Renaissance. Soon Vincent had used pencil and watercolor to render an exact likeness of a milk jug, filling a sheet of paper with the bold image. His first outdoor subject, also from his school days, was a sawmill drawn with charcoal from life. From 1875, some of Vincent's letters are illustrated. He said that it was instinctive to add a drawing when he was writing. A copy of an etching by Corot was his timid start.

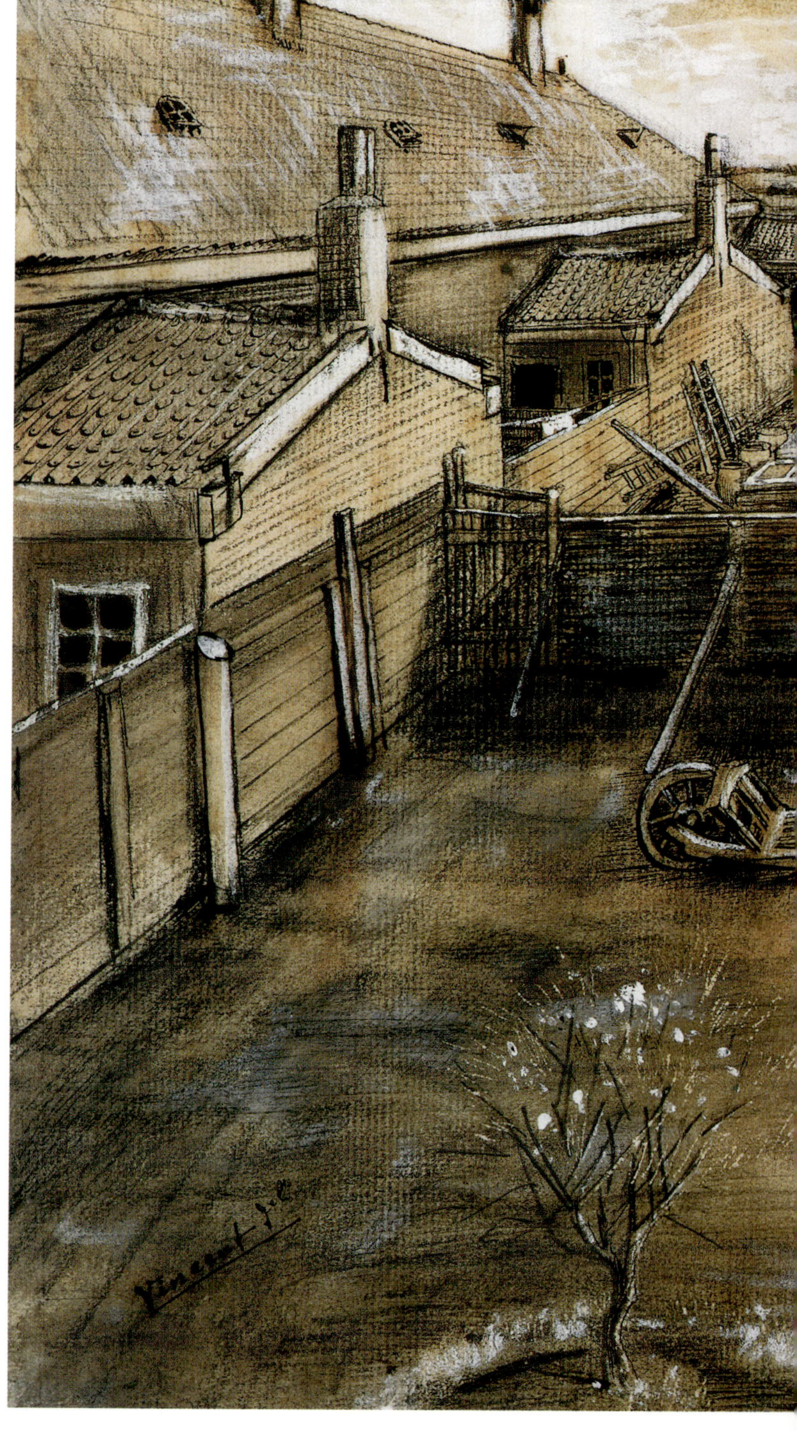

Vincent believed that drawing was "the backbone of painting, the skeleton that supports all the rest," so he drove himself pitilessly "to be master of my pencil or my crayons." One witness reported that "while eating, he made drawings in his lap....All his spare time was given to drawing." At the heart of his learning method was copying. Indeed, Vincent

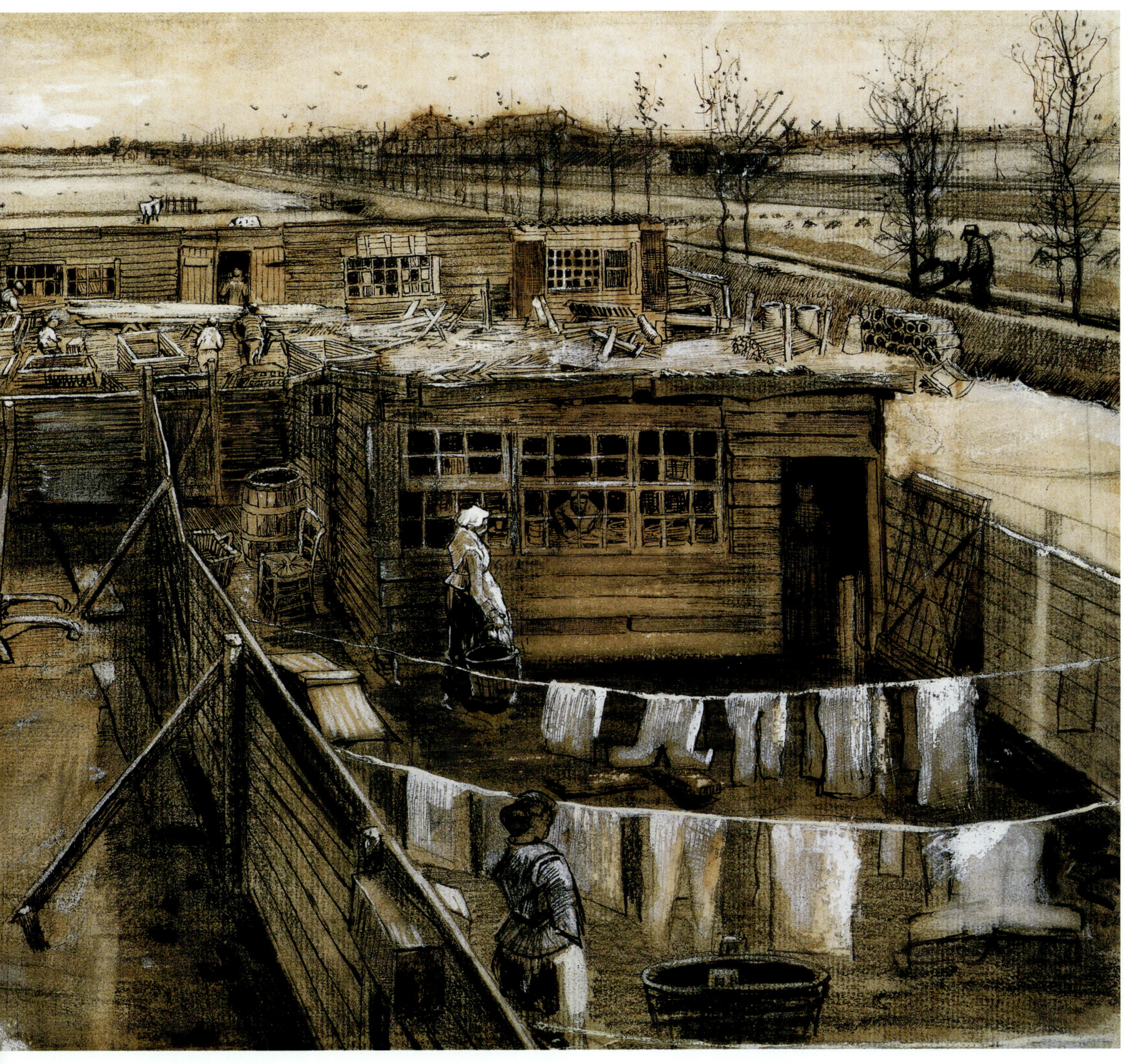

had probably learned other subjects like penmanship and arithmetic through imitation and repetition. It "makes my hand as well as my mind more supple and strong," he wrote. When not drawing, he read books on anatomy, proportions, and perspective, but confessed to Theo that the books were "terribly irritating."

Vincent frequently mentioned his habit of repetition to Theo, as in a letter from 1882: "Today I made a drawing of a baby's cradle with a few touches of color in it....I hope I shall be able to draw that little cradle persistently a hundred times more, not counting what I did today." Vincent frequently copied wood engravings of paintings by his hero, Jean François Millet, the celebrated painter of peasant scenes. He owned twenty-four such engravings. Even as a mature painter, Vincent continued the practice of copying, saying, "I know no other way." He frequently copied his own work as well as that of other artists like Millet, Rembrandt, and Delacroix.

Vincent also practiced another kind of drawing:

VIEW ON SCHENKWEG, 1882
PEN, PENCIL, BRUSH, HEIGHTENED WITH WHITE ON OLD DUTCH LAID PAPER, 11 X 19 INCHES
KRÖLLER-MÜLLER MUSEUM, OTTERLO, THE NETHERLANDS

"I...improvise...at random on a piece of paper, but I do not attach any more value to this than to a rag or a cabbage leaf." Still other drawings were done as souvenirs of the places and people he saw. One of these, full of detail and the promise of spring, is the view from his window in The Hague, when he was informally studying with Anton Mauve. Pen and ink "brought a new kind of black" to the scene, he wrote, and a brushed-on wash captured the shine of the sun and gave it a Dutch look. He imagined that the men beyond the fence in the carpenter's yard were "lighting the fires to make coffee in the little cottages." Most difficult for him was calculating the vast perspective: "Behind it all, a wide stretch of soft, tender green, miles and miles of flat meadow; and over it a gray sky, as calm, as peaceful, as Corot or Van Goyen." He used a perspective frame to help him plot the orthogonal projections. Another drawing of the scene in winter followed when he decided that the spring version was not "strong and animated enough."

Though he was a hard critic of his own work, Vincent recognized the progress he made. The drawings "are not good, but they are beginning to look like something," he wrote. "I no longer stand helpless before nature as I used to." From the start of his commitment to art, Vincent wanted to go beyond surface appearances, to observe "very accurately the physical exteriors of people in order to get at their real mental make-up." His frustration with attempting to achieve this is evident in his description of drawing as "working through an invisible iron wall that seems to stand between what one feels and what one can do." With evangelical zeal, he pledged to make something good, "drawings which touch some people...something straight from my own heart...serious sorrow." As he wrote to Theo, "It isn't there yet, but I aim at it, and struggle for it. I want something serious—something fresh—something with soul in it! Forward—forward!"

In 1882—the year that Vincent made the drawing of the carpenter's workshop from his window—he began to paint in earnest. He wrote to Theo that it brought him joy. "While painting, I feel a power of color in me that I did not possess before." With a newly acquired knowledge of modern color theories, he delighted in expressing his feelings with the

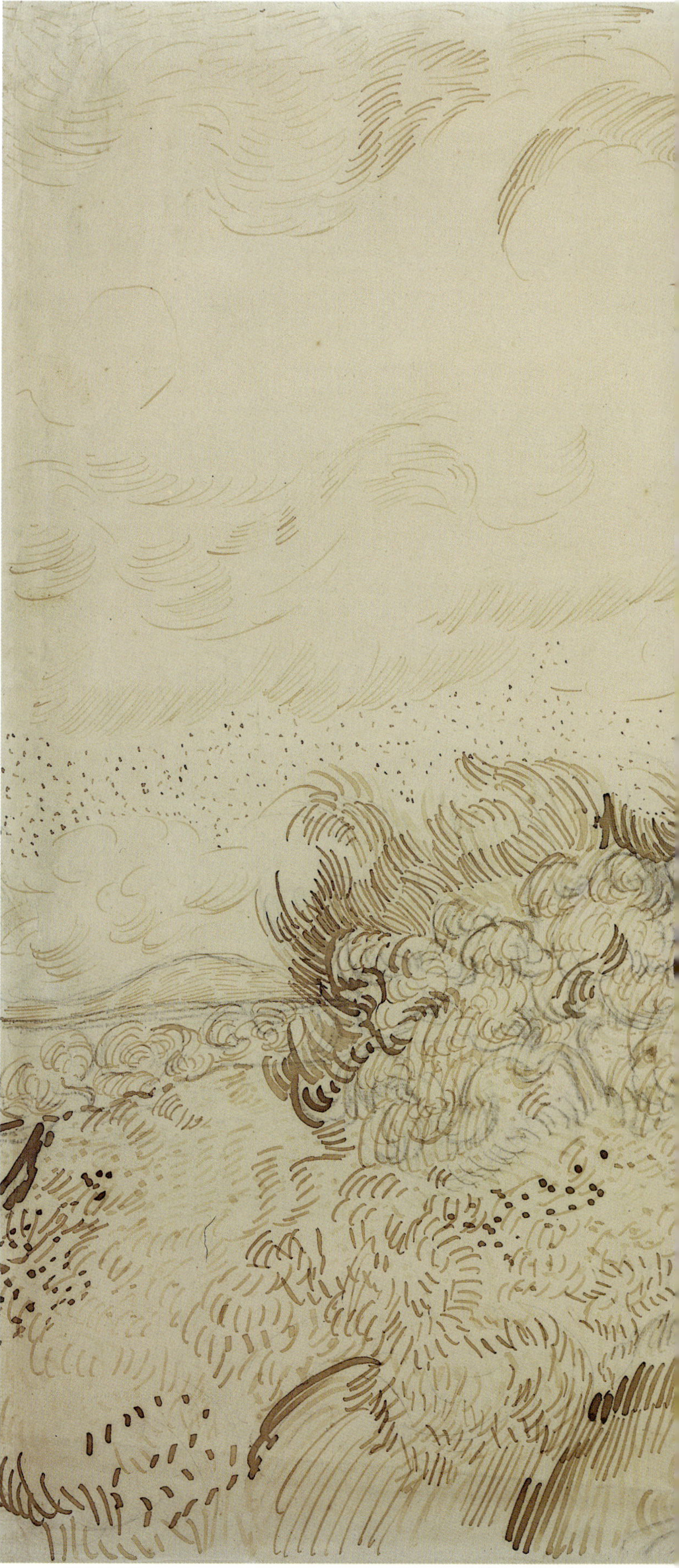

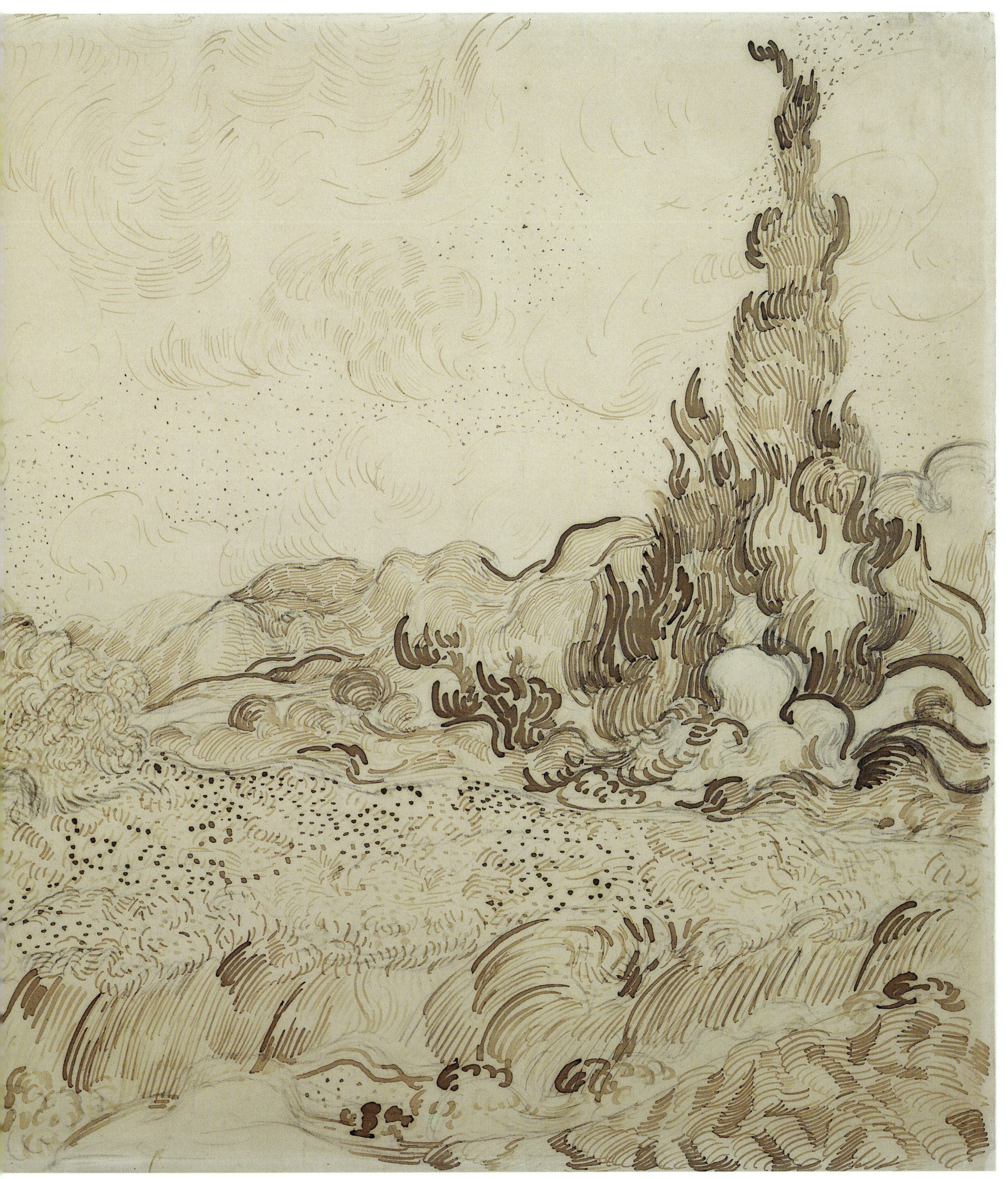

WHEAT FIELD AND CYPRESSES, Saint-Rémy, 1889
Black crayon, pen, reed pen and brown ink on yellowed paper, 19 x 25 inches
Van Gogh Museum (Vincent van Gogh Foundation), Amsterdam, the Netherlands

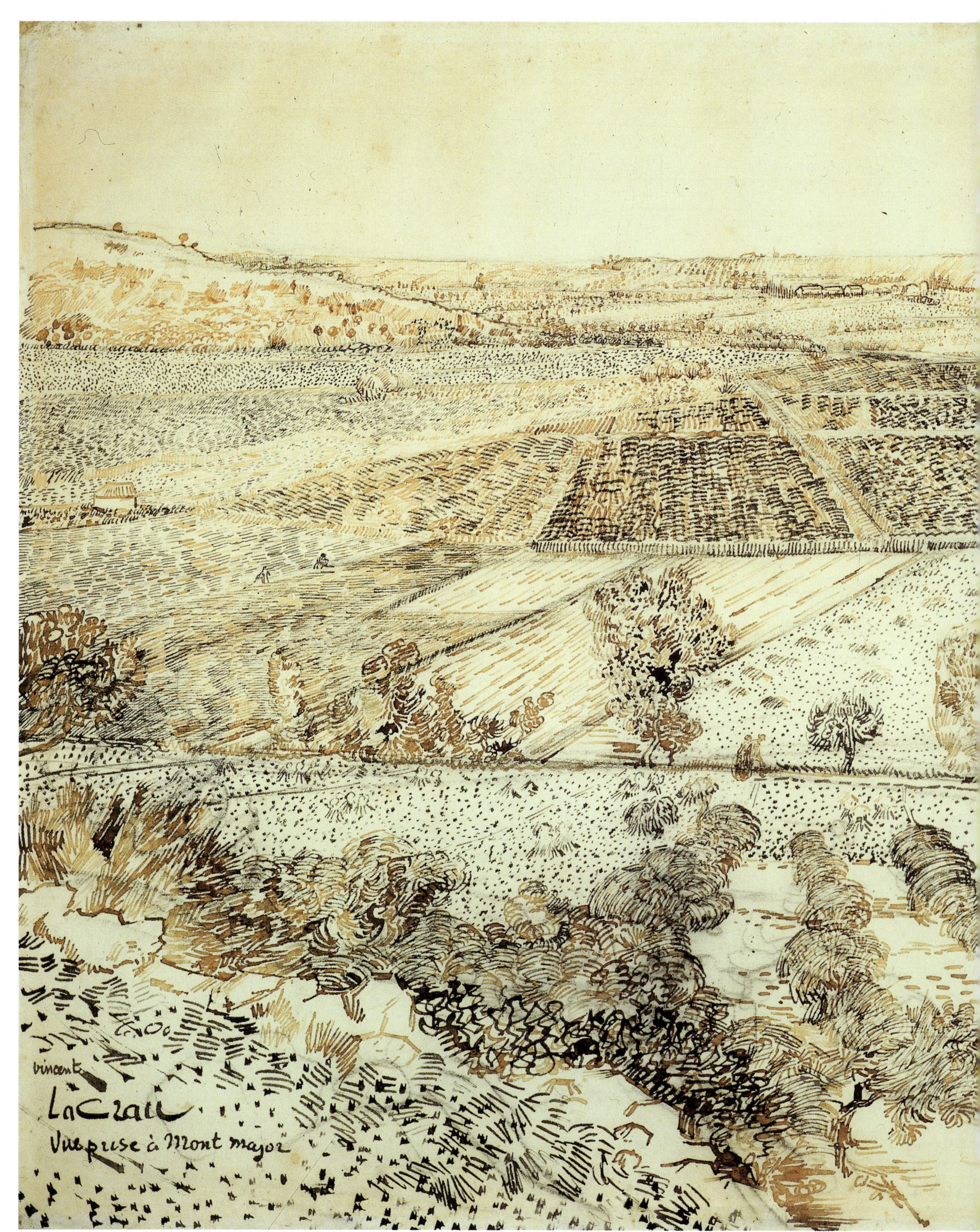

LA CRAU SEEN FROM MONTMAJOUR, Arles, 1888
Black chalk, pen, reed pen, brown and black ink on watercolor paper, 19 x 24 inches
Van Gogh Museum (Vincent van Gogh Foundation), Amsterdam, the Netherlands

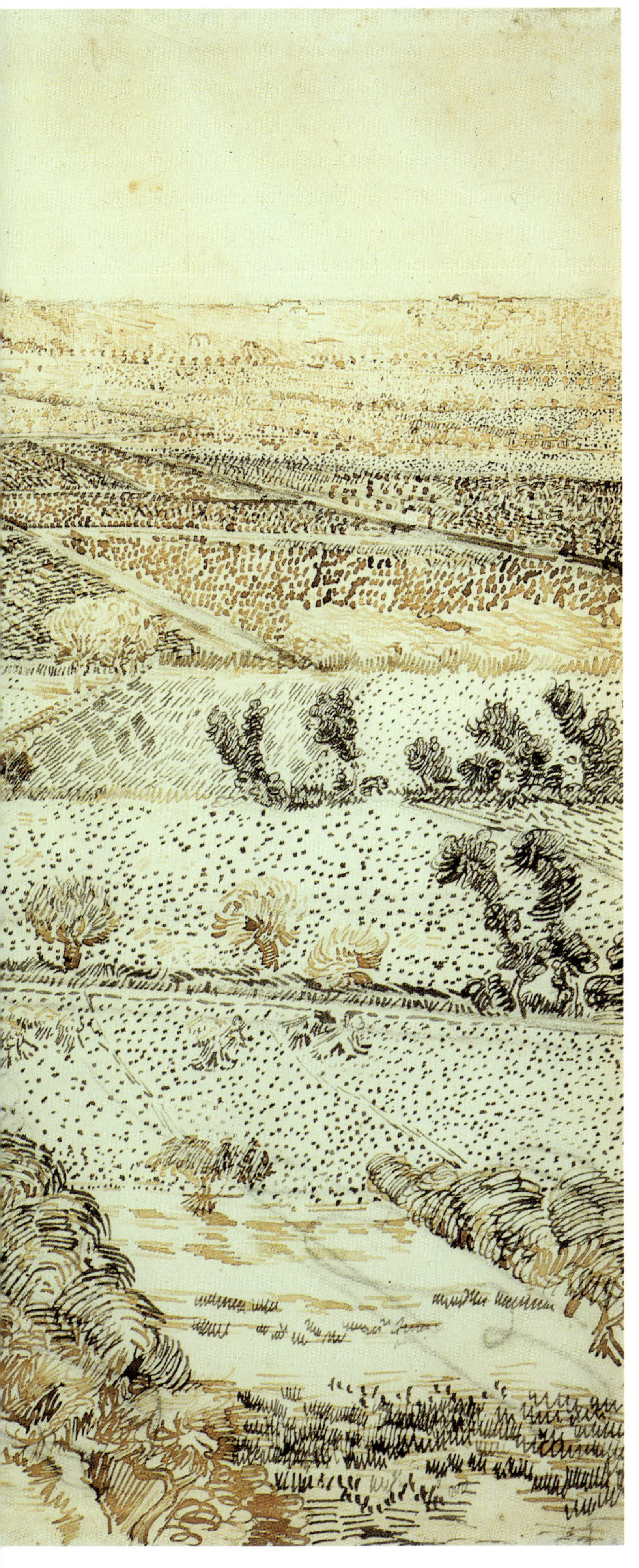

"hidden harmonies or contrasts" of color. Painting came easier to him than he expected. "In a word," he told Theo, "it is more gratifying than drawing." But Vincent did not maintain this state of euphoria. Within a year, he was self-critical, reflecting a pattern of emotional ups and downs that plagued him throughout his life. "It is a fact that now all my work is too meager and too dry," he concluded at the end of July 1883, but by September, he was inspired enough to write: "The country is so beautiful that I cannot describe it. As soon as I can paint a little better—then!"

In 1883, Vincent had daily access to a model and was greatly preoccupied with drawing her. He wanted "to progress so far in the knowledge of the nude and the structure of the figure that [he] might be able to work from memory." He believed that if he studied the figure assiduously enough—that is, if he could memorize it—he could "seize the essential" and "simplify it." He wanted to intentionally neglect "those details which do not belong to the real character, and are only accidental."

There was always a subject in front of Vincent that he wanted to paint. He seldom had to wait for inspiration: "Just dash something down when you see a blank canvas staring you in the face with a certain imbecility." Although he did not know about the French Impressionists until later, he had learned an approach to painting similar to theirs: "It is wrong to go brushing away on the same spot," he told Anton Kerssemakers, a tanner who learned art from Vincent and in 1912 published an account of his experiences with the artist. "You must set it all down at once and then leave it alone; don't be afraid and don't try to make it pretty." He also instructed Kerssemakers, "Take care you never forget to half-shut your eyes when you are painting in the open air."

Vincent often prepared for a painting by making drawings of the subject first—a memorization as well as a planning process. He then painted the scene on the spot. It was important to him that the result was "[n]ot always literally exact, or rather never exact, for one sees nature through one's own temperament." While painting was still new to him, he limited himself to the use of earth colors

Avez vous aussi vu les oliviers? Maintenant j'ai un portrait du Dr Gachet à expression navrée de notre temps. Si vous voulez quelque chose comme vous disiez de votre Christ au jardin des oliviers pas destiné à être compris mais enfin là jusque là je vous suis et mon frère saisit bien cette nuance.

J'ai encore de là bas un cyprès avec une étoile un dernier essai – un ciel de nuit avec une lune sans éclat à peine le croissant mince émergeant de l'ombre projetée opaque de la terre – une étoile à éclat exagéré, si vous voulez, éclat doux de rose & vert dans le ciel outremer où courent des nuages. En bas une route bordée de hautes cannes jaunes derrière lesquelles des basses alpines bleues, une vieille auberge à fenêtres illuminées orangé et un très haut cyprès tout droit tout sombre. Sur la route une voiture jaune attelée d'un cheval blanc et deux promeneurs attardés. Très romantique si vous voulez mais aussi je crois de la Provence. Probablement je graverai à l'eau forte celle là et d'autres paysages et motifs souvenirs de Provence alors je me ferai une fête de vous en donner un tout un résumé un peu voulu et étudié. Mon frère dit que Lauzet qui fait les lithographies d'après Monticelli a trouvé bien la tête d'arlésienne en question

LETTER OF VINCENT VAN GOGH TO PAUL GAUGUIN (LETTER 893 [643]:2)
Van Gogh Museum (Vincent van Gogh Foundation), Amsterdam, the Netherlands

similar to the ones that gave Dutch art of the early seventeenth century its distinctive appearance. He claimed that he greatly preferred "a picture in a lower key than nature to one which is exactly like nature." The masterpiece of this period is *The Potato Eaters,* a painting that some believe shows a divine light in the faces of the peasants. In spite of this achievement, Vincent needed to step outside of his heritage. He enrolled in the art academy at Antwerp, evidently thinking he would learn color, but he seemed to follow his own curriculum. During his two months there, he impressed a fellow student with "the rapidity with which he worked, as he did the same drawing...over again ten or fifteen times." Then he moved to Paris and lived with his brother Theo for two years.

Vincent's conversations with Theo and the artists he met were not recorded and there are only four extant letters from him during his Paris years, three written to Theo when he was in Holland for his annual visits to family members, and one to the English painter Horace Levens. This would be considered scant documentation of the most critical years in Vincent's artistic development if numerous paintings did not also exist. Vincent told Levens that he was working on landscapes and a series of color studies, all "simply flowers...seeking oppositions of blue and orange, red and green, yellow and violet." He wanted to "harmonize brutal extremes ...to render intense colour and not a gray harmony." He referred to his color exercises as gymnastics and told Levens, "I have faith in colour."

Several months were spent in Cormon's Studio, a private art school in Paris run by Fernand-Anne Piestre, or "Cormon." Vincent may have been impressed by Cormon's grandiose biblical scenes, but he did not find the school's academic exercises to be very helpful. Henri de Toulouse-Lautrec was a classmate of Vincent's at Cormon's and he joined Vincent and others in late-night discussions about art. Vincent also met Paul Signac, who taught him the principles of pointillism; Émil Bernard, who became one of his closest artist friends; and Paul Gauguin, who was to paint at Vincent's side for a period. "What I find so splendid in the moderns," Vincent declared, "is that they do not moralize like the old guard." As he saw more and more modern art, he kept an open mind, tried things out, and adopted whatever was compatible with his quickly developing artistic temperament.

The most lasting artistic impression from Vincent's Paris years was made by Japanese prints. Enthusiasm for Japanese culture had grown since Japan presented displays of its arts and crafts at the 1867 Paris World Fair. Vincent had been buying inexpensive Japanese wood block prints since 1885 and while in Paris, purchased hundreds more to form a collection for himself and Theo. He exhibited them in 1887 in a Paris café he frequented. They inspired him to return to his earlier study method of copying, but now his subjects were wood block prints by Hiroshige and Kesai Eisen. From them, he learned how to use unmixed and unbroken color without shadow, and he mastered the bold diagonals and shifts in perspective that had made Japanese prints such an important influence on the Impressionists and other moderns. He also read everything he could lay his hands on about Japan and concluded that it was an ideal place. "If we study Japanese art," he later wrote, "you see a man who is undoubtedly wise, philosophic and intelligent who spends his time how? In studying the distance between the earth and the moon? No. In studying the policy of Bismarck? No. He studies a single blade of grass." Vincent resolved to find a new Japan.

In 1888, Vincent relocated to the ancient town of Arles, just forty-five miles north of the Mediterranean Sea, and his first impressions of the place were so positive that he declared he had found his new Japan. His education in art was behind him; he had found the "frank technique," based on simplicity, which he revered. Now, everything would be "expressive force." He had no ambitions but to be more spontaneous and more exaggerated in his art. As he completed one glorious canvas after another during his first summer in the south, he warned Theo, "Everyone will think I work too fast...sometimes the strokes come with a sequence and a coherence like words in a speech or a letter...I am in the midst of a complicated calculation which results in quick succession in canvases quickly executed, but calculated long beforehand. So now, when anyone says that such and such is done too quickly, you can reply that they have looked at it too quickly."

The distance that Vincent had come as an artist was stunning. In May 1884, after drawing seriously for four years, he began a series of detailed studies of weavers—"a race apart from other laborers and artisans"—for whom he felt great sympathy. He modestly wrote, "I should be very happy if someday I could draw them, so that those unknown...types would be brought before the eyes of the people.... With his dreamy air, somewhat absent-minded, almost a somnambulist—that is the weaver. I have been living among them for two years, and have learned a little of their unique character...and increasingly I find something touching and almost sad in these poor, obscure laborers." Vincent's pen and pencil drawing *Weaver Standing in Front of a Loom* allows light to touch the weaver's work, the edge of his loom, and the wall behind it. Light is kept from the rest of the drawing by densely packed crosshatch lines. Five years later, in June 1889, with black chalk and pen, Vincent drew *Wheat Field with Cypresses.* His lines are free and open, with light penetrating even the heart of the spiraling cypress. Heaven seems to be touching earth and earth responds with a jig.

Vincent's period of greatness began with his arrival in Arles in February 1888 and ended with his suicide in the summer of 1890. He called himself a "steam engine" at painting. Sadly, Vincent's best two years as an artist were his frailest as a human being. He was hospitalized twice, was jailed once as a public nuisance, and committed himself to a mental asylum for a year. Nightmares, hallucinations, delusions, and fainting spells almost broke him mentally and physically, but he kept on painting. He described himself as solitary, with no time to think or to feel. He was wrong about the latter. As he sought to express "hope by some star, the eagerness of a soul by a sunset radiance," his paintings would become among the most feeling and deeply felt in art.

Vincent had partners during his career and after his death, but first and foremost, there was his brother Theo. On the day of Vincent's death, Theo found a last letter to him in Vincent's pocket. The artist told his brother, "I shall always consider you to be something more than a simple dealer in Corots...you have your part in the actual production of some canvases, which will retain their calm even in a catastrophe."

Theo's death followed Vincent's by six months, and the partnership with Vincent was quickly picked up by Theo's widow, Johanna. She traced Vincent's career and collected as many of his paintings as she could find, buying back ones he had bartered away. Others had already been destroyed by unappreciative recipients of Vincent's generosity. She also compiled his letters and published them with her biography of the artist.

Johanna raised her son, Vincent Willem, to revere the work of his uncle. He lovingly carried on the family partnership with his now famous relative by acting as caretaker of his paintings and drawings. He established the Vincent van Gogh Foundation to locate and acquire even more of Vincent's art and letters, as well as documents related to him, his family, and his friends. His final homage to his uncle was the planning of the museum in Amsterdam that bears Vincent's name.

> *And the moral of this is that it's my constant hope that I am not working for myself alone. I believe in the absolute necessity of a new art of color, of design, and of the artistic life.... There is an art of the future, and it is going to be so lovely and so young that even if we give up our youth for it, we must gain in serenity by it.*
>
> —Vincent van Gogh, 1888

A SUMMARY OF EVENTS IN THE LIFE OF VINCENT VAN GOGH

1853 Vincent Willem van Gogh was born March 30 in Groot-Zundert, North Brabant, the Netherlands, the first of six children of Theodorus van Gogh, a Dutch Reformed clergyman, and Anna Cornelia (née Carbentus).

1861–68 He was educated at the local public school, followed by two and a half years at a private boarding school where he made his first drawings, and two more years at a state-run boarding school.

1869–76 His Uncle Vincent, a partner in Goupil & Cie, Paris art dealers, got him a job with the firm—first in The Hague, then in London and Paris. After six and a half years, he resigned and taught school in London.

1877–79 He briefly sold books in Dordrecht and prepared for theological studies, though he took a course at an evangelical college instead. He failed the course, but began ministering to coal miners in Belgium. He drew and painted during this period.

1880 He decided to become a painter. His brother Theo began to support him. Vincent studied anatomy and perspective drawing at the Brussels Academy.

1881–82 He studied for a month with a relative, the painter Anton Mauve, in The Hague. He would not draw from plaster casts, a standard academic exercise, and left Mauve. He began to paint with oils.

1883–85 Peasant scenes and rural landscapes occupied him, culminating in *The Potato Eaters.* A paint store in The Hague exhibited some of his paintings in its windows, the first time his work was shown to the public.

1886 He took painting and drawing classes at the *Académie Royale des Beaux-Arts* in Antwerp but soon moved to Paris and lived with Theo. He studied at Cormon's Studio and met many artists. Vincent, Émile Bernard, Paul Gauguin, and Toulouse-Lautrec exhibited together at the Café du Tambourin. Vincent also showed with Georges Seurat and Paul Signac, the well-known pointillists.

1888 Vincent moved to Arles and hoped to establish an artists' colony in his "yellow house" there. Paul Gauguin visited him for two months, a period of feverish activity that ended in a breakdown. Three of Vincent's paintings were exhibited in Paris at the Salon des Artistes Indépendants.

1889 Vincent committed himself to the Saint-Paul-de-Mausole mental asylum at Saint-Rémy-de-Provence, near Arles. One of his two rooms, paid for by Theo, served as a studio. Once more, he exhibited works at the Salon des Artistes Indépendants in Paris. A Dutch art writer irritated him with inflated praise, calling him heroic and "a lone pioneer." Père Tanguy, owner of a Paris art supply shop and a friend, put on a show of several of Vincent's paintings in his store.

1890 Six of Vincent's works were exhibited in Brussels at an exhibition of the artists' group Les XX and Anna Boch, the sister of the artist Eugène Boch, bought *The Red Vineyard*, probably the only painting Vincent ever sold. Ten more works were shown at the Salon des Artistes Indépendants in Paris. Monet called the paintings "[t]he best in the exhibition." An article on Vincent's work appeared in a French publication—the first recognition of him outside the Netherlands. In May, Vincent left the asylum and went to Paris to visit Theo, his wife, and their new child, who was named after him. Soon he settled in Auvers-sur-Oise, about one hour away by train. He shot himself on July 23 and died on July 29.

1891 Theo died on January 25. In 1914, his body was moved to Auvers-sur-Oise and placed next to Vincent's. Theo's widow, Johanna Gesini (née Bonger), and later her son, became the custodians and promoters of Vincent's art, establishing the Vincent van Gogh Foundation in 1962 and the Rijksmuseum Vincent van Gogh in Amsterdam in 1973.

VINCENT VAN GOGH FIRST BEGAN TO paint in earnest after he settled at The Hague in December 1881. The city was the center of Dutch art and a relative, Anton Mauve, was the leader of a group of landscape painters who were reconciling the great Dutch traditions of the seventeenth century with outdoor painting—a new approach first practiced in France by the Barbizon painters. Vincent was drawn to the coast and the dunes, as they were, but he insisted that he "was definitely not a landscape painter; if I paint landscapes, there will always be something figural in them." He defined art as "man added to nature."

Begun as a "scribble of the woods," this pensive scene has a tender quality because of Vincent's placement of the quiet girl in white amid monumental beech trees that appear to be more animated than she is. Indeed, the hulking trees might be the source of her hesitation as she finds her way through the forest. The girl's costume brings her timid actions into view—she steadies herself by touching a tree trunk. Her other hand, clamped against her white skirt, emphasizes her step forward. Soon she will see the forest around her—which the artist has already explored.

GIRL IN WHITE IN THE WOODS
THE HAGUE, AUGUST 1882
OIL ON CANVAS, 15 1/4 X 23 1/4 INCHES
KRÖLLER-MÜLLER MUSEUM, OTTERLO, THE NETHERLANDS

➢

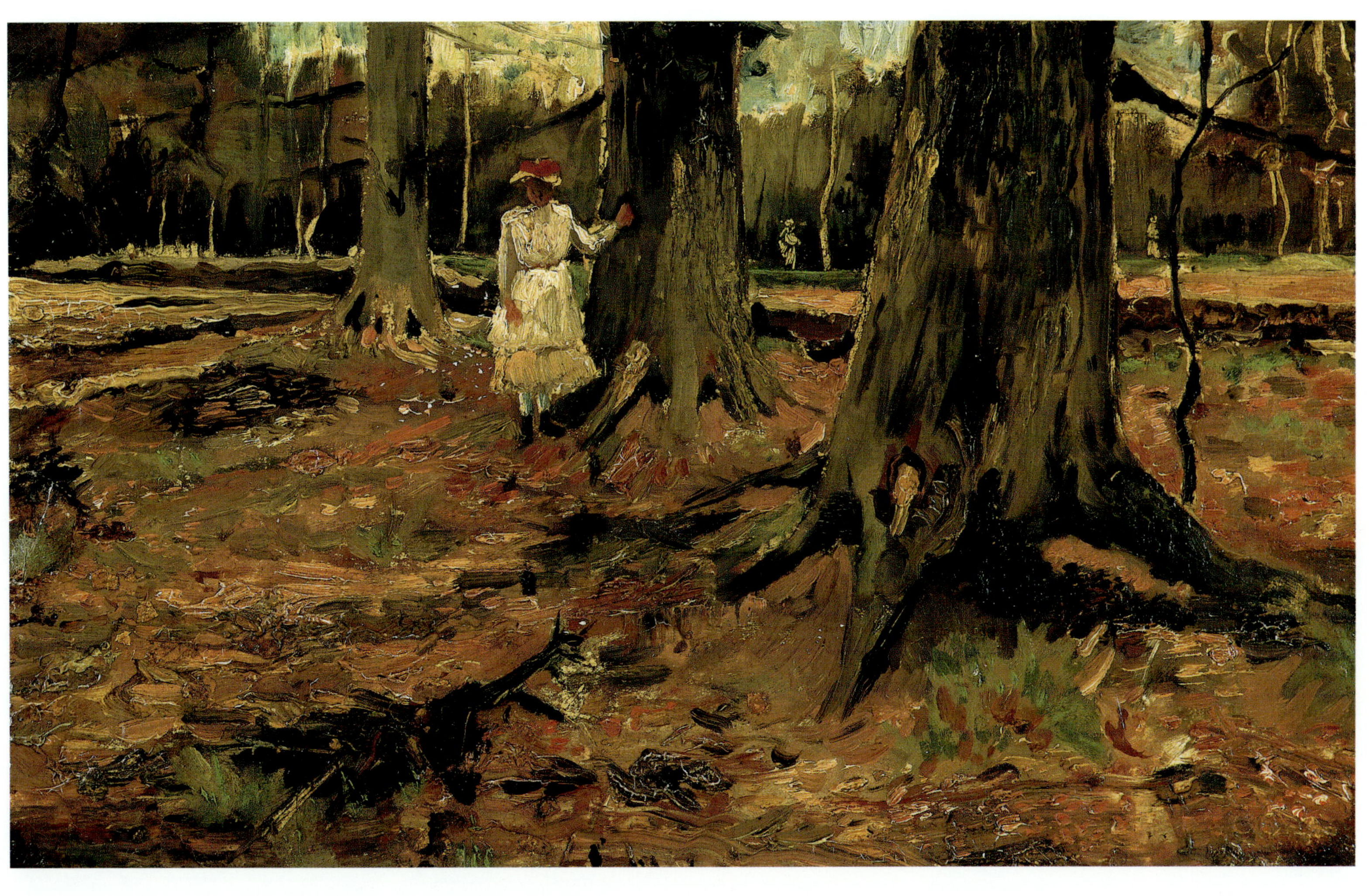

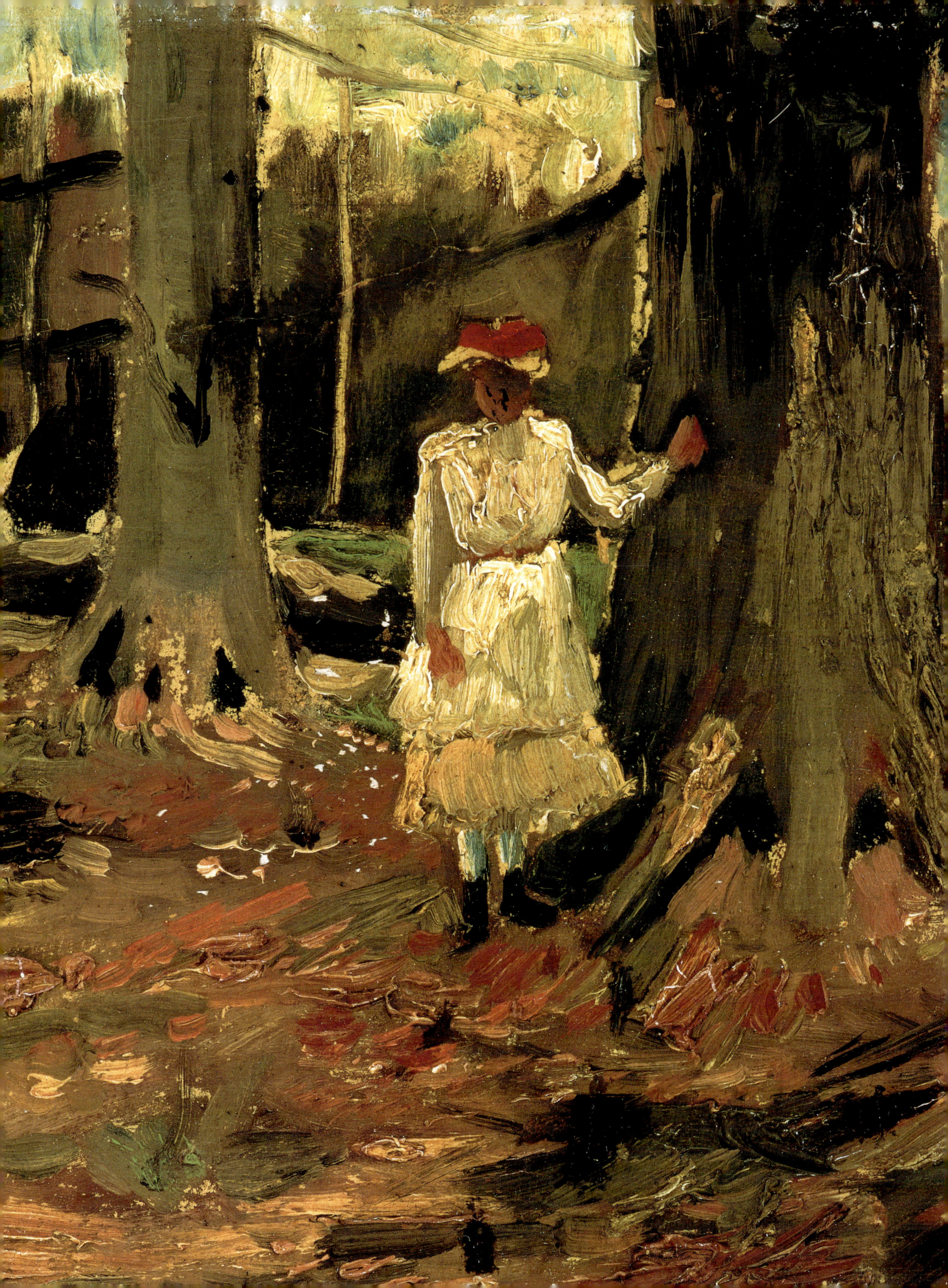

VINCENT SPENT TWO YEARS LIVING with his brother in the Montmartre district of Paris. He built a circle of artist friends from whom he learned what was new. He socialized—often through the night—but mainly he worked, completing about two hundred thirty paintings—more than in any other period of his life. He painted both out of doors and in his studio, which he rented from Toulouse-Lautrec, who received this painting as a gift from Vincent.

Wanting to master color, Vincent became intoxicated by the dot techniques of Seurat, Signac, and Pissarro. They analyzed colors, broke them into their components, and let the viewer's eye mix the divided pigments. Vincent tried out this "stippling," as he called it, as he looked out his studio window. The results are heightened colors in the foreground buildings and a faded lavender background. He combined three vantage points into what appears to be a single glance: he looked down at the building with the red window shutters, up and to the right to view the tall structure next door, and straight out for the rest.

VIEW OF PARIS FROM VINCENT'S ROOM IN THE RUE LEPIC
PARIS, SPRING 1887
OIL ON CANVAS, 18 X 15 INCHES
VAN GOGH MUSEUM (VINCENT VAN GOGH FOUNDATION)
AMSTERDAM, THE NETHERLANDS

➢

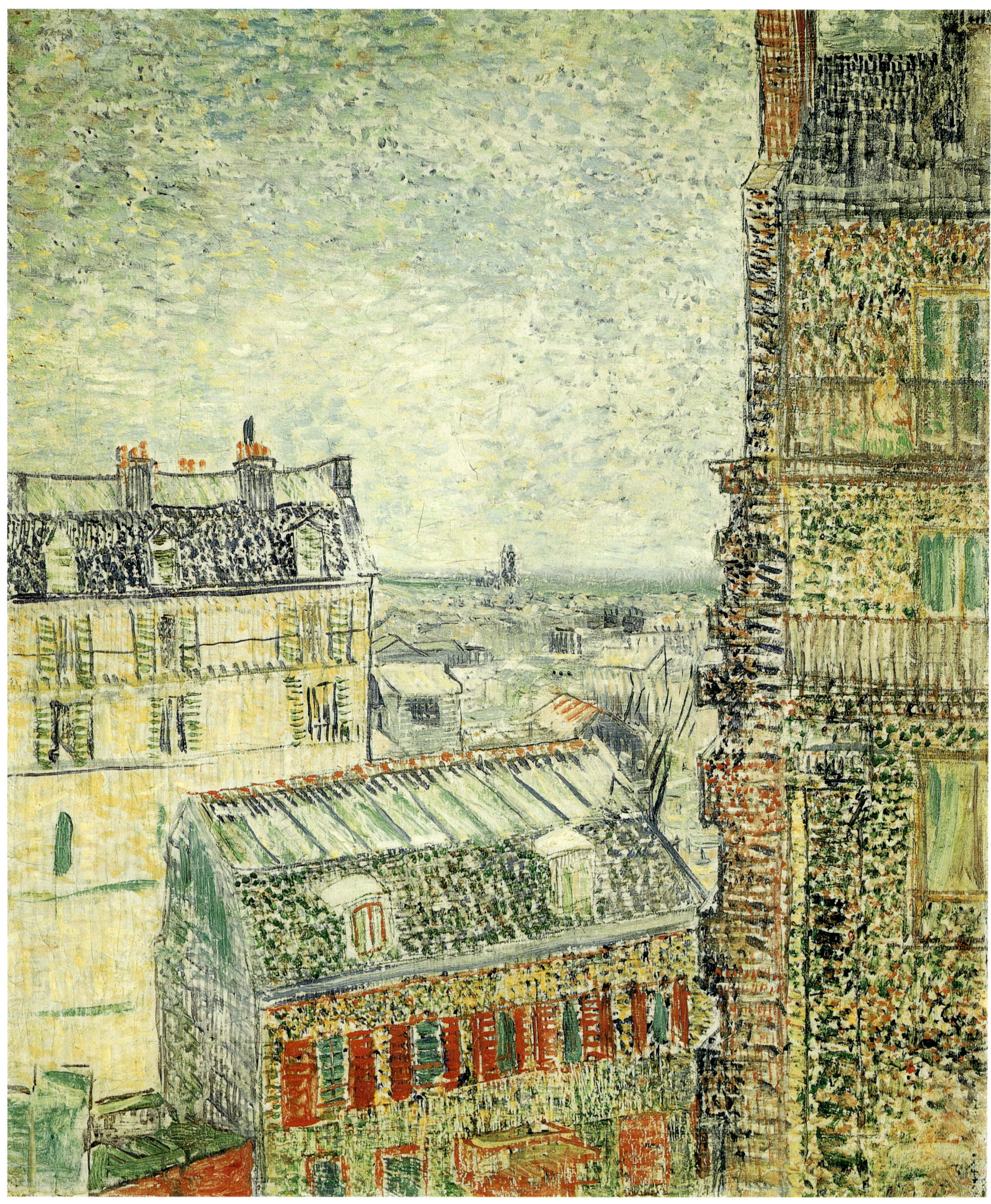

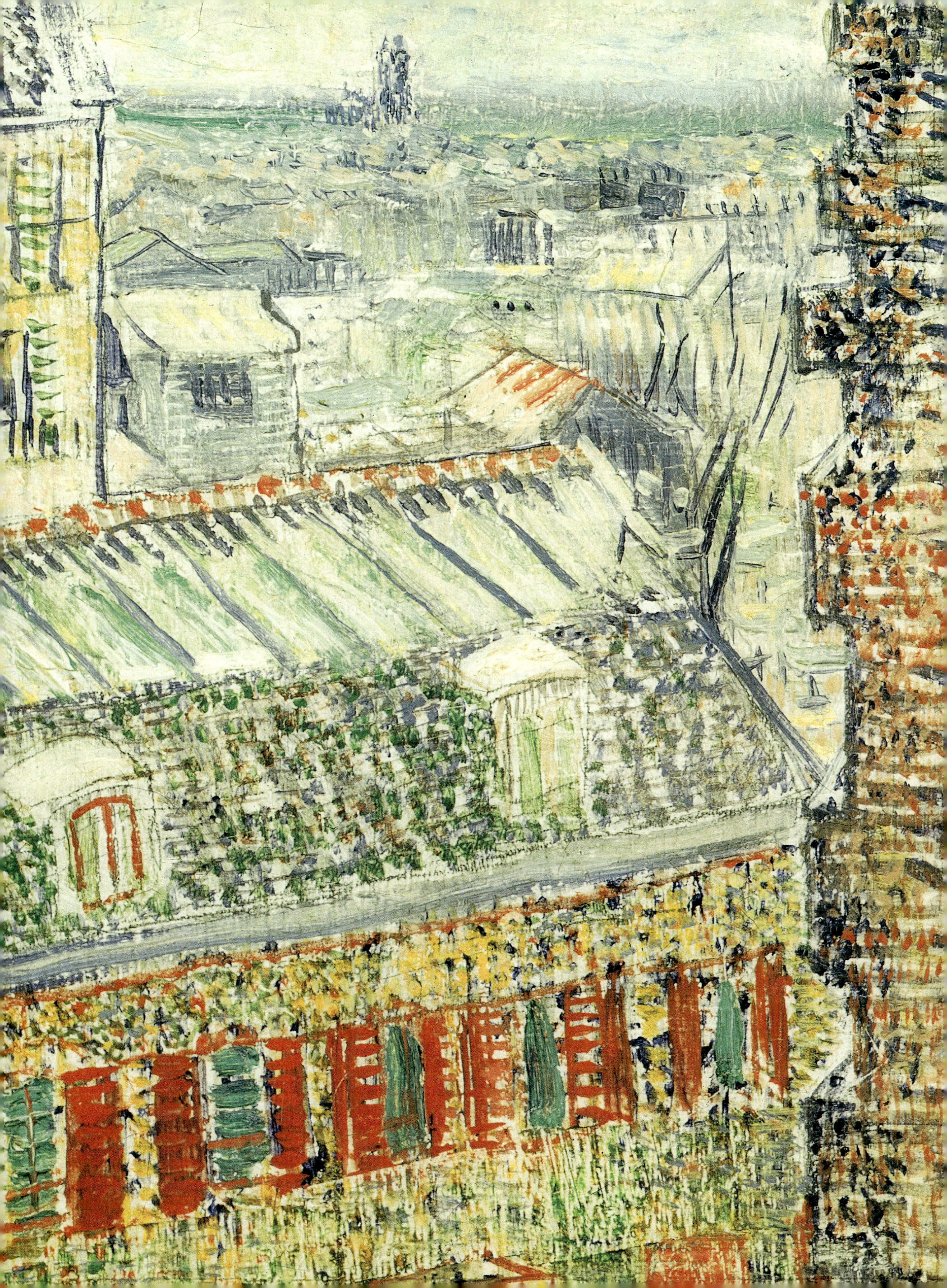

LIVING WITH HIS PARENTS IN THE poor Dutch town of Nuenen, Vincent felt unwelcome. "They are as reluctant to let me into the house as they would be to let in a big shaggy dog," he wrote to his brother Theo. In spite of the tension, Vincent's father gave him money for all the art supplies he needed, including oil paint, which he could not always afford in the past. Vincent rented a studio from the sexton of the local Roman Catholic Church and began *The Potato Eaters.* He prepared studies of heads, figures, interiors, and details, challenged by the dim light in the hovels where his sitters lived. The canvas was painted in his cramped studio—very likely from memory. While he was working on it, his father died suddenly. Recent differences had not dimmed Vincent's love for his father and he was deeply affected by the loss.

In a preparatory version of *The Potato Eaters,* a kerosene lamp is the only source of illumination. The final canvas shows light glowing from the faces of each of the five figures. The peasants' regular meal of boiled potatoes is interrupted by the aroma and pouring of coffee. This luxury is offered up in an almost sacramental way, but the woman on the left seems concerned that her brother will succumb to it before he gets adequate nourishment from the bowl in front of him. Vincent, like his father, had dedicated himself to serving the poor. *The Potato Eaters* represents the artist's final ministration to them, showing these poor, obscure laborers to the world in their authenticity as noble souls. As the summation of everything he had learned and felt, Vincent hoped the painting would be the start of his career. Two years later, writing from Paris to his sister Wilhelmien, he remembered *The Potato Eaters* as "the best of all my work."

THE POTATO EATERS
NUENEN, APRIL OR SEPTEMBER–OCTOBER 1885
OIL ON CANVAS, 32 1/4 X 45 INCHES
VAN GOGH MUSEUM (VINCENT VAN GOGH FOUNDATION)
AMSTERDAM, THE NETHERLANDS

➢

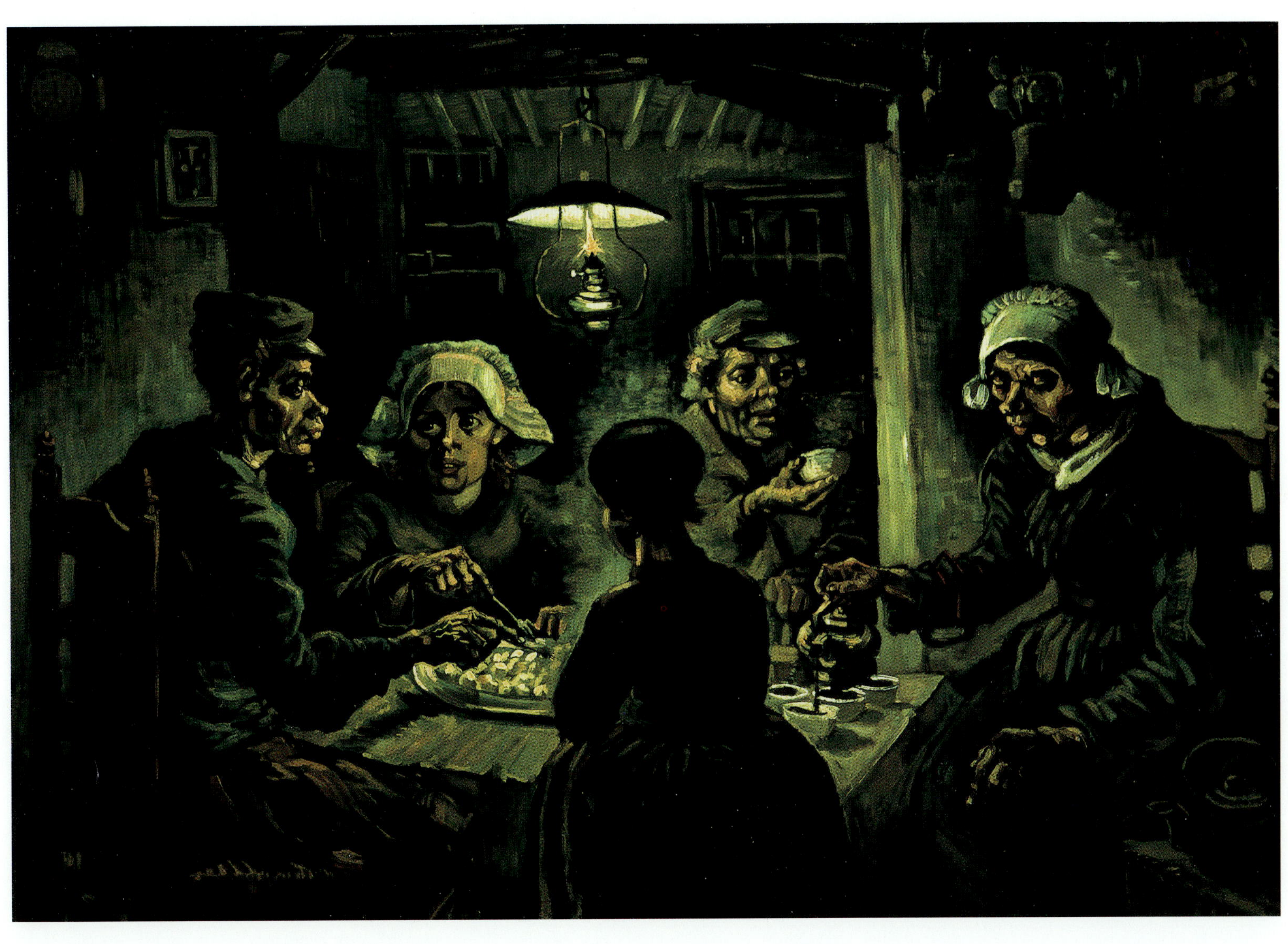

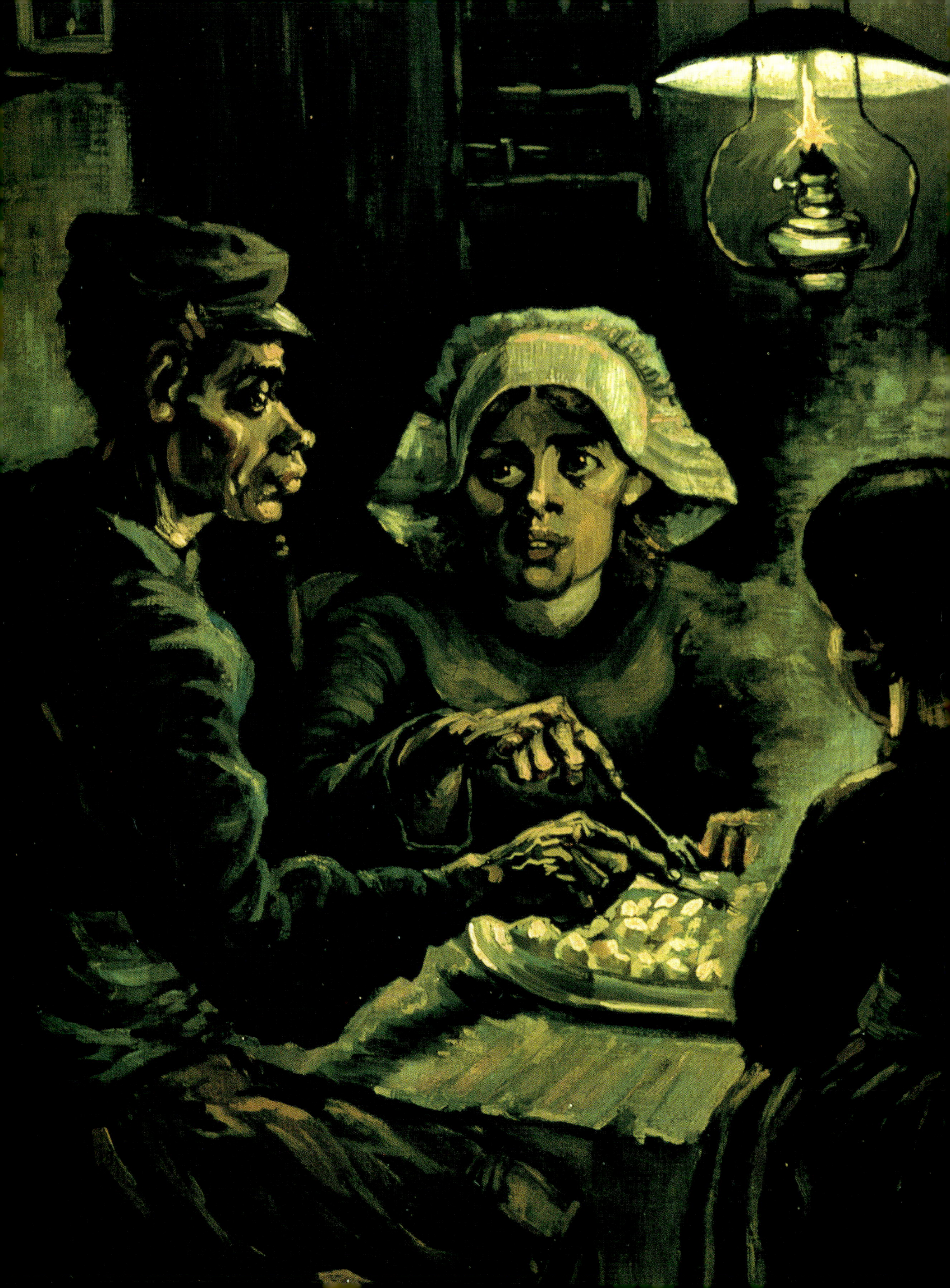

VINCENT COLLECTED BIRDS' NESTS ON walks and painted at least five canvases featuring them. Each of the others shows three nests against black, for he wanted the viewer to recognize the nests as a collection outside of their natural state. Here, two more nests are added and the background is light enough to emphasize their varied shapes and textures and the pattern of the reaching tree branch that serves as the armature for the mossy nest on the left.

In a letter in which Vincent described his paintings of nests to his brother Theo, he also explained complementary colors Perhaps he switched from a black background to glowing orange against fresh green as a color demonstration. Always thinking of who might buy his paintings, Vincent explained to Theo that "some people who are good observers of nature might like them because of the colors of the moss, the dry leaves and grasses, clay, etc."

STILL LIFE WITH FIVE BIRDS' NESTS
NUENEN, SEPTEMBER–OCTOBER 1885
OIL ON CANVAS, 15 1/4 X 18 1/4 INCHES
VAN GOGH MUSEUM (VINCENT VAN GOGH FOUNDATION)
AMSTERDAM, THE NETHERLANDS

➢

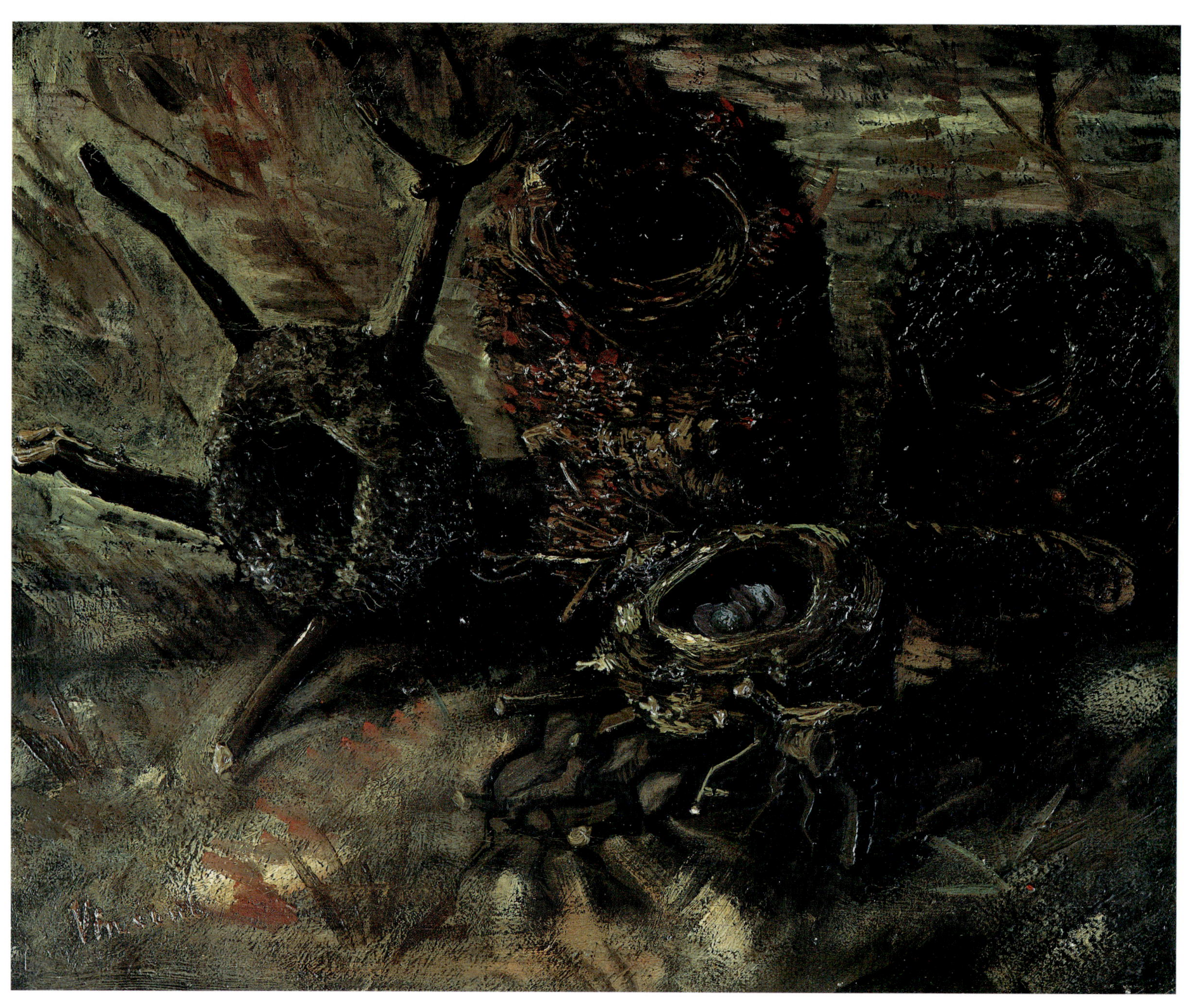
Vincent

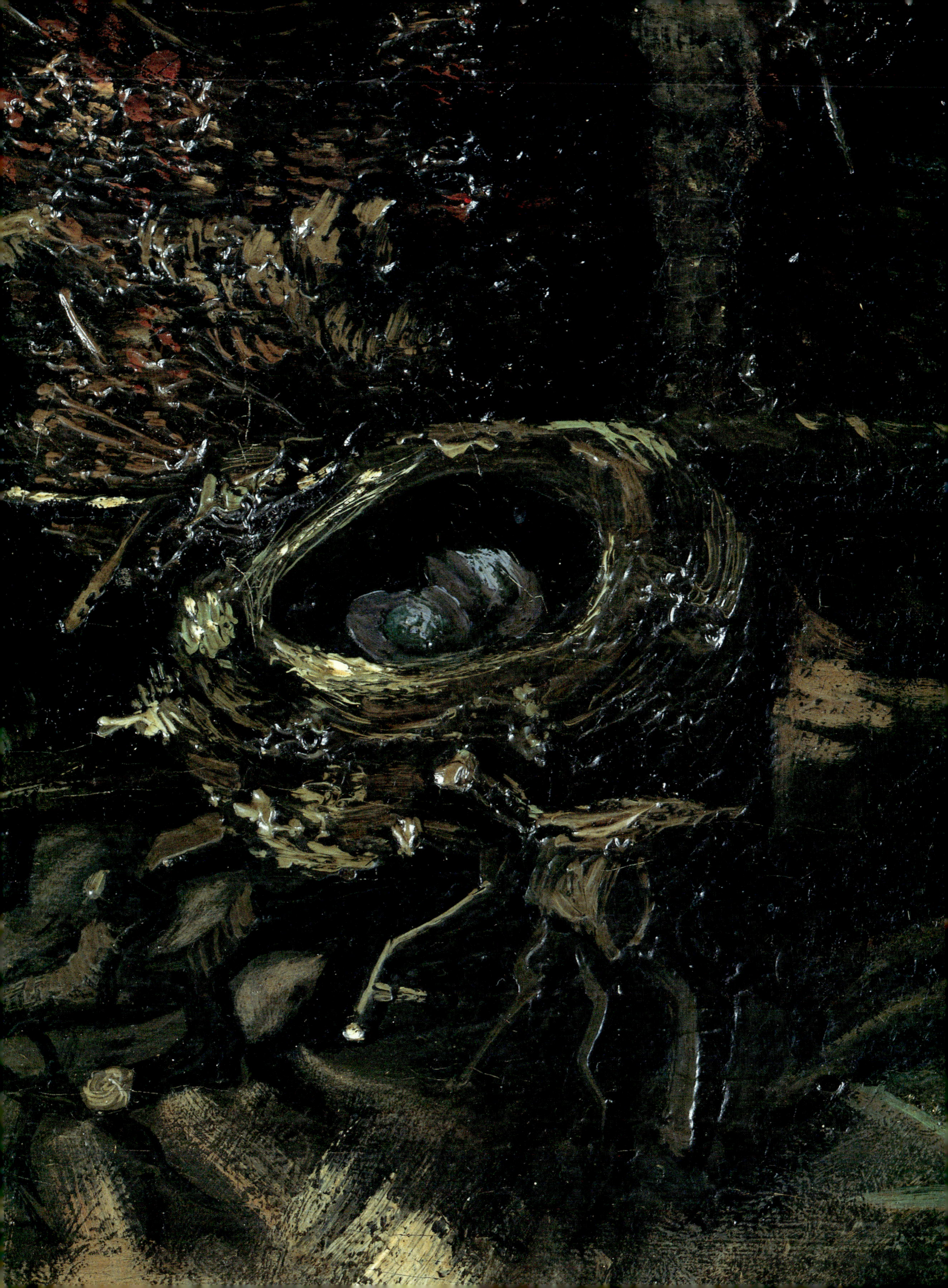

In a letter to their mother, Theo described Vincent as being very popular, with "acquaintances who send him a fine bunch of flowers to paint every week." While in Paris, he produced over forty flower still-life paintings, trying to "freshen" his colors from the earth tones he was used to in the Netherlands. Here, the blossoms in his vase wait for the ones he dropped on the table top, but completing the bouquet could not make the composition more lush and rococo than it already is at this accidental moment. The flowers aim, thrust, and jerk in many different directions, lending a nervous energy to the painting. The floral drama is heightened by a black background on one side and a slightly turbulent one on the other that is colored like the glazed vase.

VASE WITH POPPIES, CORNFLOWERS, PEONIES
AND CHRYSANTHEMUMS
Paris, Summer 1886
Oil on canvas, 39 x 31 inches
Kröller-Müller Museum, Otterlo, the Netherlands

➢

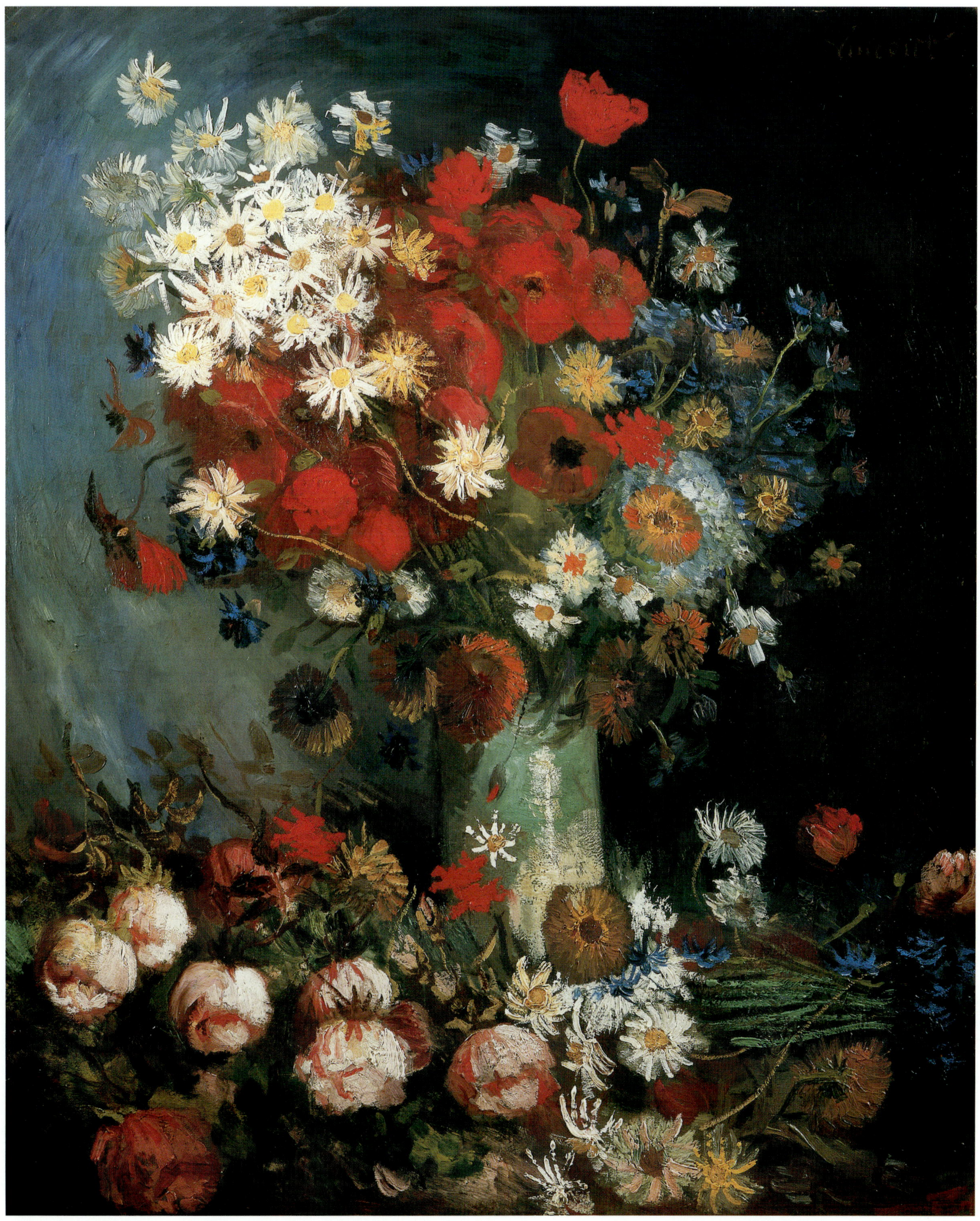

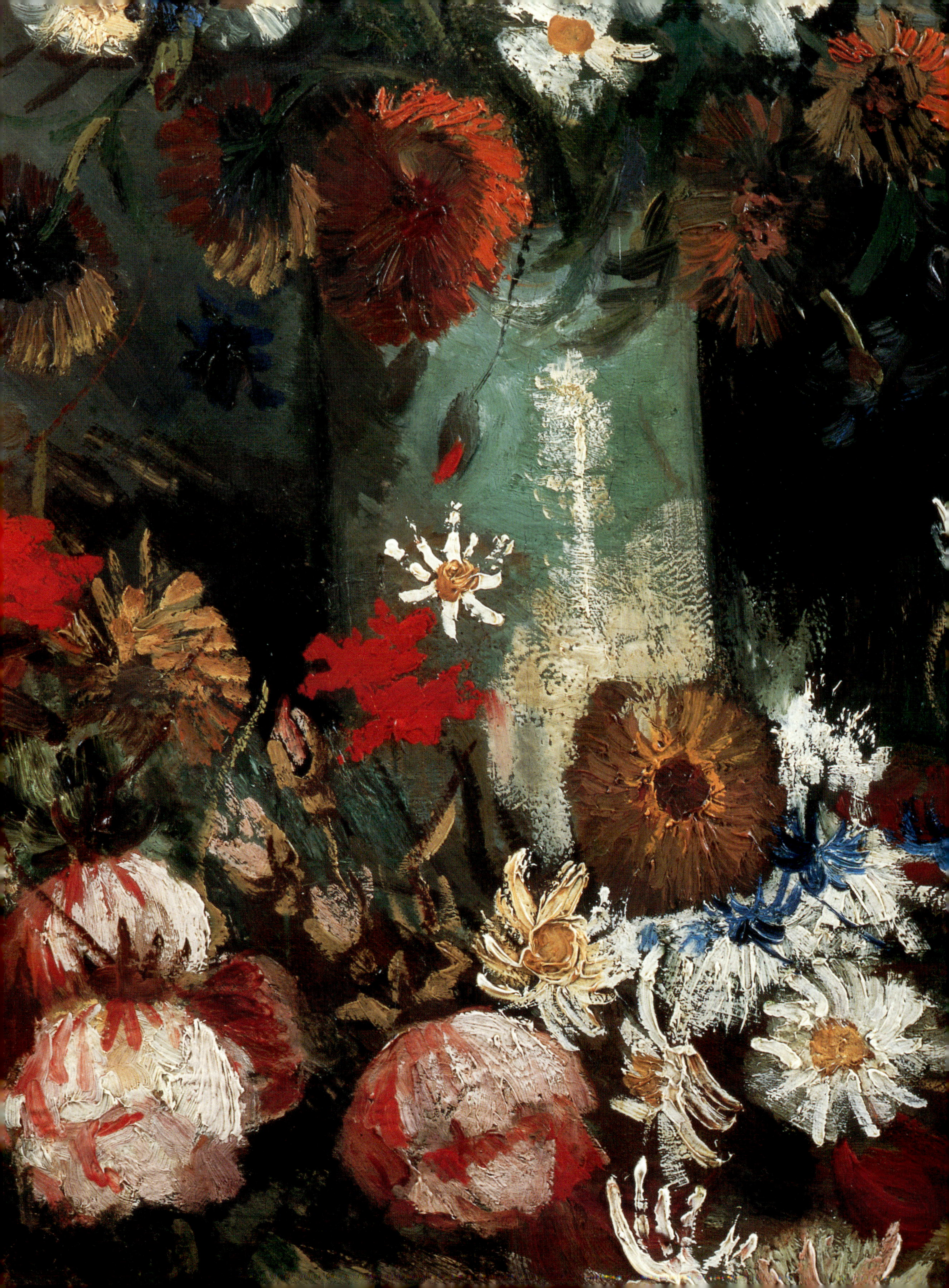

COLOR THEORY AND CONVENIENCE motivated Vincent to paint floral still lifes. Flowers and vases were in his studio, waiting to be used as models, and ideas about color never stopped running through his mind. He dotted the background with the complementary color of the nodding fritillaries, knowing that the opposition would give the blossoms greater vibrancy. The radiating table mat under the vase increases the impression that paired colors give objects a special force of their own. Using Dutch art tricks as old as Rembrandt, Vincent painted his vase with shades of yellow and brown to give the impression of golden brass. Neither the vase nor the flowers make the composition symmetrical, for Vincent preferred a more dynamic balance.

FRITILLARIES IN A COPPER VASE
Paris, April–May or Summer 1887
Oil on canvas, 29 x 23 3/4 inches
Musée d'Orsay, Paris/Art Resource, New York

➢

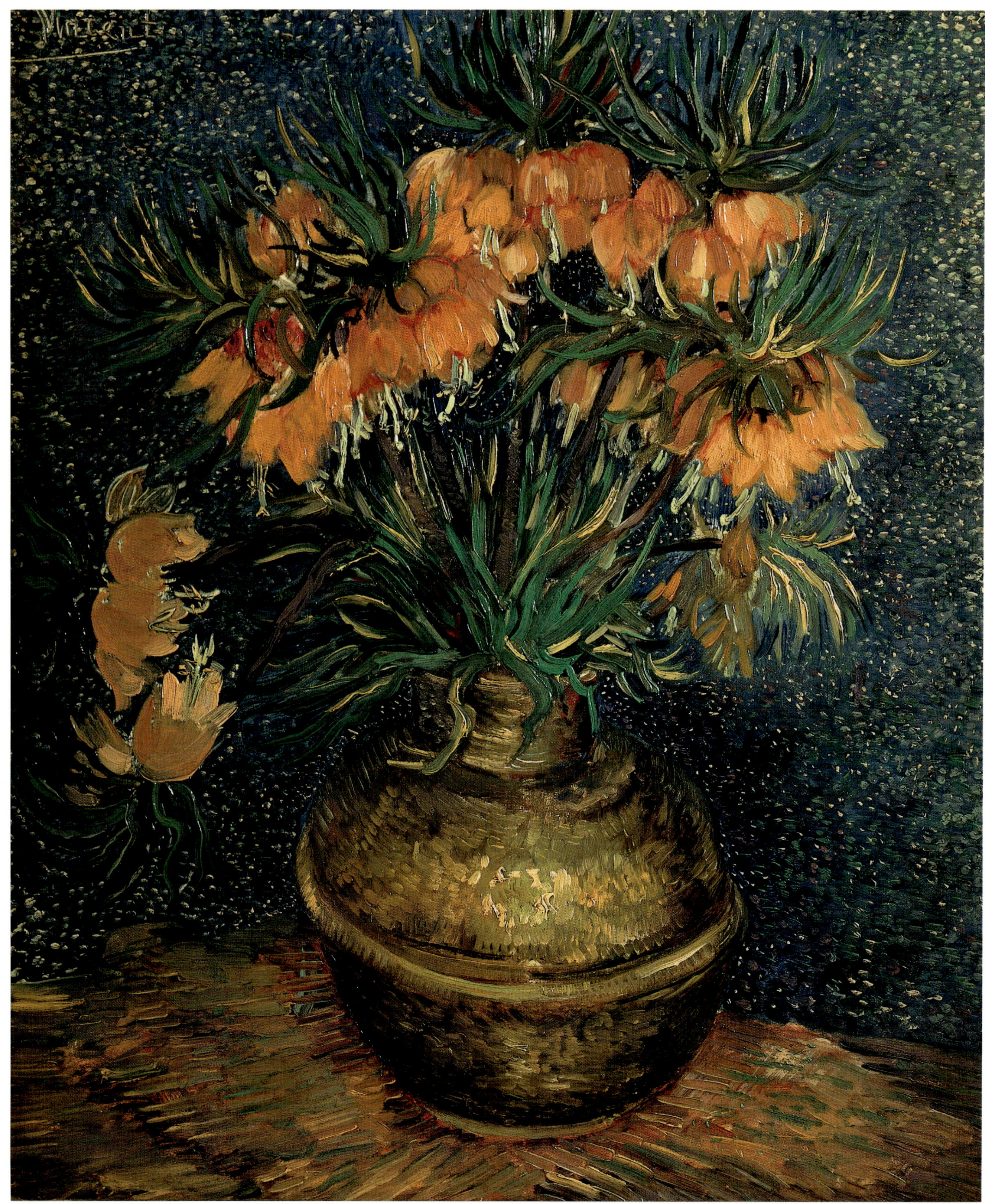

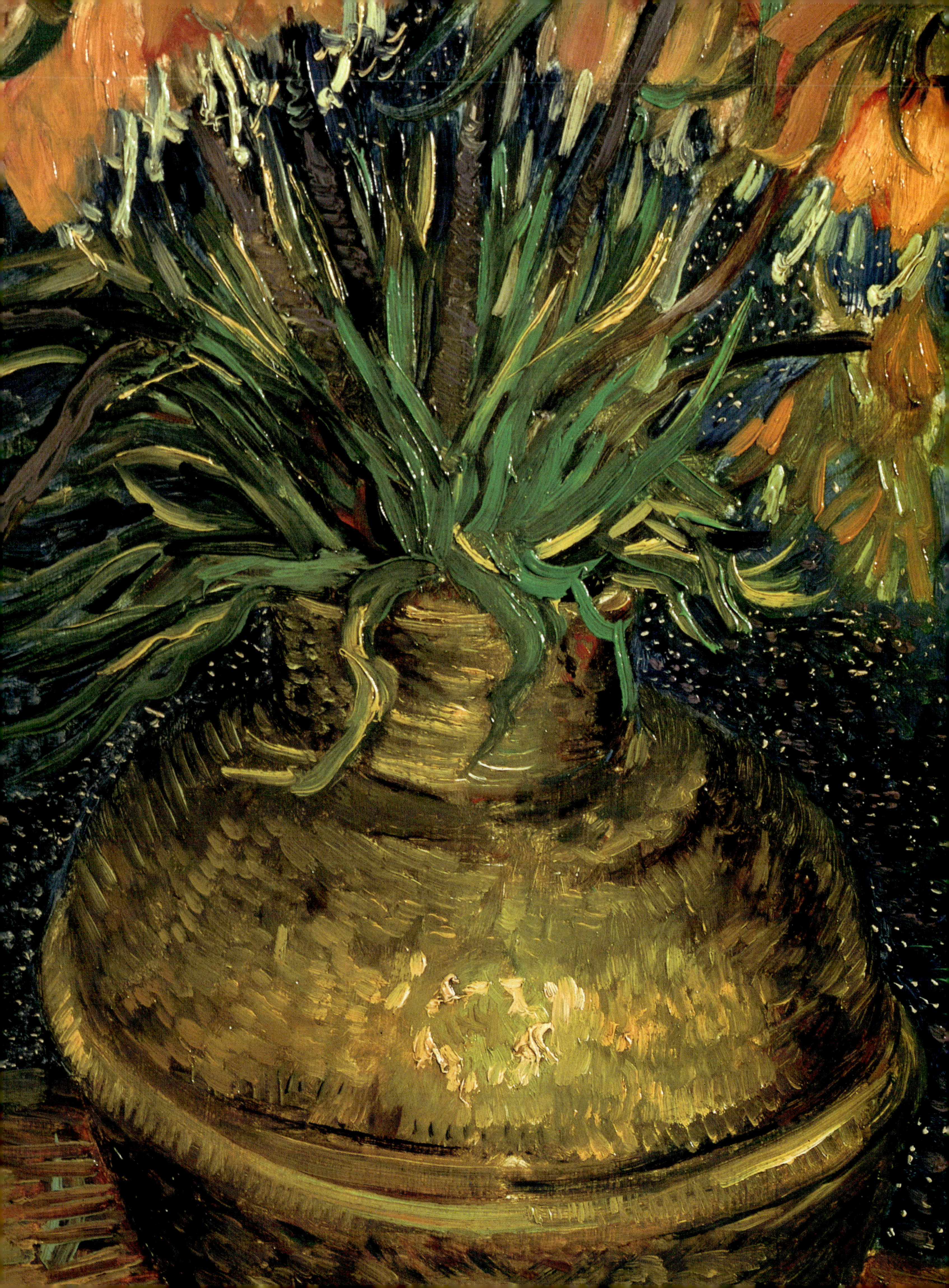

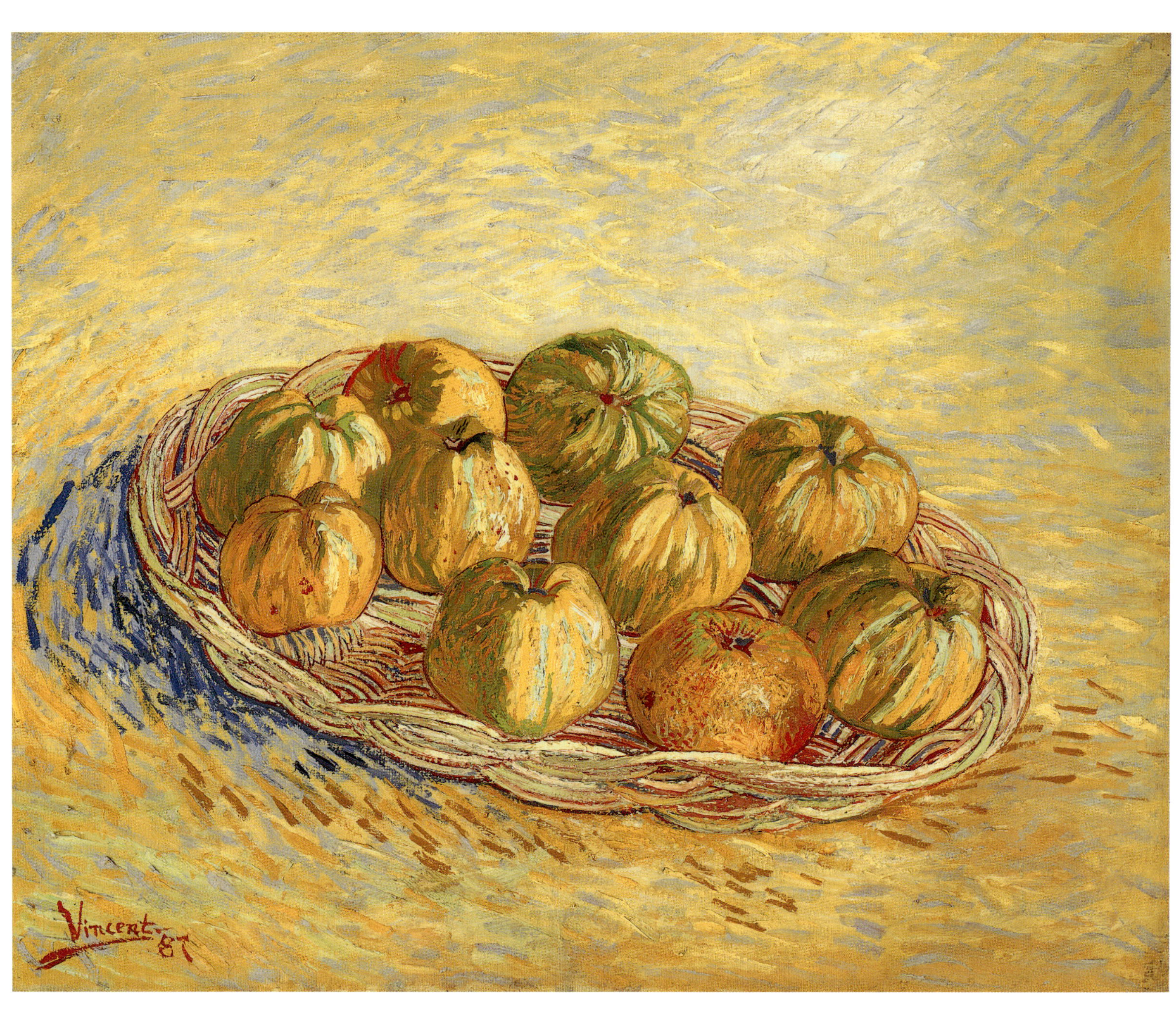
Vincent 87

THE LAVENDER SHADOW AND SCATTERED strokes of yellow show that Vincent made his own technique out of the Impressionist and pointillist influences all around him. The view from above and the simplicity of the arrangement of ten apples in a plain shallow basket reflect his fascination with Japanese composition. Every single apple has its own character—some are heightened with bright red paint. Vincent seems to have borrowed the brush patterns for the background from the weave of the basket. As the color lightens beyond the basket and apples, it suggests infinity.

STILL LIFE WITH BASKET OF APPLES
Paris, Autumn 1887
Oil on canvas, 18 x 21 3/4 inches
The Saint Louis Art Museum
Gift of Sydney M. Shoenberg Sr.

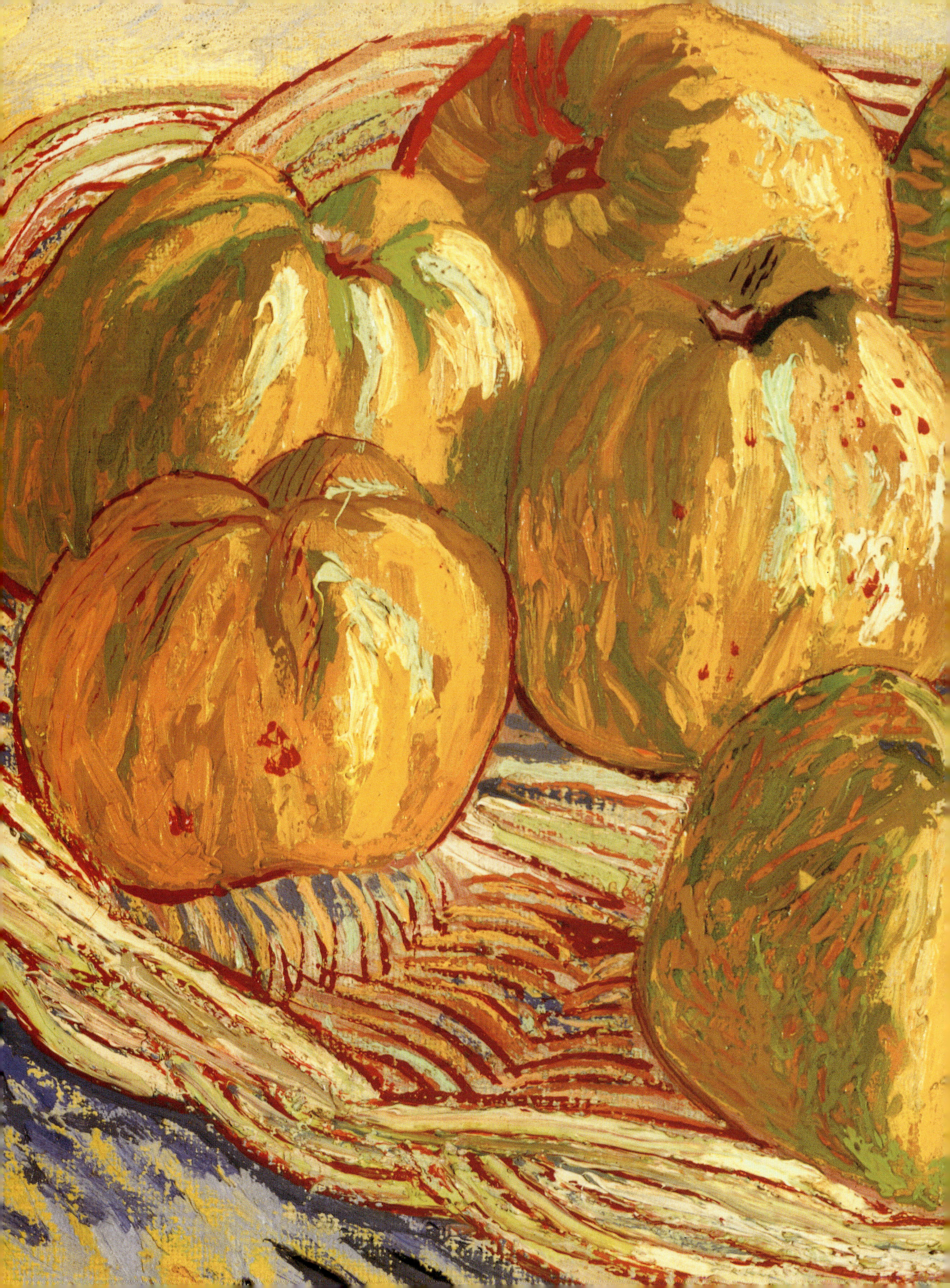

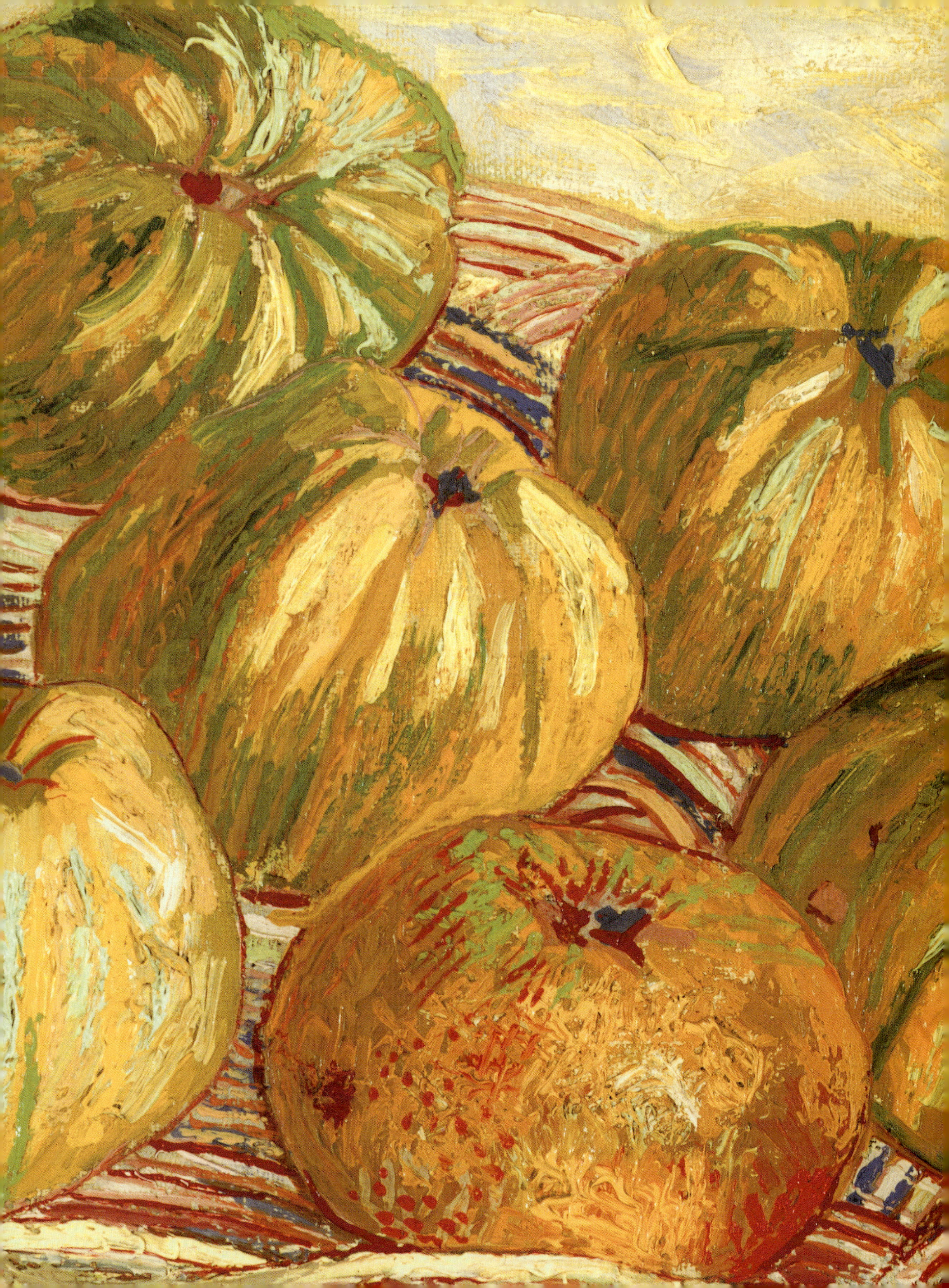

VINCENT BOUGHT HIS PAINTS FROM Julien "Père" Tanguy, who earned his sobriquet through his kindness to struggling artists. He often used his back room as a gallery for the artists' latest work, and he also featured Vincent's paintings in his store window. Like an icon of a Buddha, he sits in stillness in front of selections from Vincent's and Theo's collections of Japanese prints. He himself owned none. As though Vincent wanted to give Père Tanguy the prints around him, he linked him to them by a simple compositional device. The triangle of Mount Fujiyama, which he placed above Tanguy's head, is repeated in the shape of his beard, the neckline of his jacket, and the space between his legs. Vincent was the first to use Japanese prints as a subject for paintings, and here his synthesis of Eastern and Western art combines the broken color of modern Parisian painters with the flat, unmodulated color of the Japanese.

PORTRAIT OF PÈRE TANGUY
Paris, Autumn 1887
Oil on canvas, 36 1/4 x 29 1/2 inches
Musée Rodin, Paris/Art Resource, New York

➢

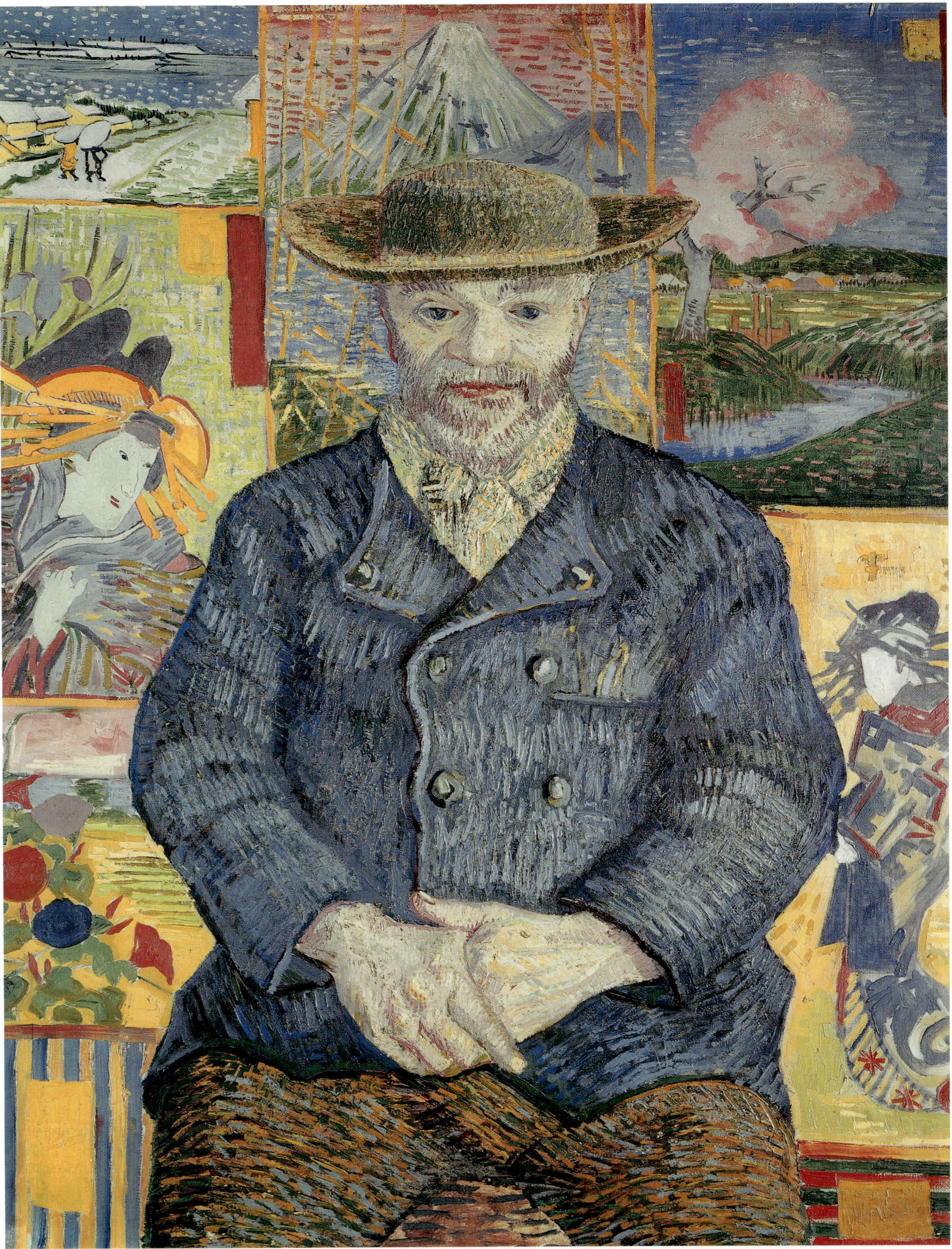

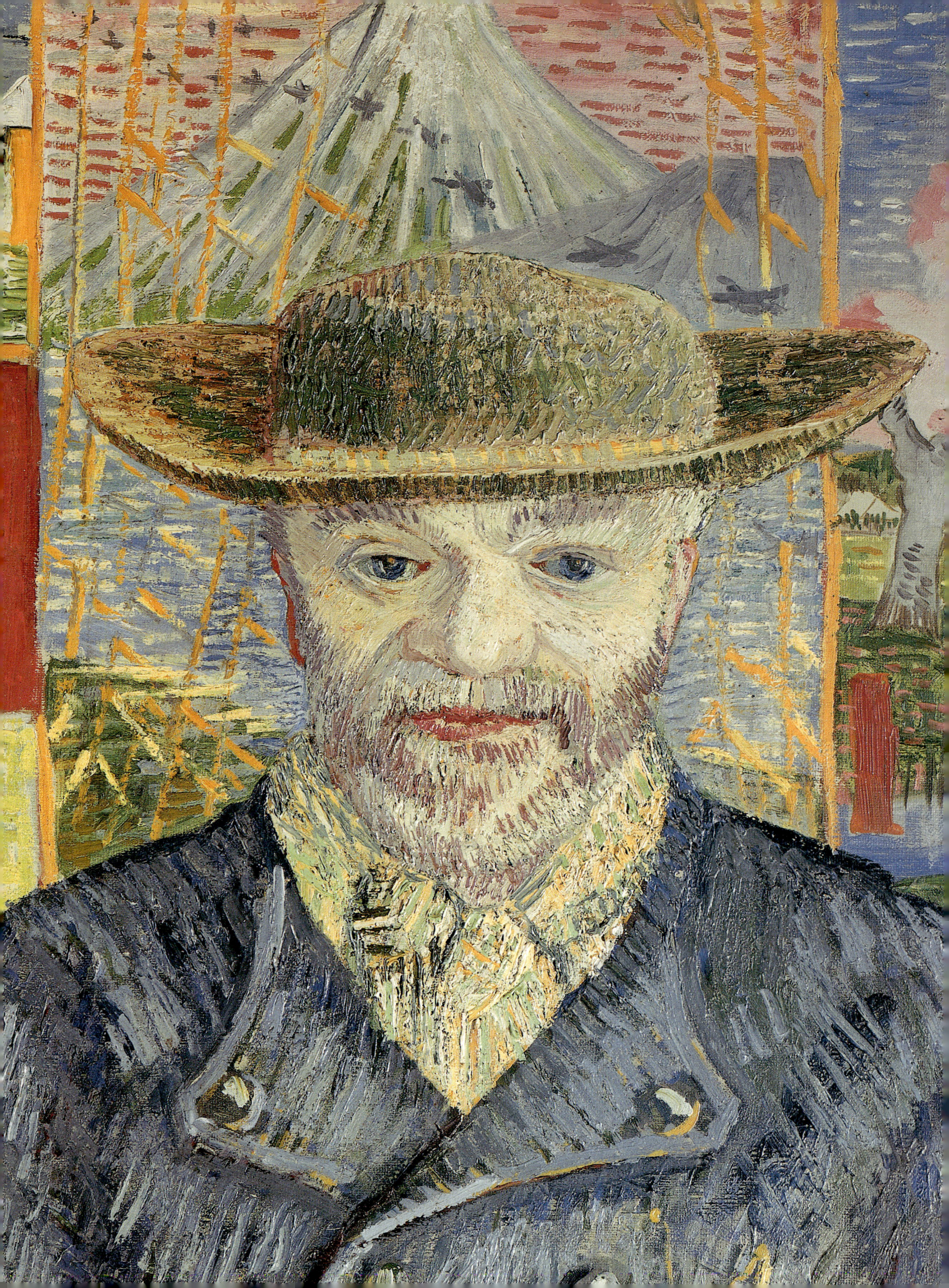

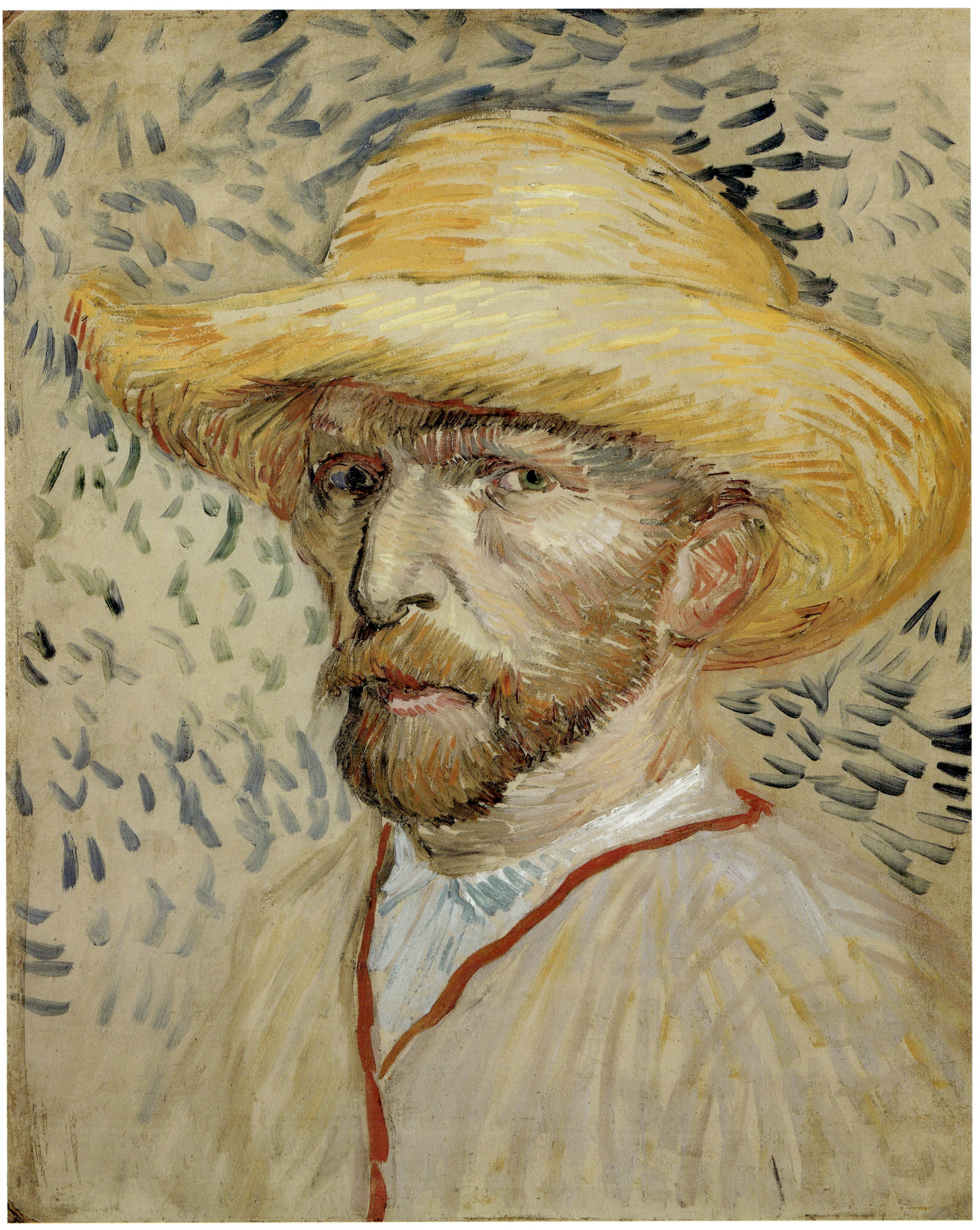

VINCENT VAN GOGH LEFT THIRTY-seven self-portraits, all but ten done while he was in Paris. In six of them, he showed himself wearing a straw hat, the brim stylishly turned back as though to signal that the subject was not a peasant. Self-portraits were a cheap investment—they required only a mirror, canvas, and paints. Vincent worked from his own features, "in default of a model, because I can manage to paint the coloring of my own head, which is not to be done without some difficulty."

The artist once confessed that he neglected his appearance, but here he simply forgot part of it. It is an unfinished painting. "The question," he wrote in 1885 about painting the human being, "is only whether one starts from the soul or from the clothes." The soul won out here, and Vincent might have found it wanting. He smoked, drank, quarreled too much, and did not sleep enough. His face was haggard and his eyes and mind tired from the constant stimulation he felt in the midst of the art world of Paris. The strong outlines of his nose and right cheek emphasize the boniness of his face, while the preliminary orange line of his lapel is more like a stream of lost lifeblood than a textile edging. Vincent once thought that neglect was "sometimes a good way to assure the solitude necessary for concentrating on whatever study preoccupies one." Now it was a sign that he needed a change.

SELF-PORTRAIT WITH STRAW HAT
PARIS, SUMMER 1887
OIL ON CARDBOARD, 16 1/4 X 13 INCHES
VAN GOGH MUSEUM (VINCENT VAN GOGH FOUNDATION)
AMSTERDAM, THE NETHERLANDS

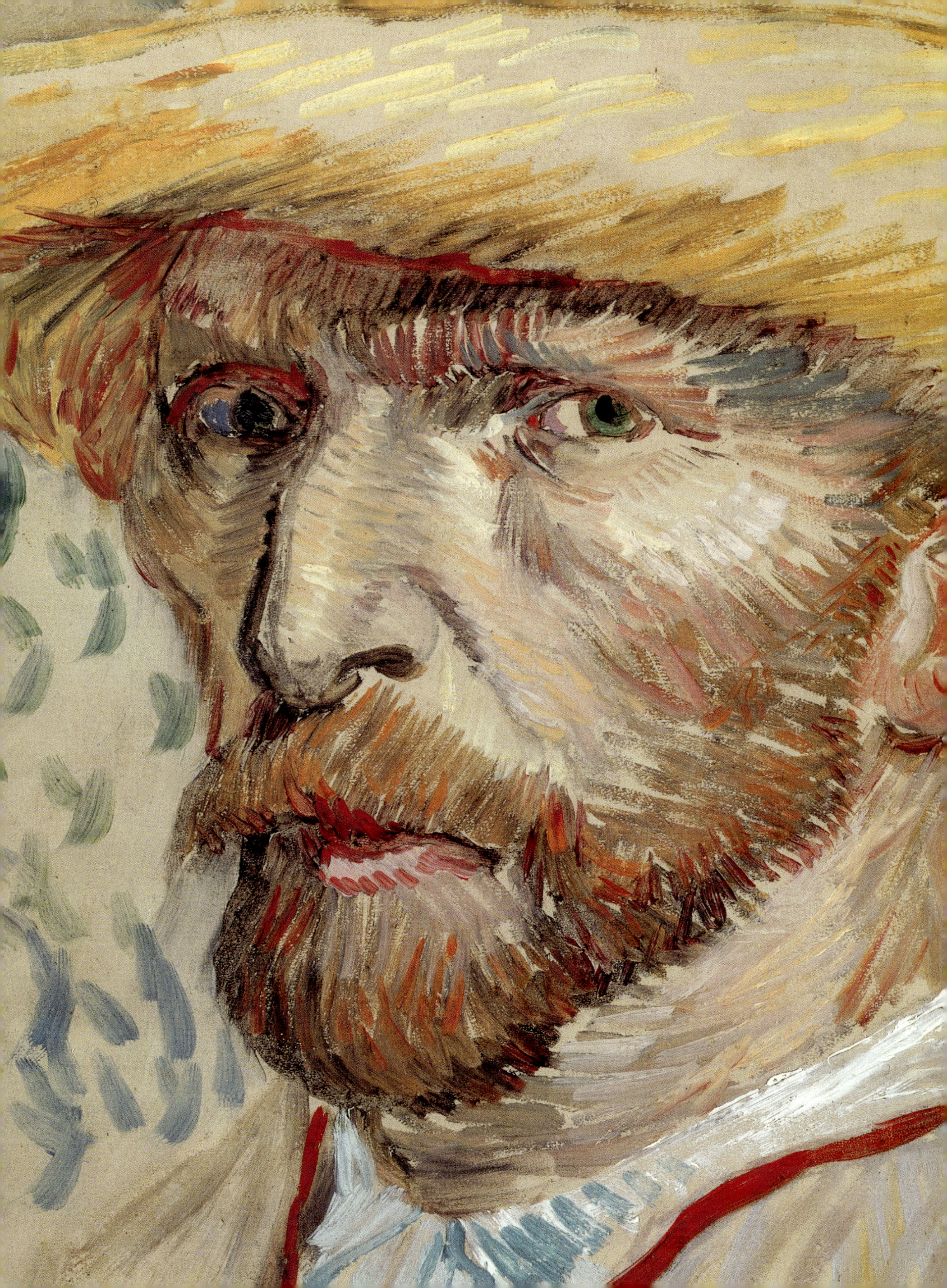

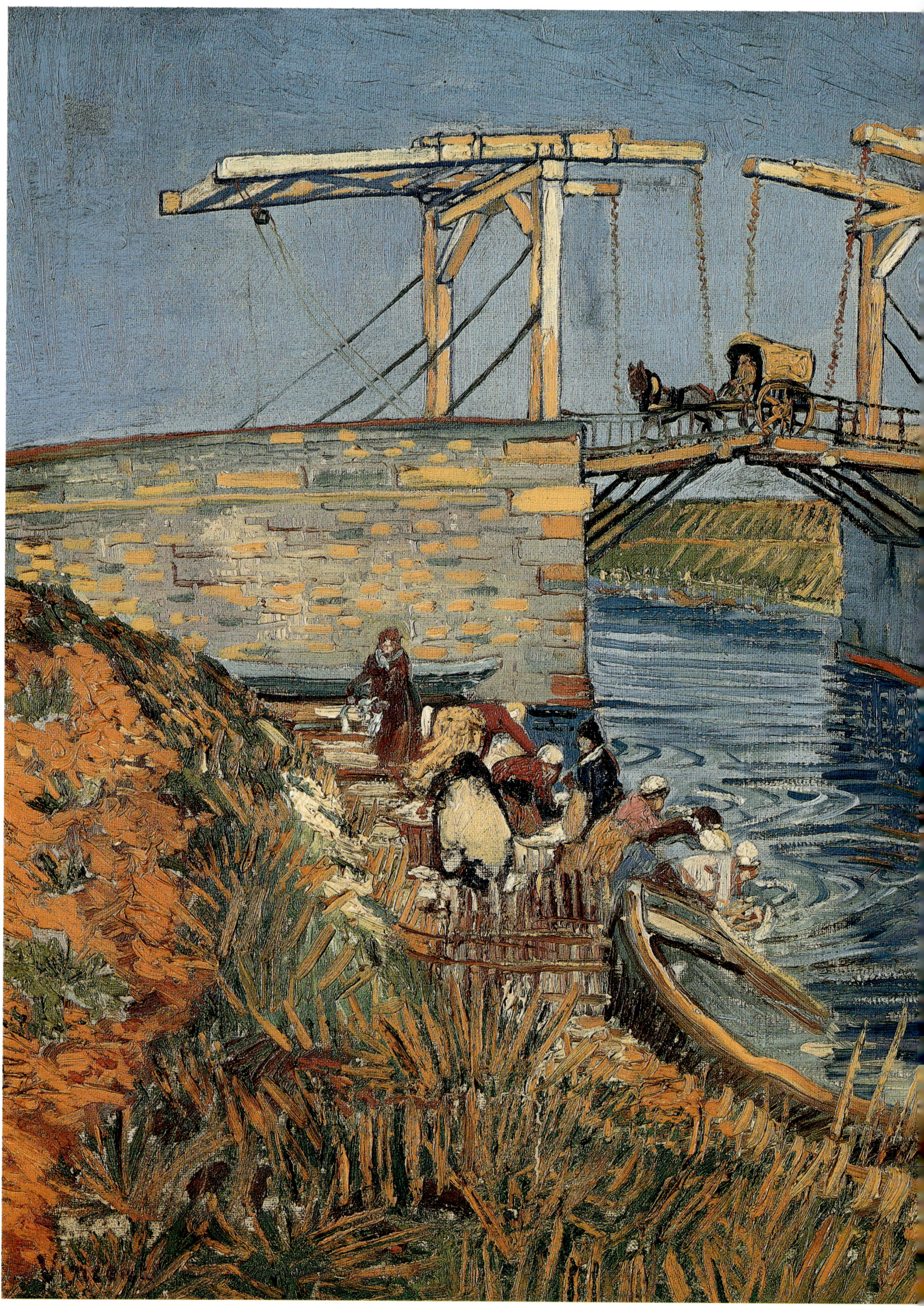

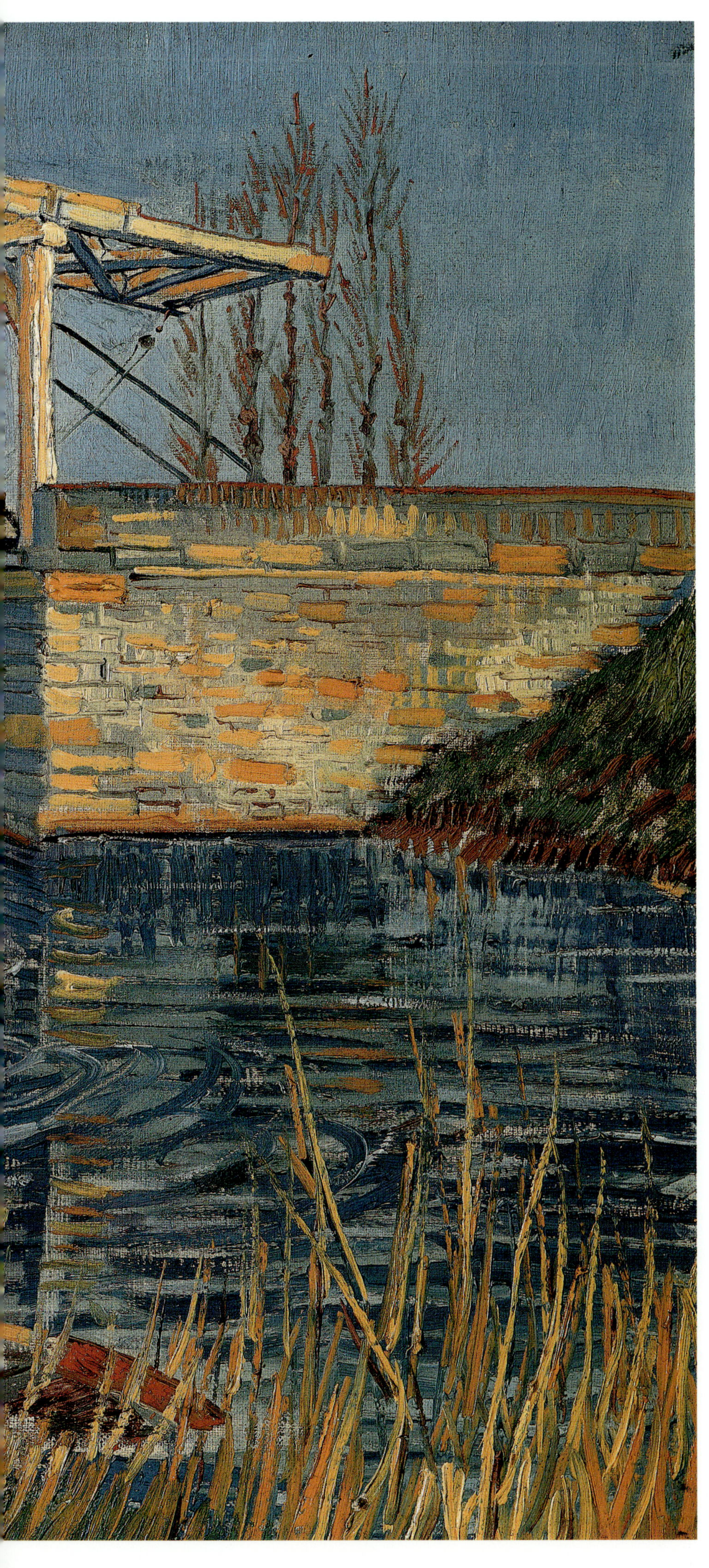

In February, Vincent arrived in Arles exhausted, yet he quickly completed twelve studies for paintings. "I am seeing new things, I am learning, and I take it easy, my body doesn't refuse to function," he reported to Theo. He painted still lifes in the guest house where he lived and sometimes tramped into the frosted fields to paint snow scenes.

A Rhone River canal flowed south of the town to the Mediterranean. Vincent was attracted to a drawbridge that spanned the canal (Langlois, for whom it was named, had been a bridge guard). It was like a bridge he had painted in brown tones in the Netherlands about three years earlier, but his memory of the north must have quickly been blinded by the bright orange ground, the green grass, and the blue water and sky of this nostalgic spot.

To prepare studies for painting the scene, Vincent used his perspective frame to draw the width of the structure. Five variations of the bridge exist—one from the road, one from the opposite shore, and three that required Vincent to climb down the bank of the canal. There he painted the women washing their laundry on the shore near a wrecked and flooded barge. Their scrubbing and rinsing creates patterns in the water, arcs that contrast with the spikey grass in the foreground. This vignette is the human center of the painting for Vincent, so he allowed it to diminish the scale of the bridge itself. Only the presence of a cart and horse suggest its true proportions.

THE LANGLOIS BRIDGE AT ARLES WITH WOMEN WASHING
Arles, March 1888
Oil on canvas, 21 1/4 x 25 1/2 inches
Kröller-Müller Museum, Otterlo, the Netherlands

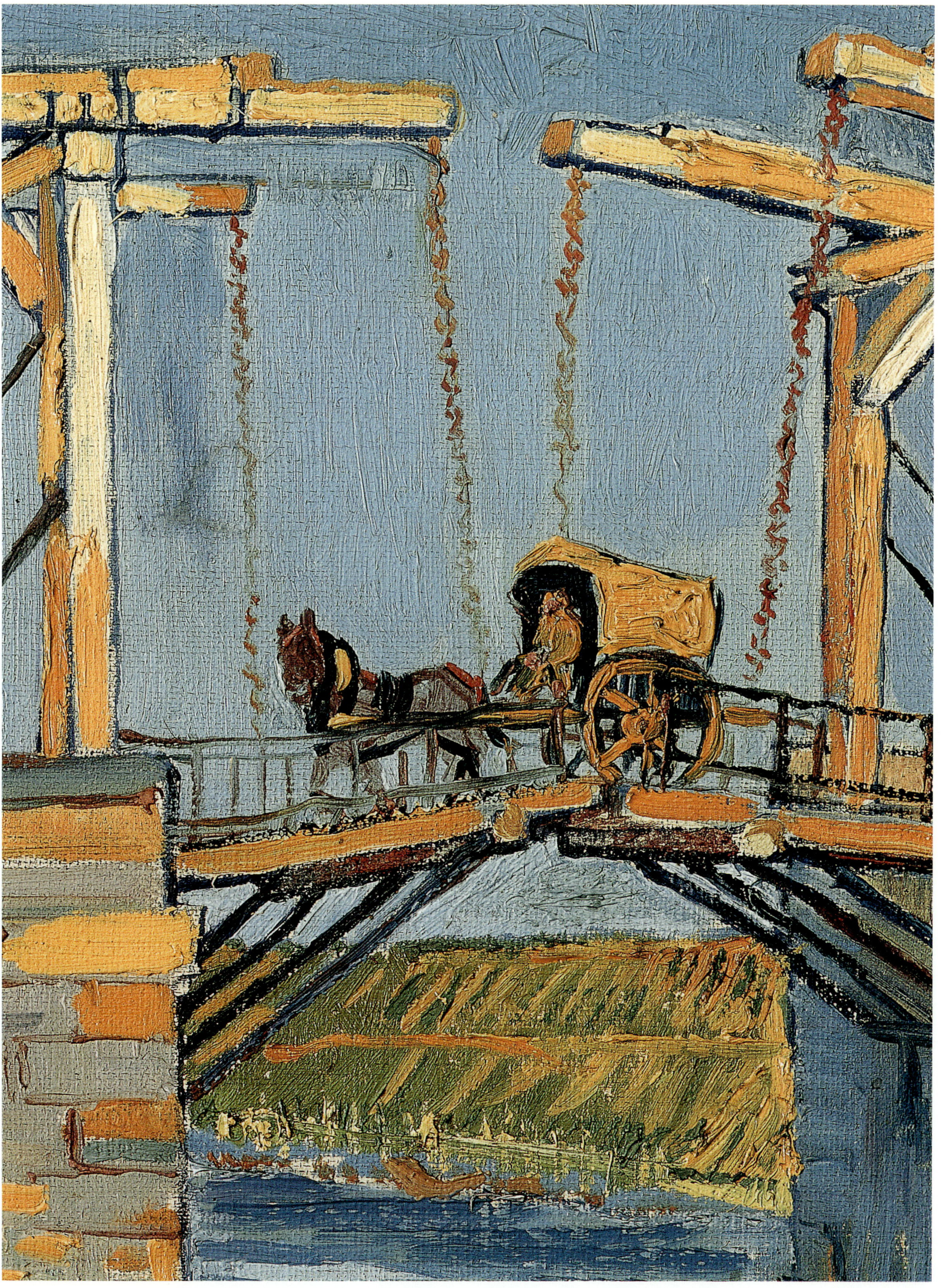

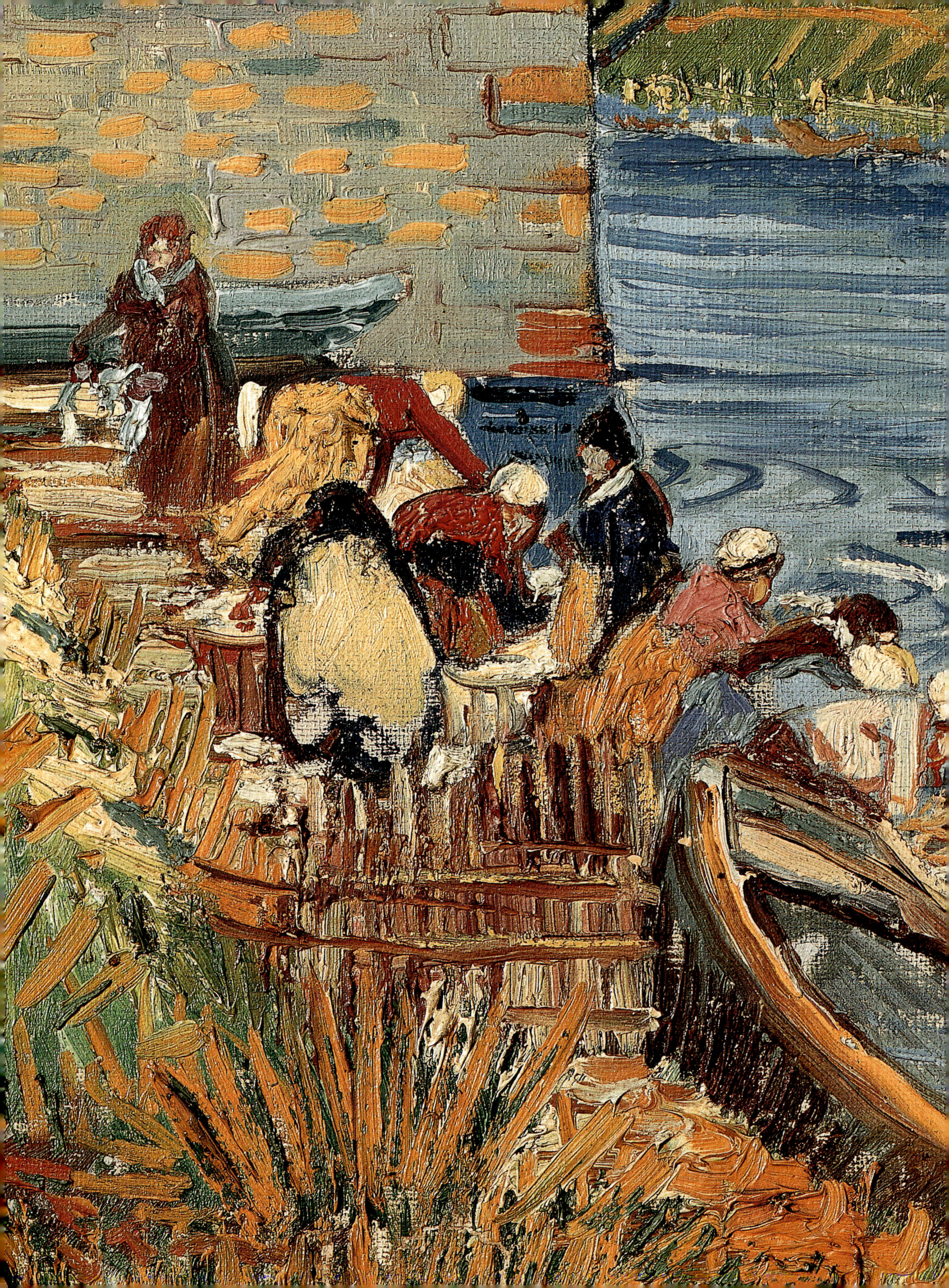

FINALLY SPRING CAME, AND IT WAS a staggering experience for Vincent. "Work in these magnificent natural surroundings has restored my morale," he wrote, but added, "some efforts are too much for me: my strength fails me." Indeed, the fullness of nature sometimes eluded Vincent's painting abilities. To capture the effect of light on the tree blossoms in the orchard required him to return twice to the canvas to rework it. He reduced the shadows of the trees that fall across the grassy ground to irregular black hatch marks—different only in color from the pale green and yellow brush strokes that represent new grass. The trees occupy a wavy strip of green, bordered by lavender outcroppings of stone and a yellow and lavender fence woven of fresh rushes. This orchard landscape is presented on a diagonal to animate the dance of the trees.

Vincent completed fifteen blossoming orchard scenes. They were his most impressionistic paintings, and he thought they were his most Japanese. He was anxious when he started for he had no oil paints, but Theo came through. Then Vincent began to worry that the wind would take all the blossoms. Feverishly, he completed his unique series.

ORCHARD IN BLOSSOM
Arles, April 1888
Oil on canvas, 28 1/2 x 36 1/4 inches
Van Gogh Museum (Vincent van Gogh Foundation)
Amsterdam, the Netherlands

➢

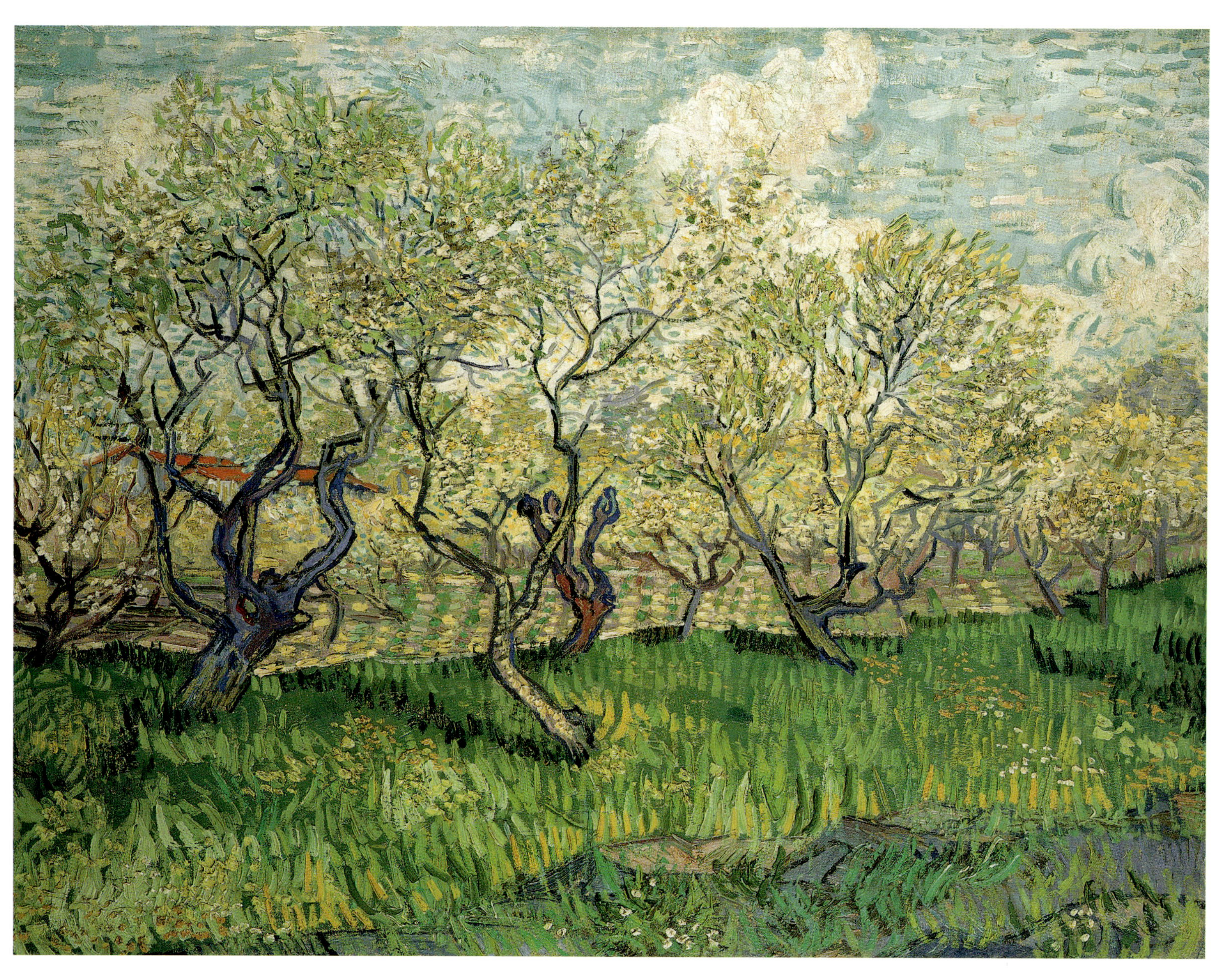

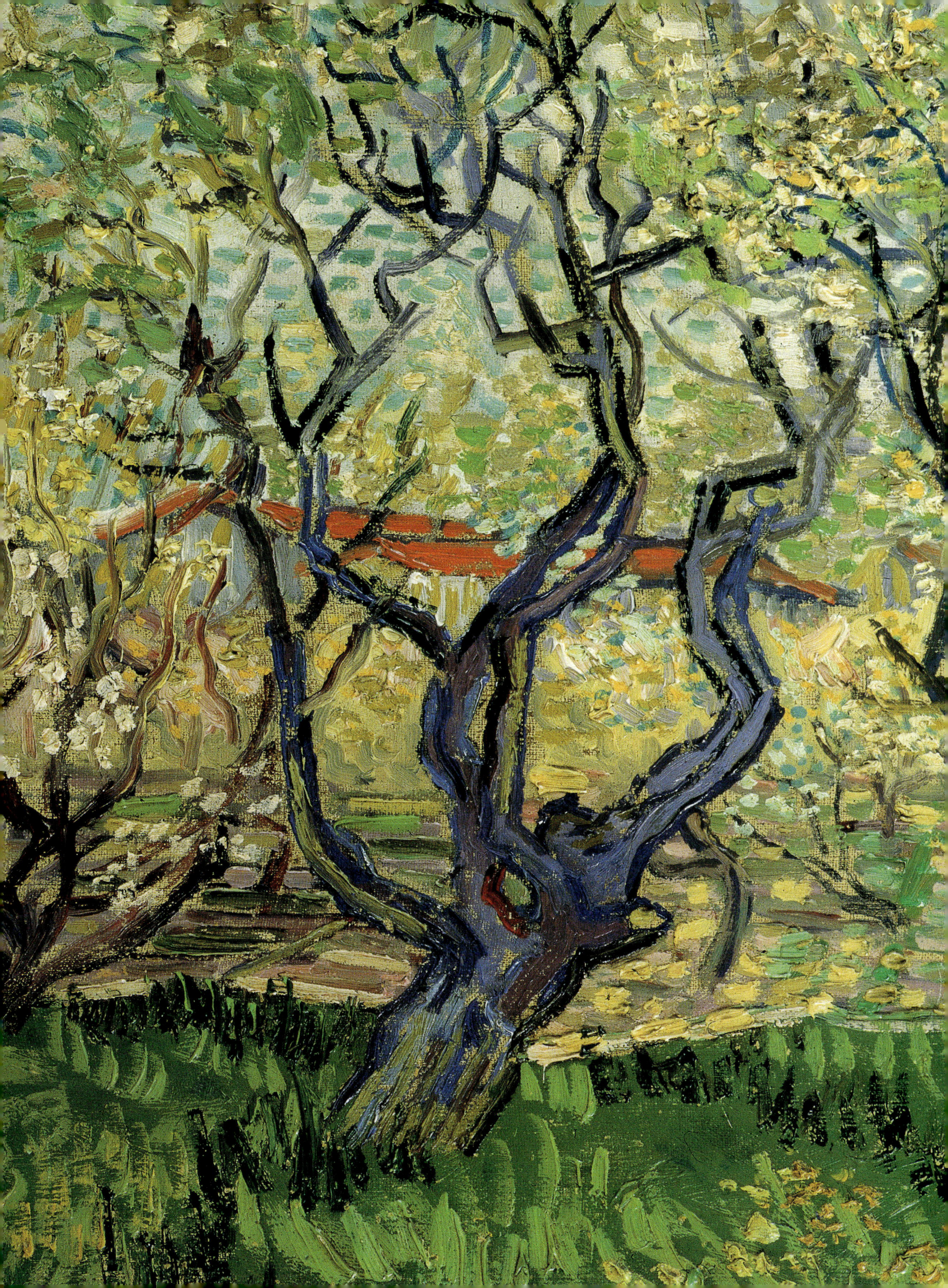

DUTCH PAINTERS OF THE SEVENTEENTH century celebrated the flatness of their country with low horizon lines and big skies. They sometimes presented a magical view of the landscape by imagining themselves on high, looking out for miles on end. Vincent did that here, explaining that he was emulating the paintings of Philips Koninck (1619–88), a Dutch master of panoramas. Vincent climbed Montmajour, purple in the left background, and drew pictures of rocks, a ruined monastery, and views across the fields. With no high places on the opposite side of the broad stretch of farmlands, he constructed his aerial view in his imagination.

Vincent painted horizontal rows of crops, a fence, and vegetation that propel the eye from the bottom of the canvas to a blue cart, dead center in the composition. The diagonal edges of farm plots and dirt roads lead to the range of mountains in the background, while red is used as a punctuation to slow the journey. Farm activity in the fields is another aspect of the painting that should be appreciated.

HARVEST AT LA CRAU, WITH MONTMAJOUR IN THE BACKGROUND
Arles, June 1888
Oil on canvas, 28 1/2 x 36 1/4 inches
Van Gogh Museum (Vincent van Gogh Foundation)
Amsterdam, the Netherlands

➢

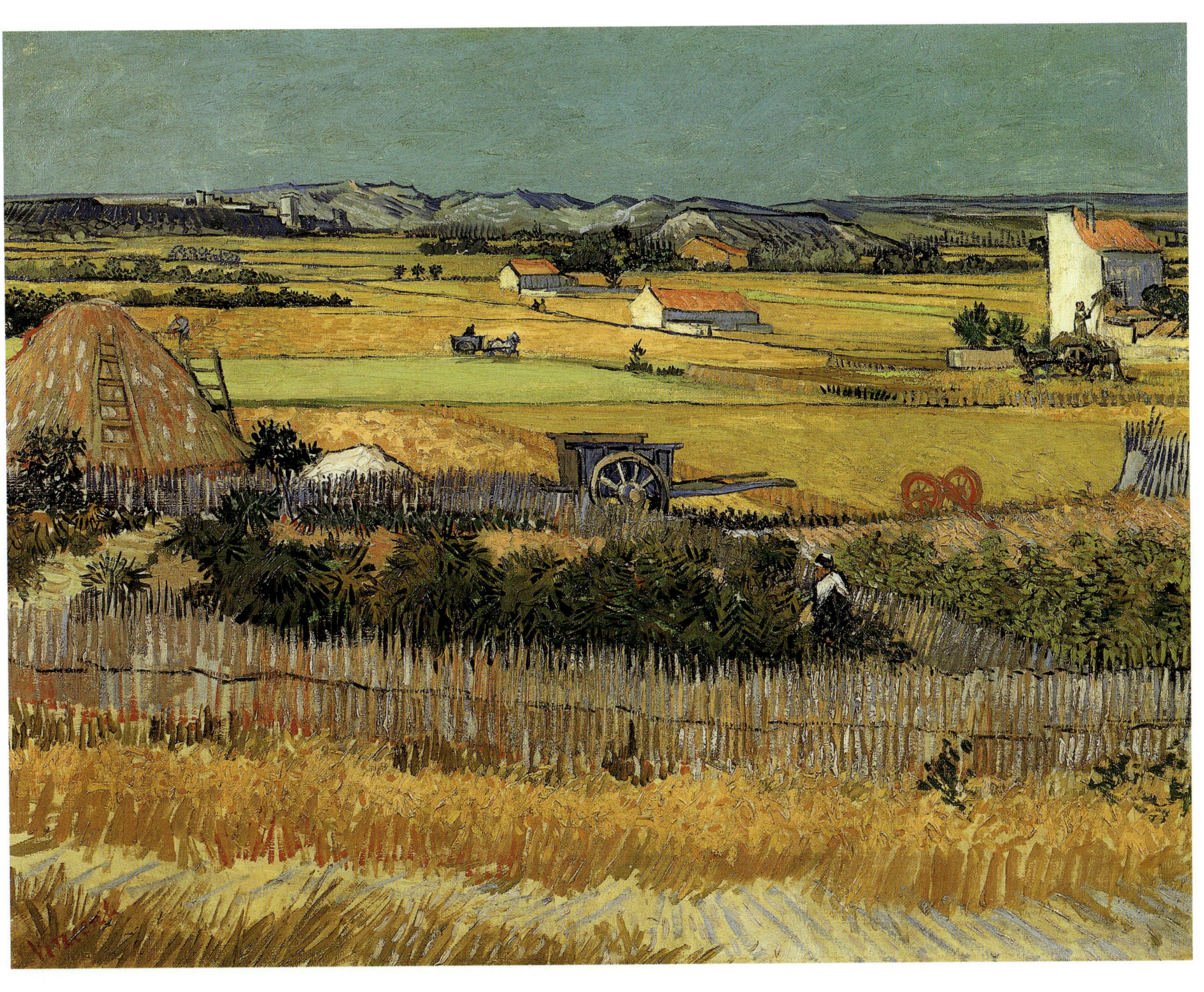

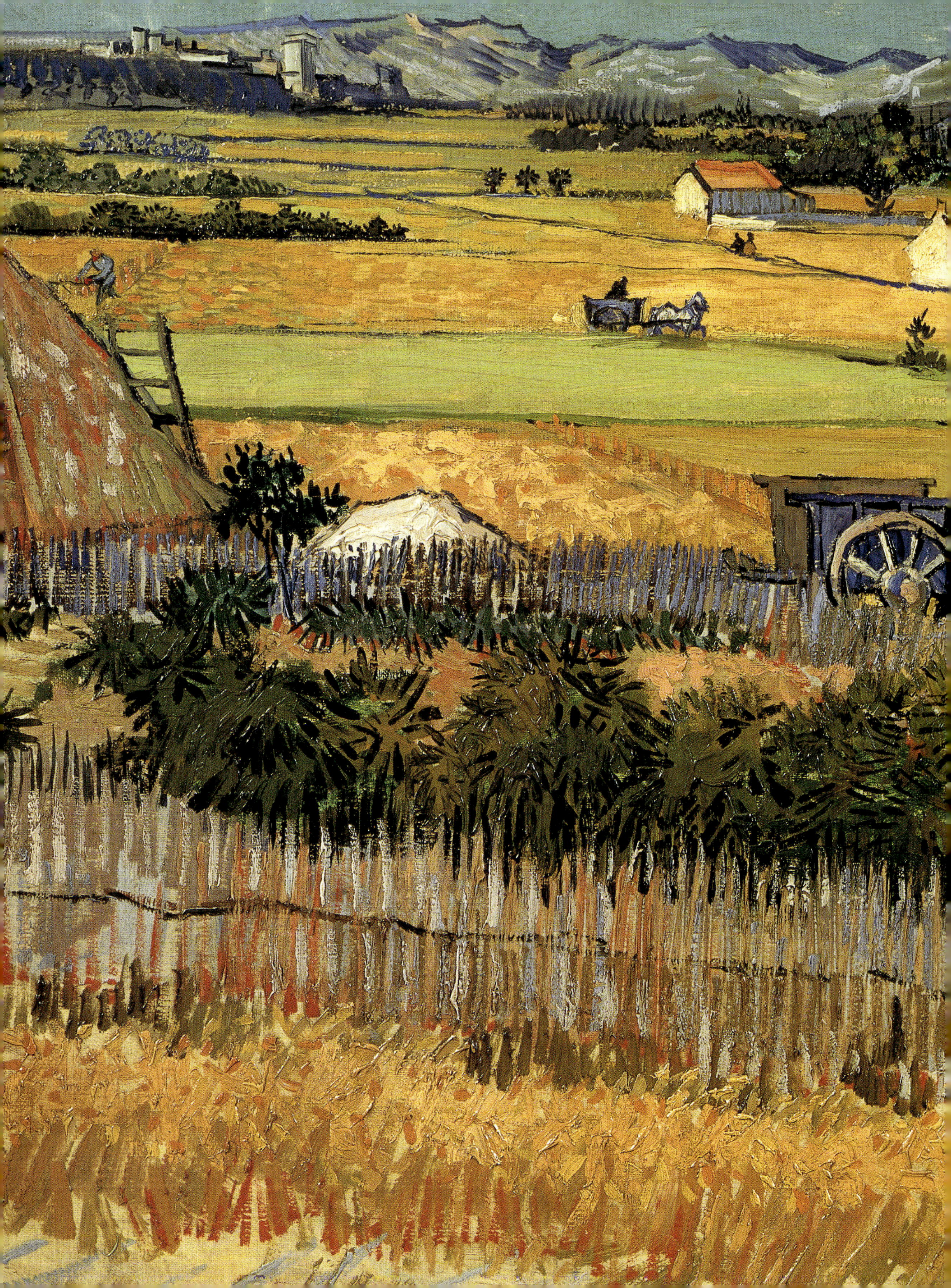

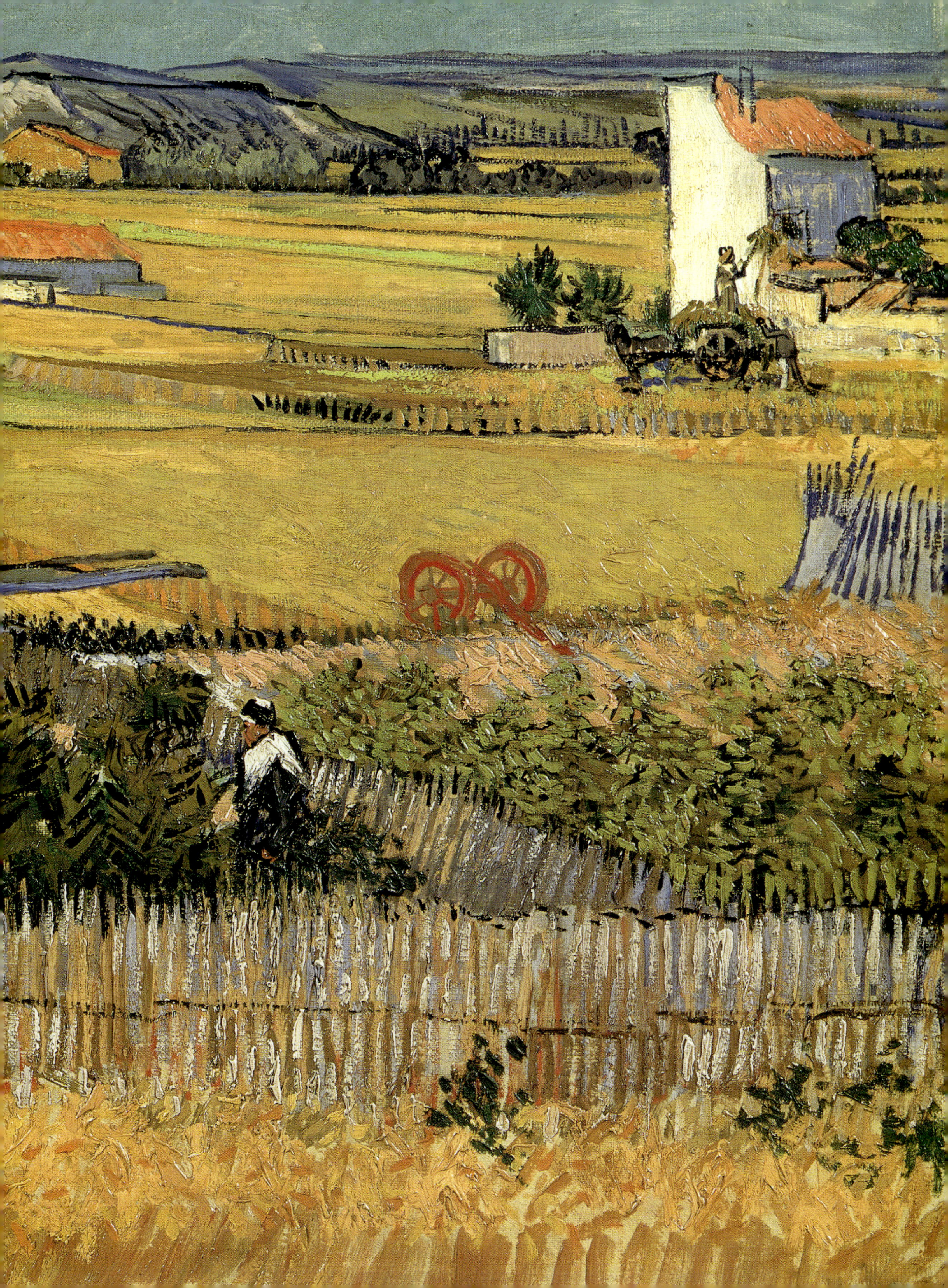

THE PAINTINGS AND PRINTS OF JEAN François Millet (1814–75) celebrated the peasant and the solemnities of the soil. In his letters, Vincent mentioned Millet more often than any other artist, and he visited places associated with his life. *The Sower* is Vincent's sprightly version of one of Millet's dignified figures.

As a young man, Vincent told an artist friend that "only after a year or a couple of years shall I have gained the ability to do a sower who is sowing." By this he meant *not posed.* He believed that goodwill was needed to paint figures, "and this to a high degree. One must have a warm sympathy with human beings, and go on having it, or the drawing will remain cold and insipid."

The clods of earth are painted, as Vincent put it, "for the most part frankly violet." The field of wheat beyond is "yellow ochre with a little carmine. The sky, chrome yellow, almost as bright as the sun itself, which is chrome yellow No. 1 with a little white, whereas the rest of the sky is chrome yellow No. 1 and 2 mixed. So very yellow." Vincent located the path and the sower off center, going in different directions, as a way of centering the sun. The painting "torments me," he wrote to Theo.

THE SOWER
ARLES, JUNE 1888
OIL ON CANVAS, 25 1/4 X 31 3/4 INCHES
KRÖLLER-MÜLLER MUSEUM, OTTERLO, THE NETHERLANDS

➢

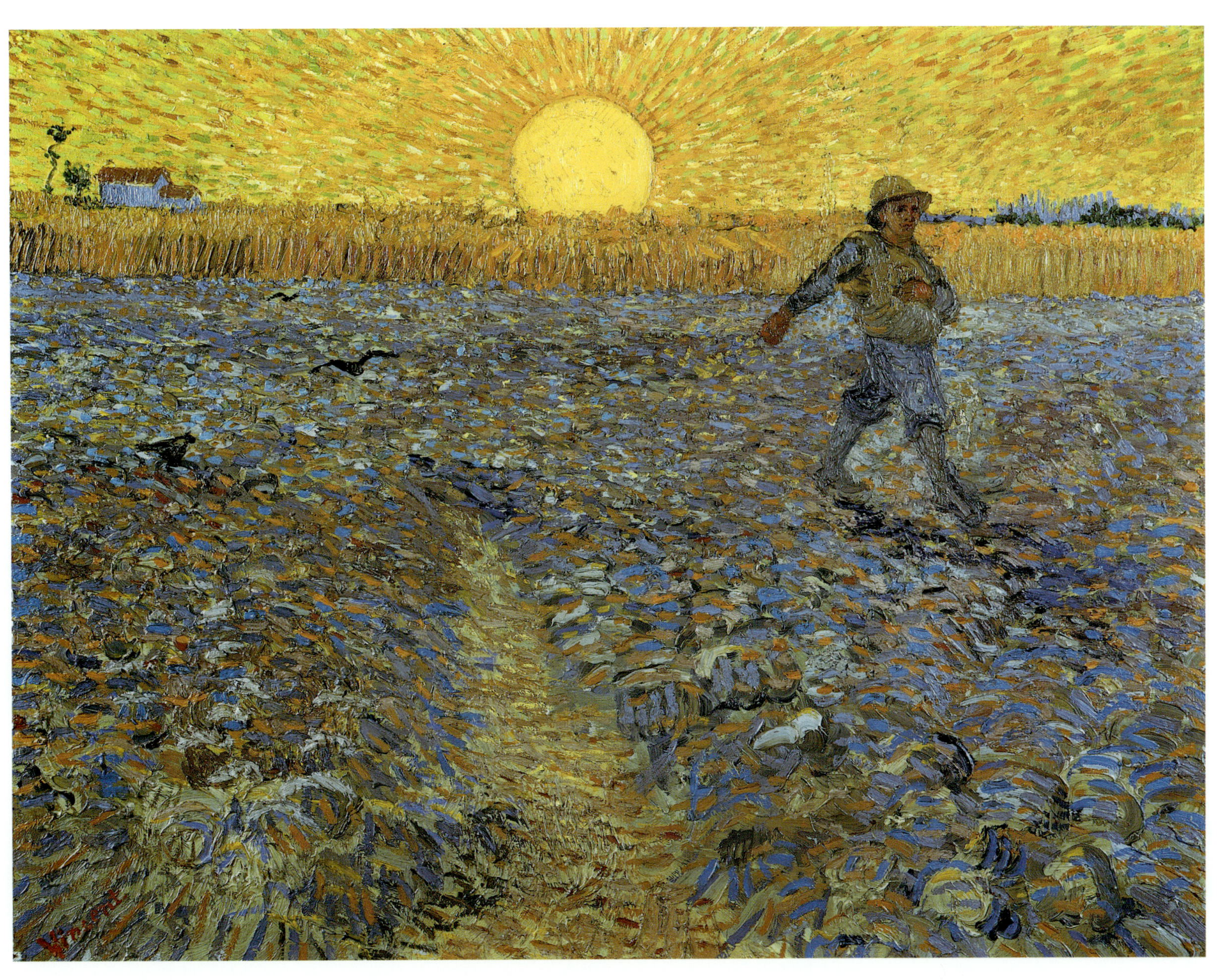

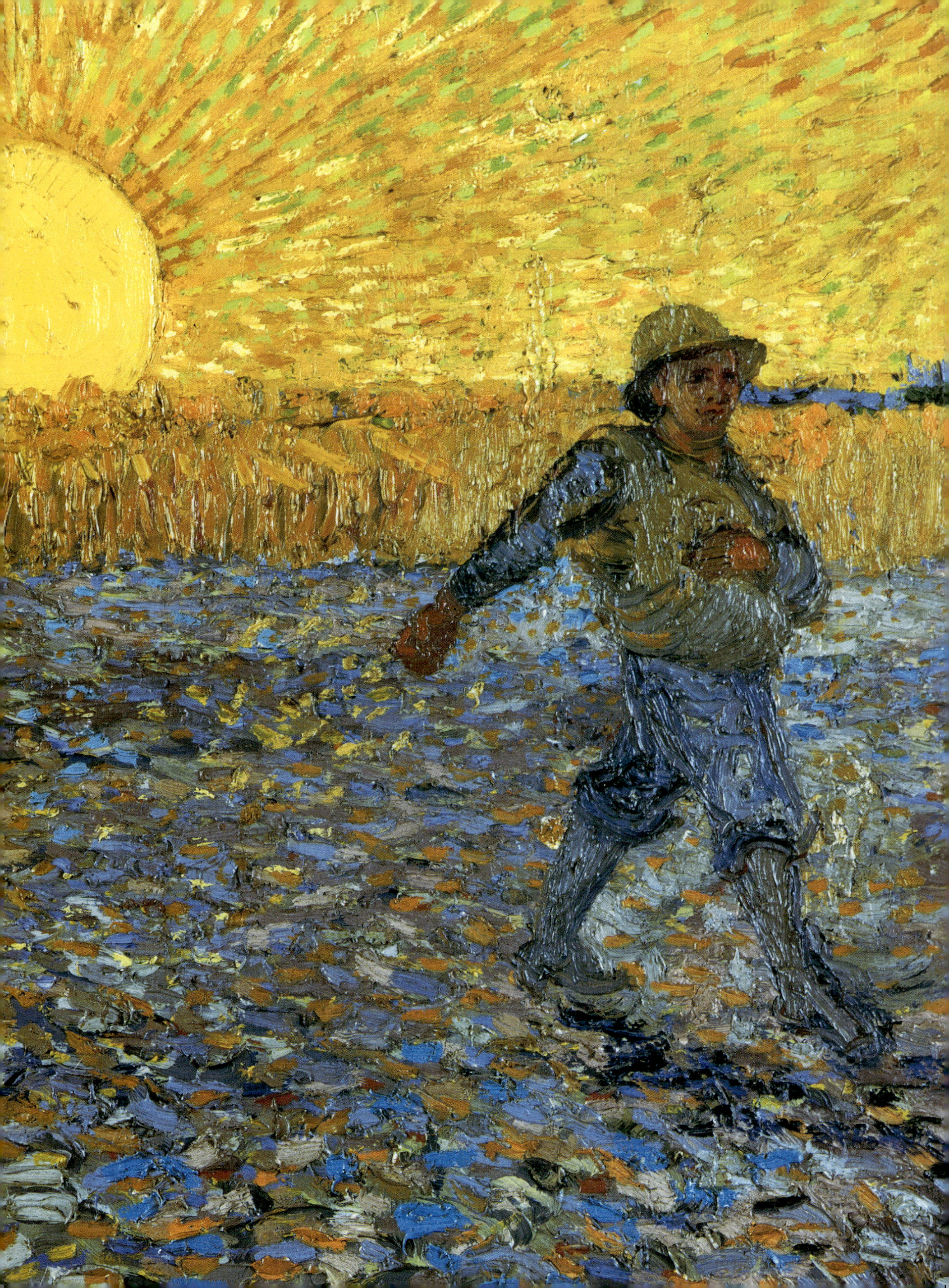

VINCENT CONCEDED THAT THE PAINTing of haystacks in a farmyard was "too bizarre." He accentuated the Haystacks' awkward presence by creating a likeness between them and the houses in the upper left background. They are painted the same golden color and both the ricks and the dwellings have green "windows." The contrast between straight lines and curved ones distinguishes the work of the farmer and the work of the builder and emphasizes a kinship between the two.

Because Vincent reduced shadows to a broken line along the base of each haystack, the piles of wheat do not appear solid. The tipped perspective—looking down at the earth and across to the ricks and houses—adds to the instability of the piles of hay. The one in the background, with ladders against it, appears to be levitating slightly and its partner might be about to skid forward.

The ricks were left over from the harvest of the year before. By the time the artist discovered them at the start of summer, weather had broken through the upper layers of hay.

Vincent deeply admired Millet's paintings in which haystacks seem to have emotional and symbolic connections to the peasants who live off the fields. Peasants are not seen in Vincent's painting, though the stepladders and nearby dwellings suggest that they might soon appear. In fact, the haystacks are most likely the subject of Vincent's painting solely for their shape and color.

HAYSTACKS IN PROVENCE
ARLES, JUNE 1888
OIL ON CANVAS, 28 3/4 X 36 1/2 INCHES
KRÖLLER-MÜLLER MUSEUM, OTTERLO, THE NETHERLANDS

➢

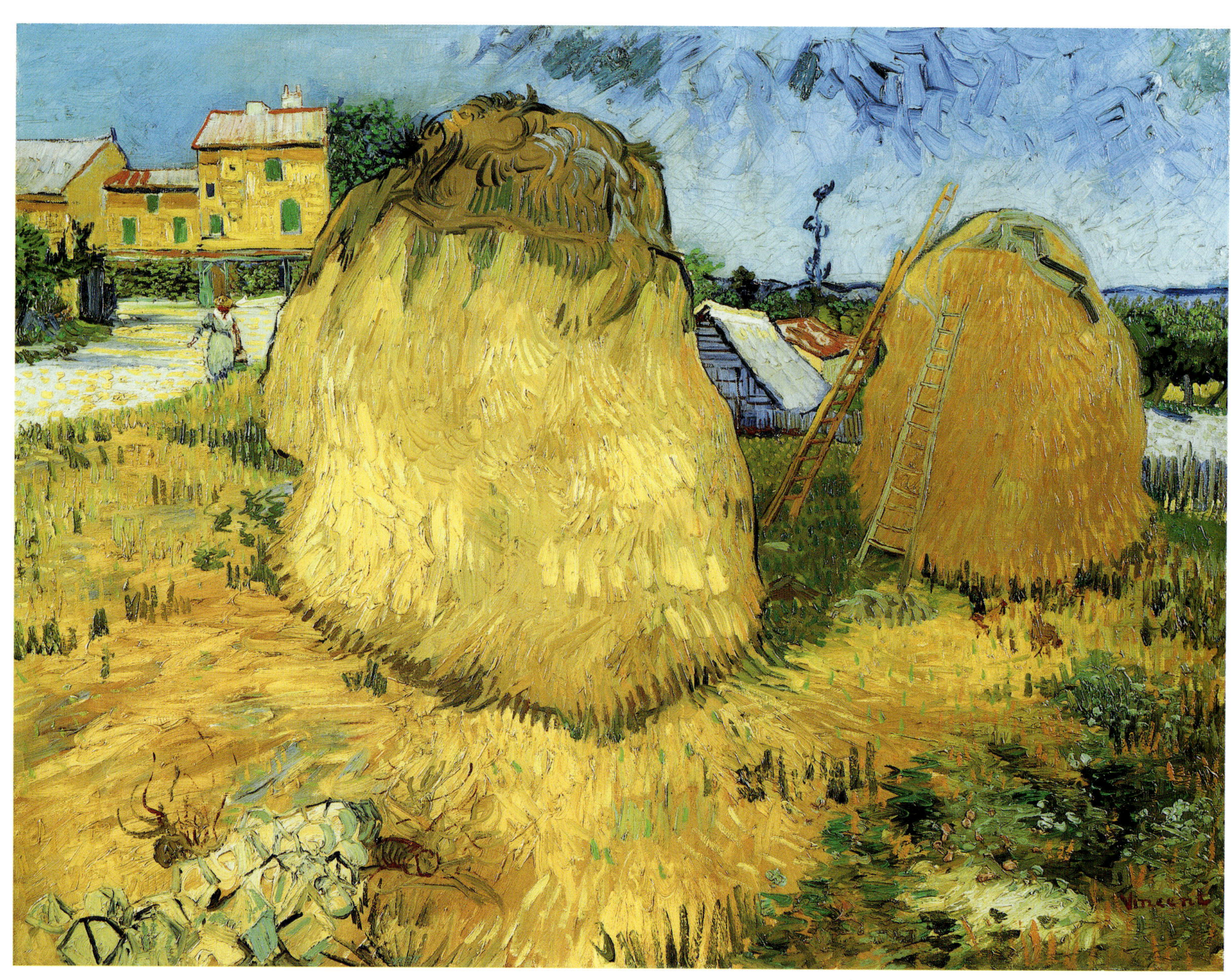
Vincent

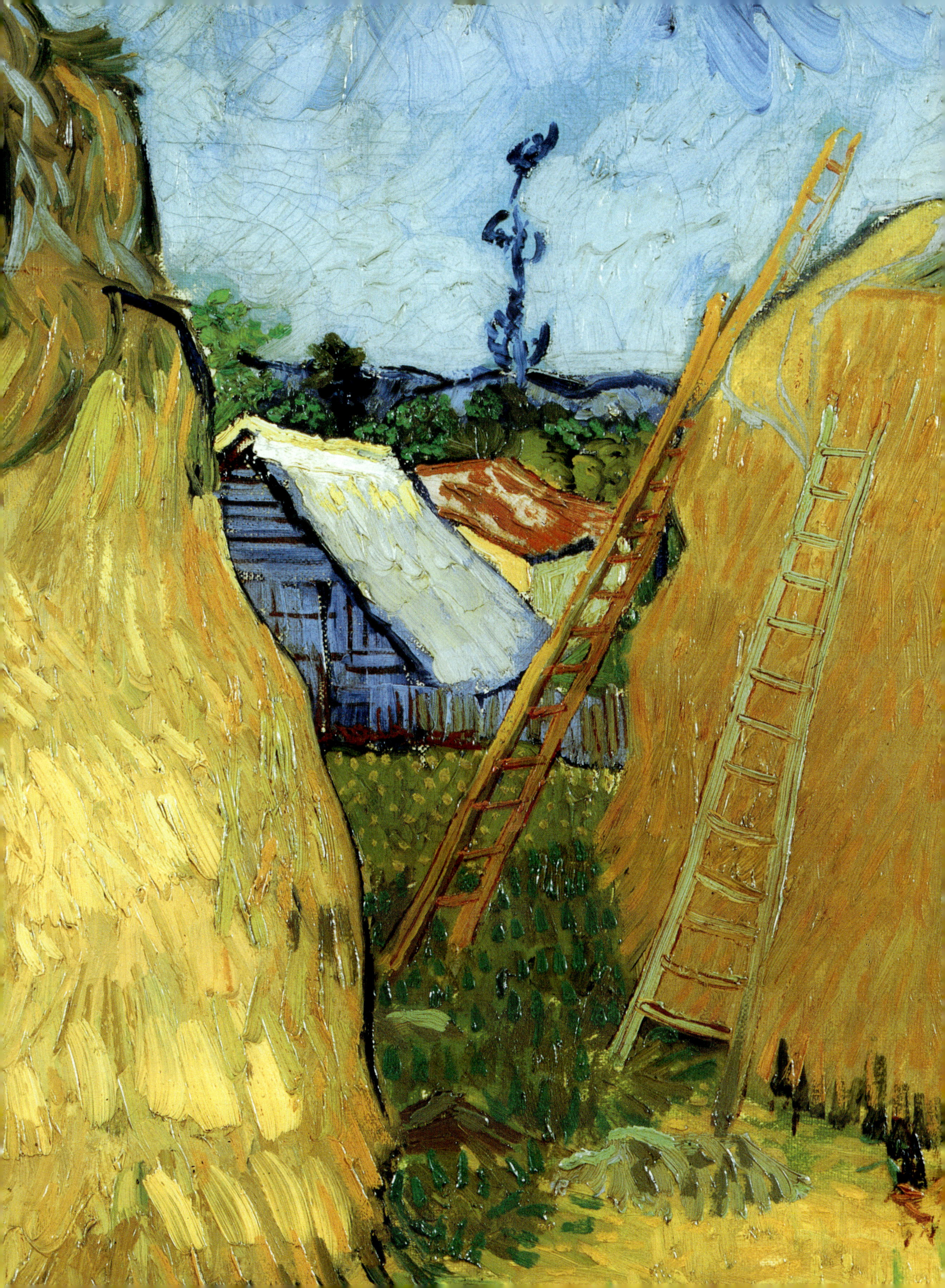

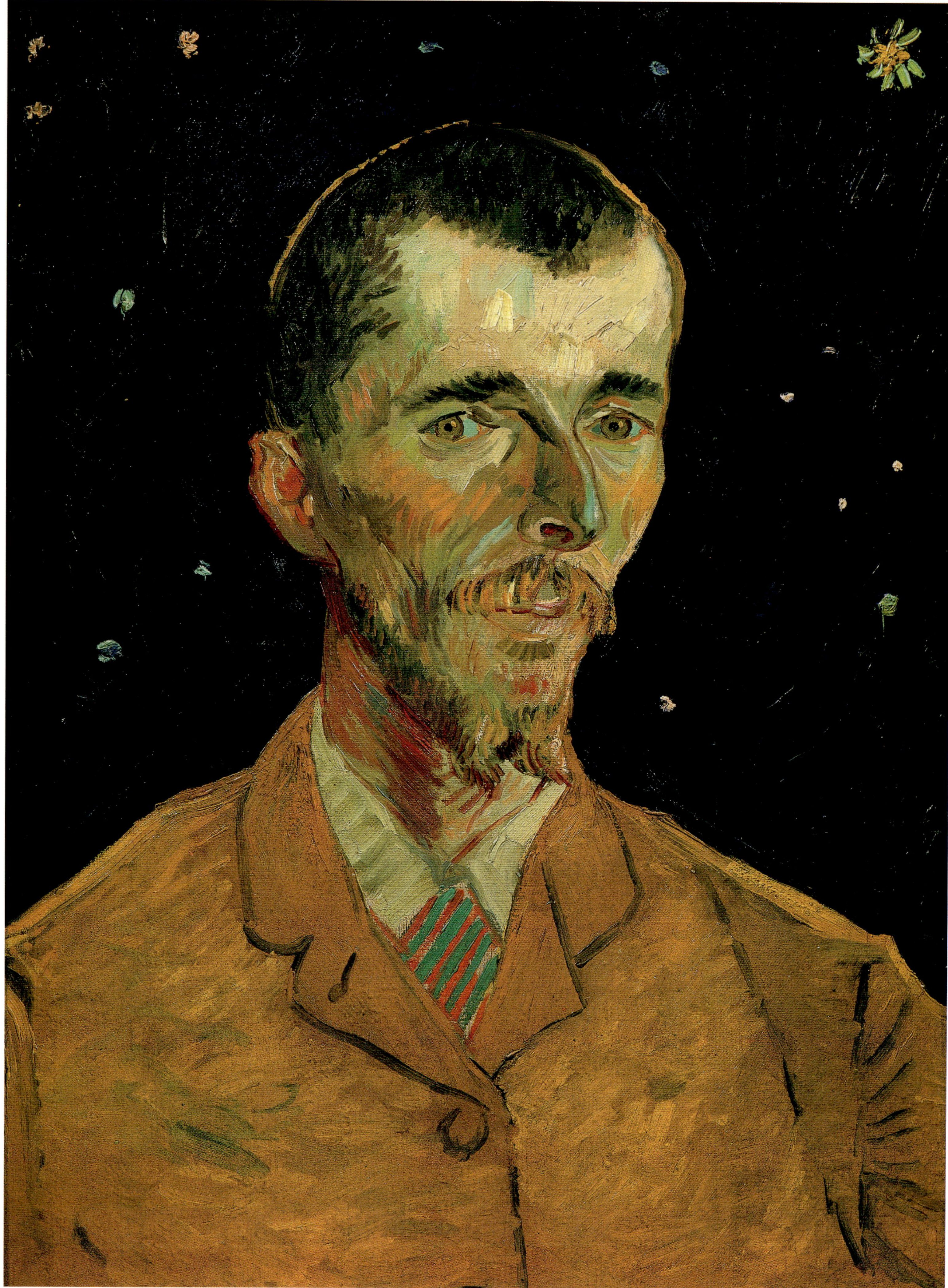

EUGÈNE BOCH (1855–1941), A BELGIAN writer and painter, lived at times in the village of Fontvielle near Arles. His sister, Anna, also an artist, purchased *The Red Vineyard,* the only painting by Vincent known to have been sold during his lifetime. Vincent admired Eugène, though he felt that as an artist he was too preoccupied with the technique of Impressionism to be himself. During their few times together, Boch's eyes were opened to new subject matter. Perhaps inspired by Vincent, he painted in the coal mining district where Vincent had once been a preacher.

When he first met Boch, Vincent wrote that he had an appearance he very much liked: "A face like a razor blade, green eyes, and a touch of distinction." Later, without mentioning his name, he told Theo of an artist friend "who dreams great dreams, who works as the nightingale sings," who most certainly had to be Boch.

Boch sat twice in one day for Vincent and the result was The Poet, a picture Vincent said he had envisioned for a long time. Imagining the painting before he ever began it, he told Theo he would substitute the ordinary background for "infinity...of the richest, most intense blue that I can contrive, and by this simple combination of the bright head against the rich blue background, I get a mysterious effect, like a star in the depths of an azure sky."

PORTRAIT OF EUGÈNE BOCH
ARLES, SEPTEMBER 1888
OIL ON CANVAS, 23 1/4 X 17 3/4 INCHES
MUSÉE D'ORSAY, PARIS/ART RESOURCE, NEW YORK

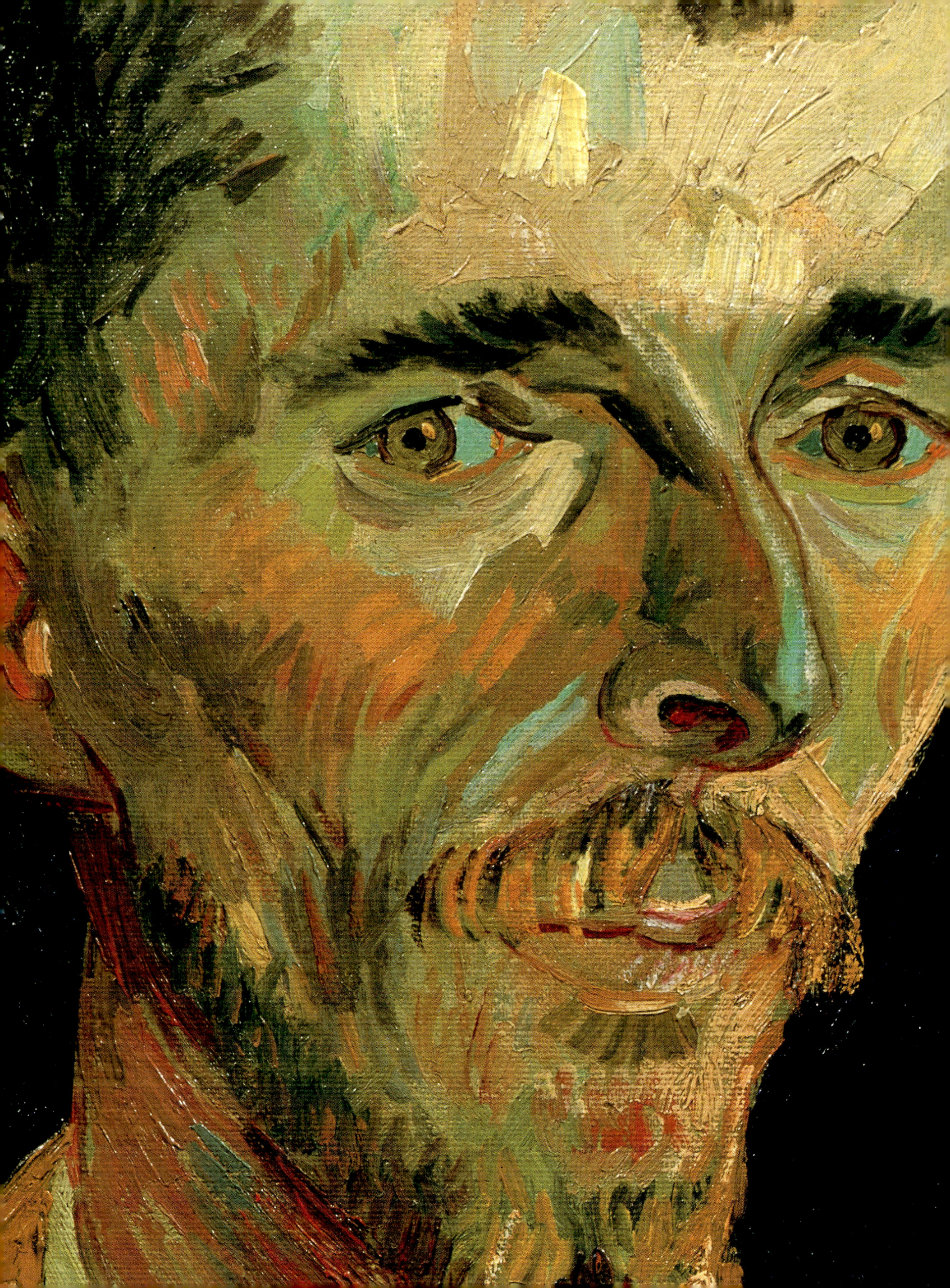

VINCENT OFTEN ATE BY GASLIGHT IN the night café. He explained to Theo that it was a fairly common type of restaurant that stayed open all night, where "[n]ight prowlers can take refuge...when they have no money to pay for a lodging. He described the room as very queer...gray all over; the floor is of gray bitumen like a street pavement, gray paper on the walls."

Painting the night café was on Vincent's mind for a month before he began, and he seemed elated as he started the job. "To the great joy of the landlord...of the visiting night prowlers and of myself, for three nights running I sat up to paint and went to bed during the day." He changed every color he saw. "I have tried to express the terrible passions of humanity by means of red and green....[T]he café is a place where one can ruin oneself, run mad, or commit a crime." He called the place "a devil's furnace of pale sulphur."

"The clash and contrast of the most alien reds and greens" is an environment of Vincent's imagination, not of fact. It is not the view of "the stereoscopic realist," as he put it, but of an expressionist whose work, decades later, would excite another generation of "ardent temperaments." The aureoles emanating from the kerosene jets, however, represent an optical phenomenon associated with Vincent's lack of sleep during the long night hours at his canvas in the café. The tipped up floorboards are pictured through a Japanese perspective.

THE NIGHT CAFÉ IN THE PLACE LAMARTINE IN ARLES
Arles, September 1888
Oil on canvas, 27 1/2 x 35 inches
Yale University Art Gallery
Bequest of Stephen Carlton Clark, B.A. 1903

➢

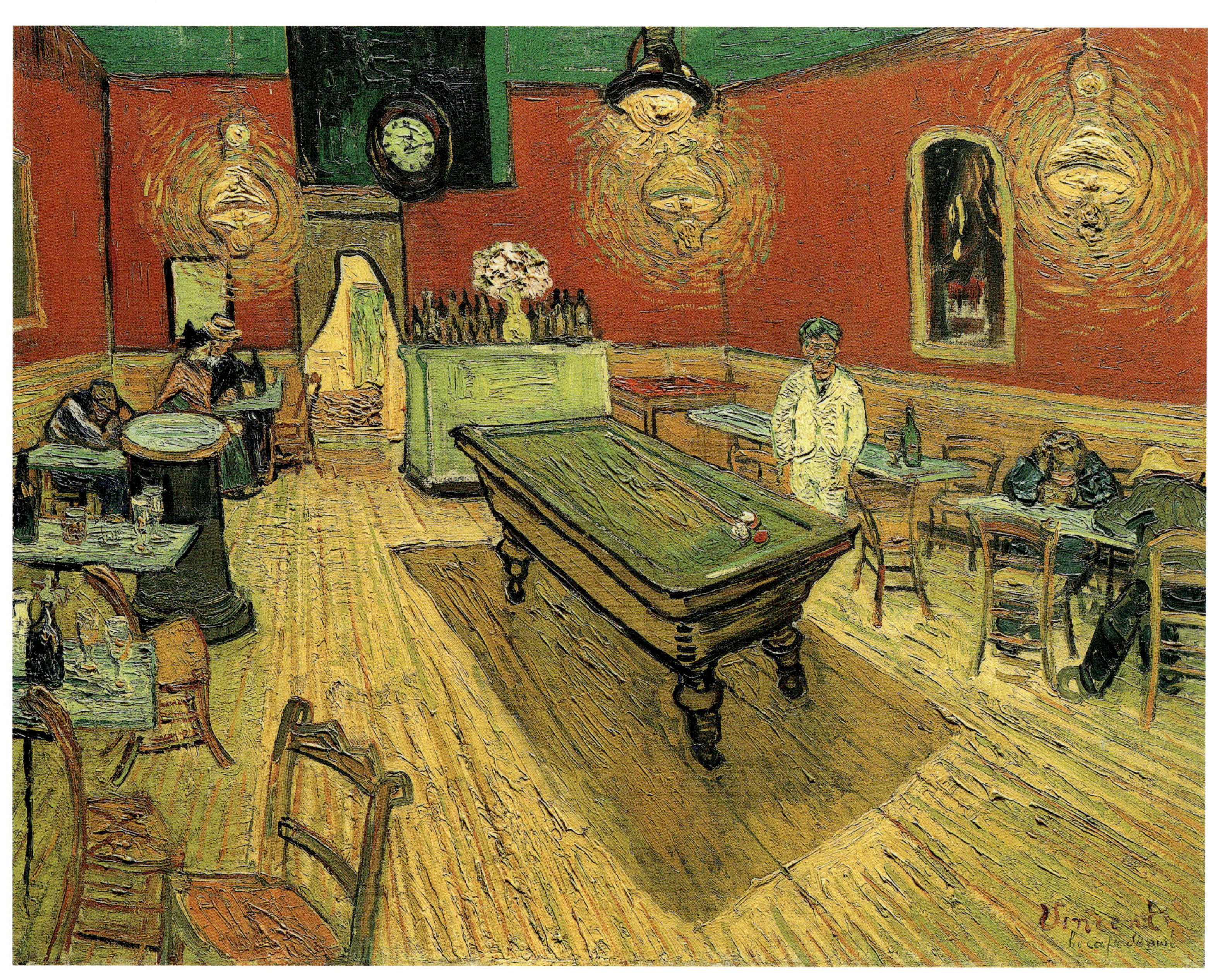
Vincent

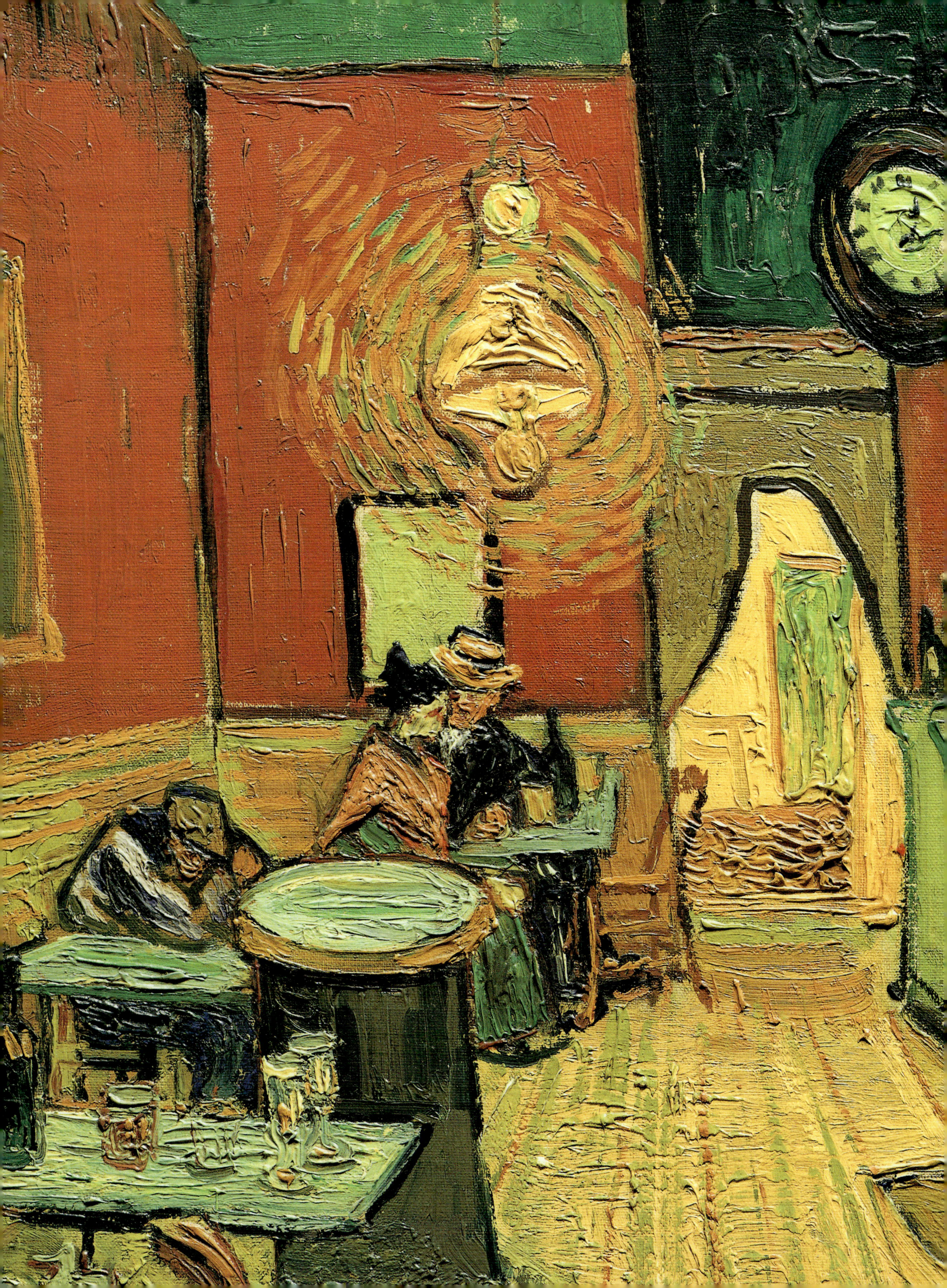

VINCENT HAD THOUGHT ABOUT PAINTing a starry night for months. "It is something I should like to try to do," he wrote to one of his artist friends. The painting shows the town of Arles, sputtering with "red gold and bronzed green" gas jets and their "ruthless" reflections in the blue river. Above is Ursa Major, the constellation known as the Great Bear, "a sparkling of pink and green on the cobalt blue field of the night sky."

Small boats go from the town to the green projection of land at the bottom of the painting where a man and a woman walk from the mooring. The artist viewed them from above, perhaps through a second-floor window of an inn or a night café. When Vincent wandered after dark looking for night subjects, he carried his usual gear plus a supply of candles. If he decided to paint in the open air, he lit his work by securing candles to the brim of his straw hat and along the top edge of his canvas. But Vincent wrote that he painted this scene by the light of a gas jet.

Vincent used a composition that he had probably seen in Dutch seventeenth-century paintings, for it was a standard format for views of towns across a body of water. He wrapped the river around the triangular spit and stretched the town into a gentle arc so all of it can be seen. This panorama left room for an immense sky that manages not to dwarf anything—even the couple in the foreground.

STARRY NIGHT OVER THE RHONE
ARLES, SEPTEMBER 1888
OIL ON CANVAS, 28 1/2 X 36 1/4 INCHES
ON LOAN TO MUSÉE D'ORSAY, PARIS/ART RESOURCE, NEW YORK

➢

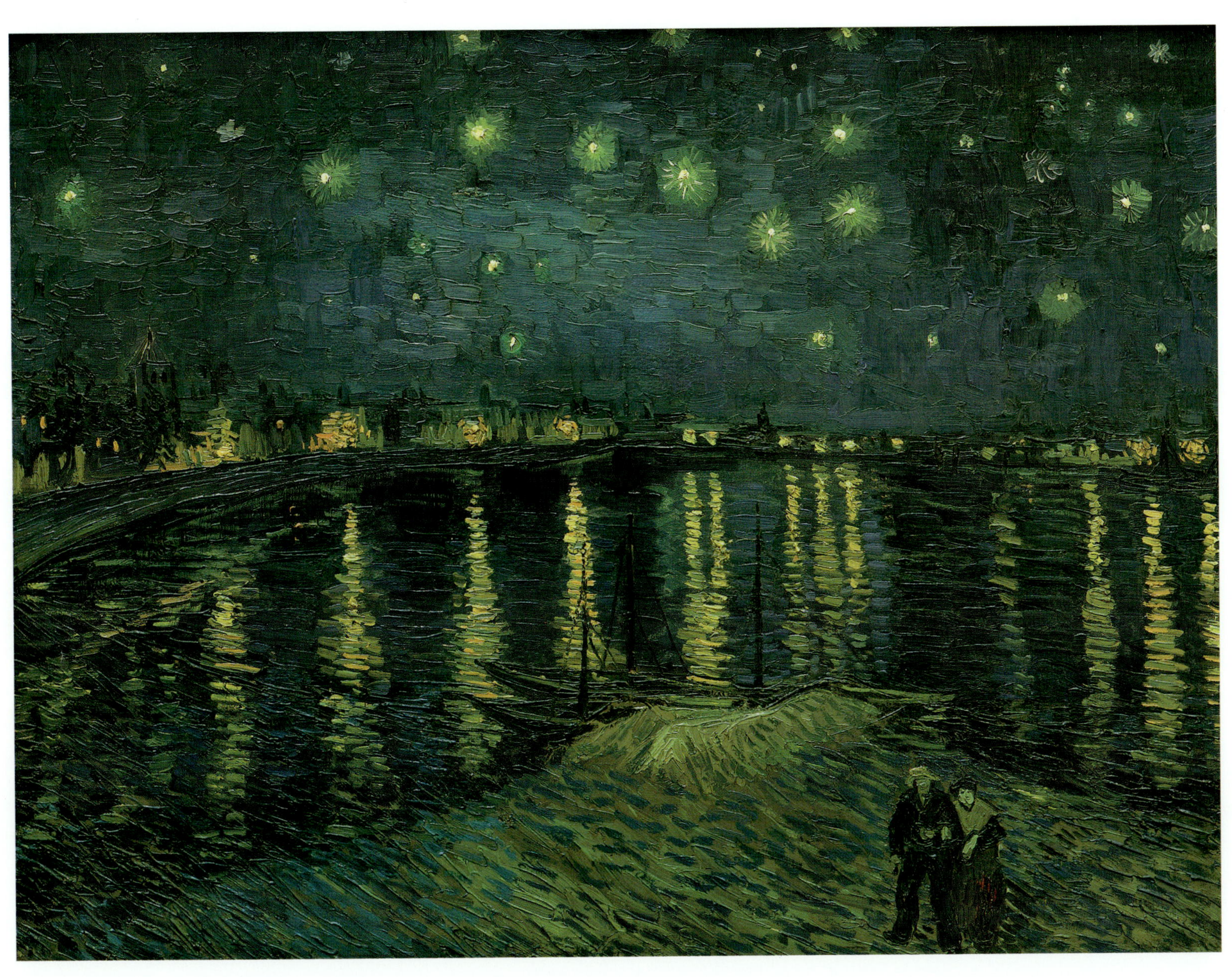

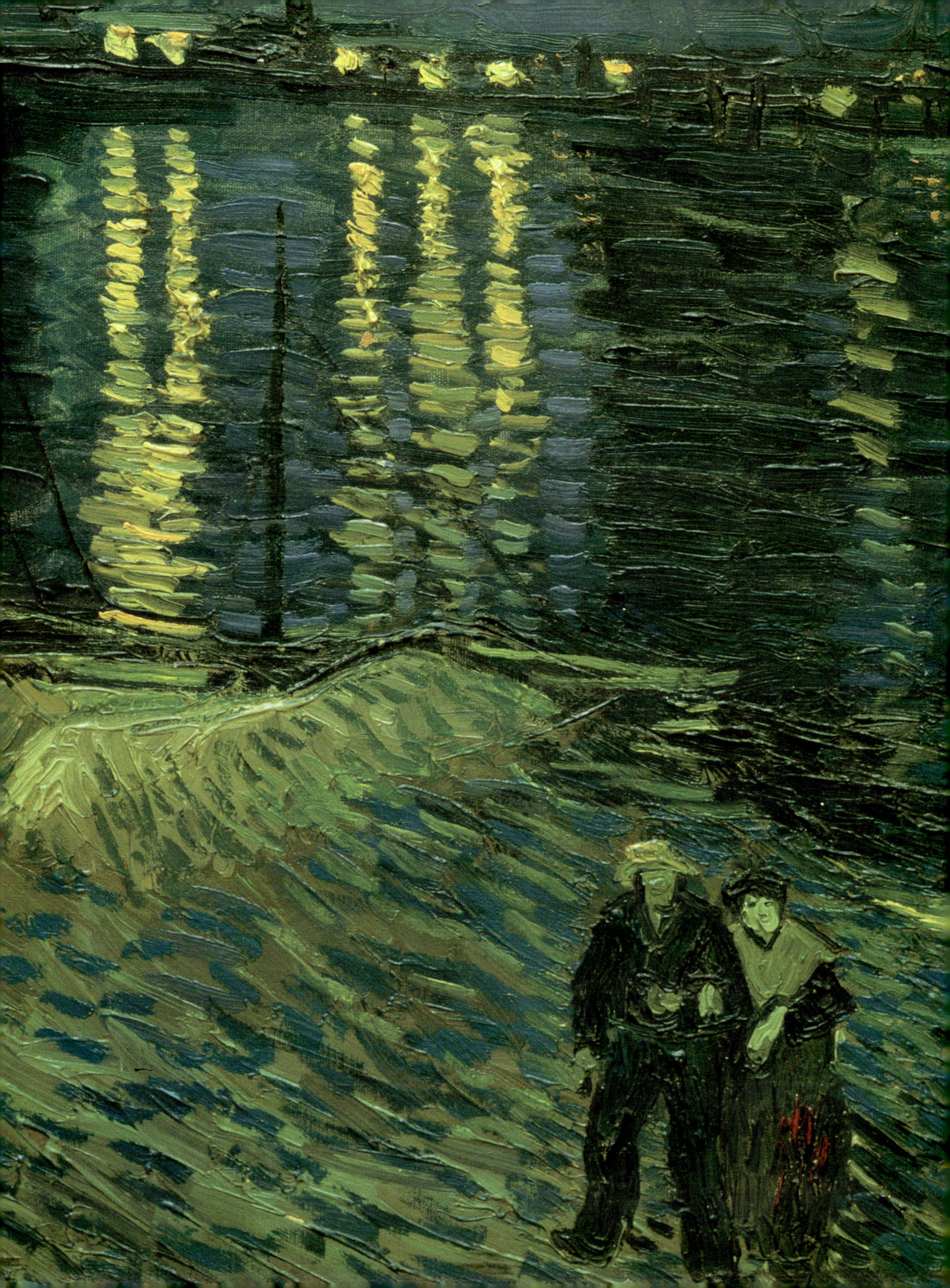

VINCENT TOLD HIS SISTER WILHELMIEN that she would probably think the study of his "empty bedroom with a wooden bedstead, the most unbeautiful thing of all." To Vincent, however, his room in Arles was immensely important. It was in the only house he ever had for himself, the "yellow house" that would welcome Gauguin, Signac, and other artists seeking the sun. Vincent carefully furnished the rooms and decorated them with his own paintings and framed prints. As seen in this later version, his personal space seems to be inviting company. There are two chairs and two fluffy pillows on the bed, creating a place for the mate Vincent never had.

While he lived in the yellow house, Vincent painted over two hundred canvases and produced over a hundred drawings and watercolors—a body of work that many consider his best. He often felt "nearly half dead" from his work, but he would sleep "sixteen hours at a stretch" and feel considerably restored. Just eleven months after creating the study of his bedroom, he painted two copies of it, though at this time his studio was a cell in a mental hospital at Saint-Rémy-de-Provence, near Arles. This version of his bedroom differs from the original study only in being more colorful. The tipped-up floor, outlined objects, and lack of shadows were conventions from Japanese prints that Vincent often utilized. They allowed more to show and they developed out of Vincent's way of seeing, as he wrote: "It's looking at things for a long time that ripens you and gives you deeper understanding."

VINCENT'S BEDROOM IN ARLES
SAINT-RÉMY, SEPTEMBER 1889
OIL ON CANVAS, 22 1/4 X 29 INCHES
MUSÉE D'ORSAY, PARIS/ART RESOURCE, NEW YORK

➣

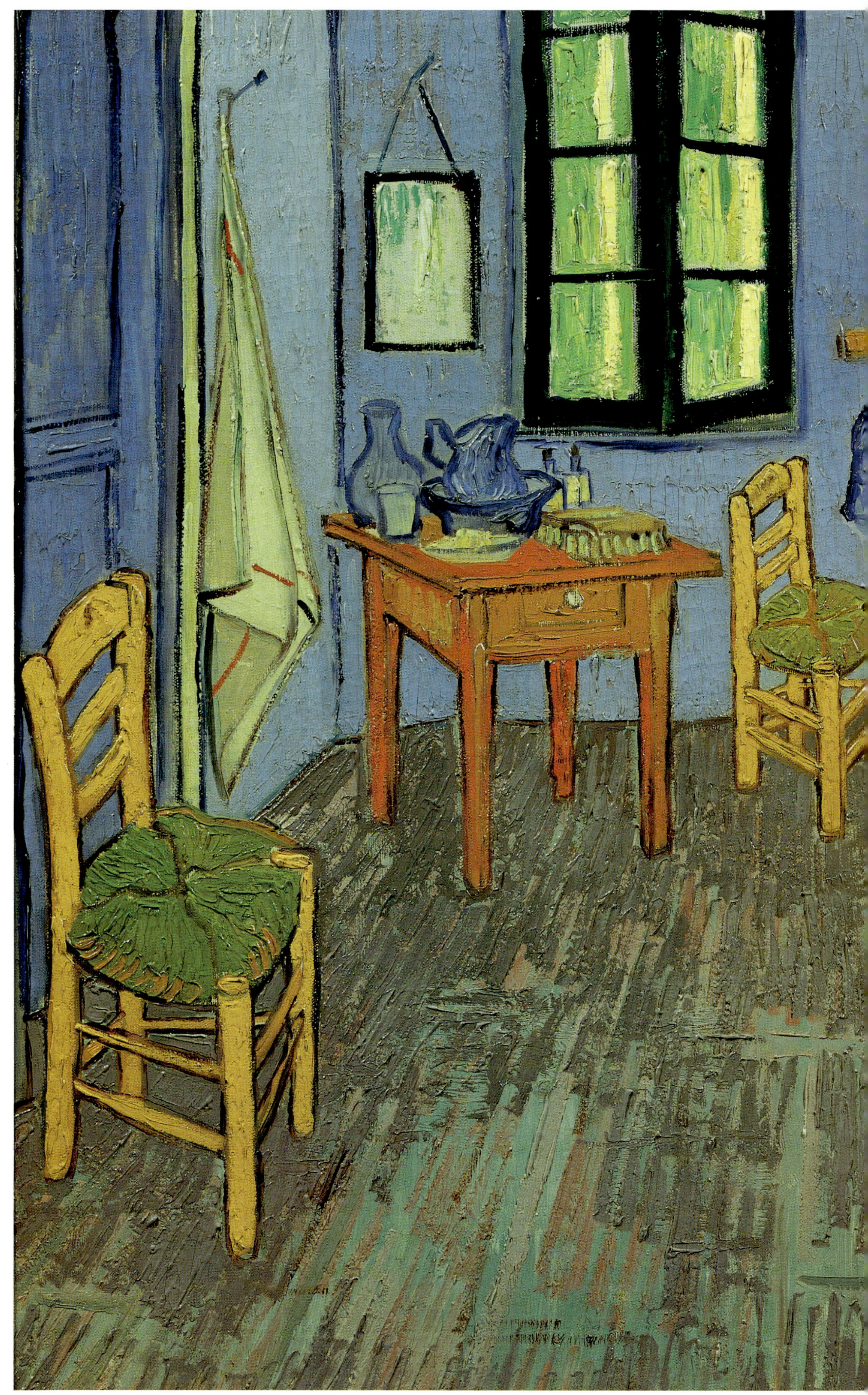

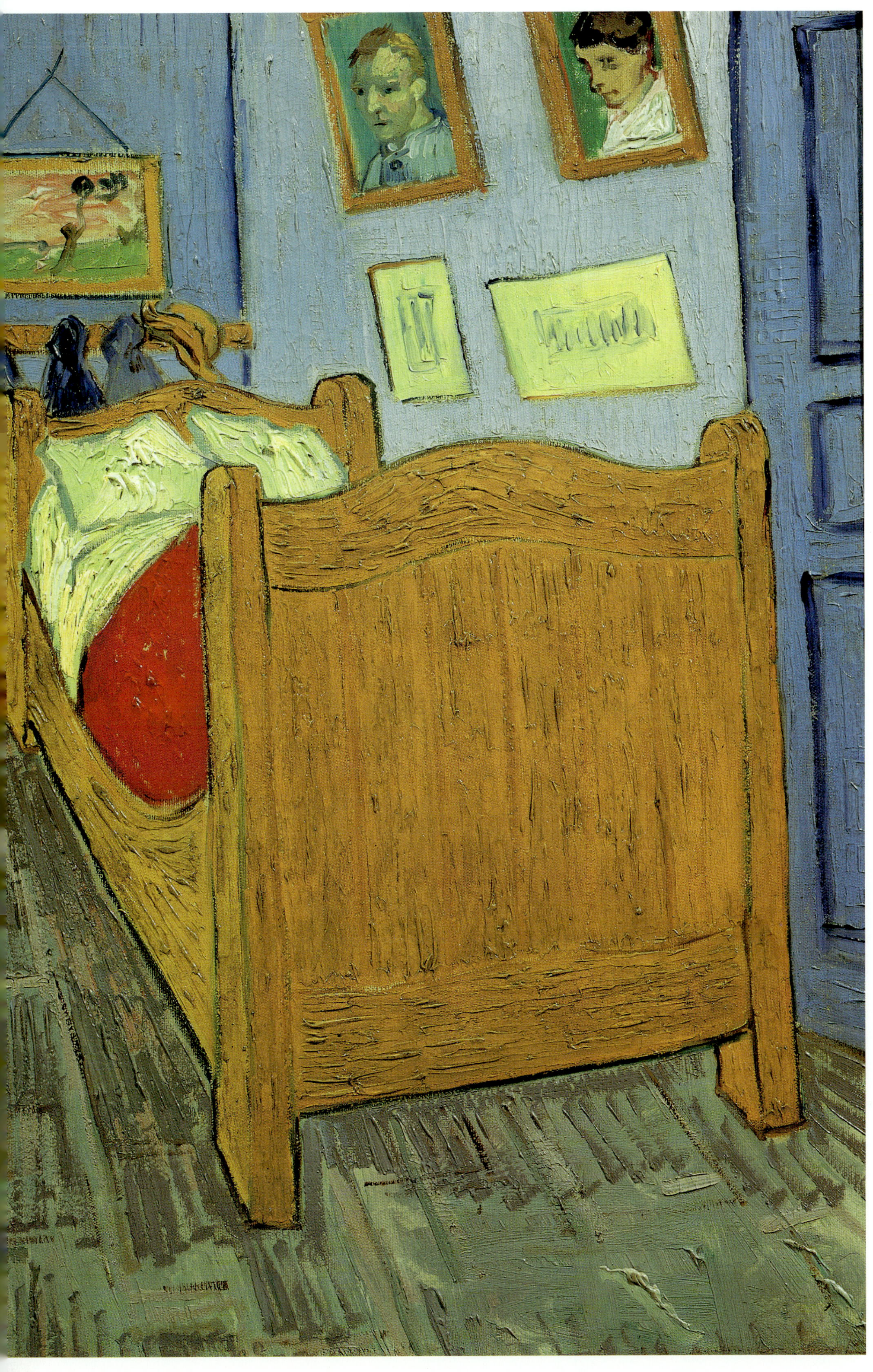

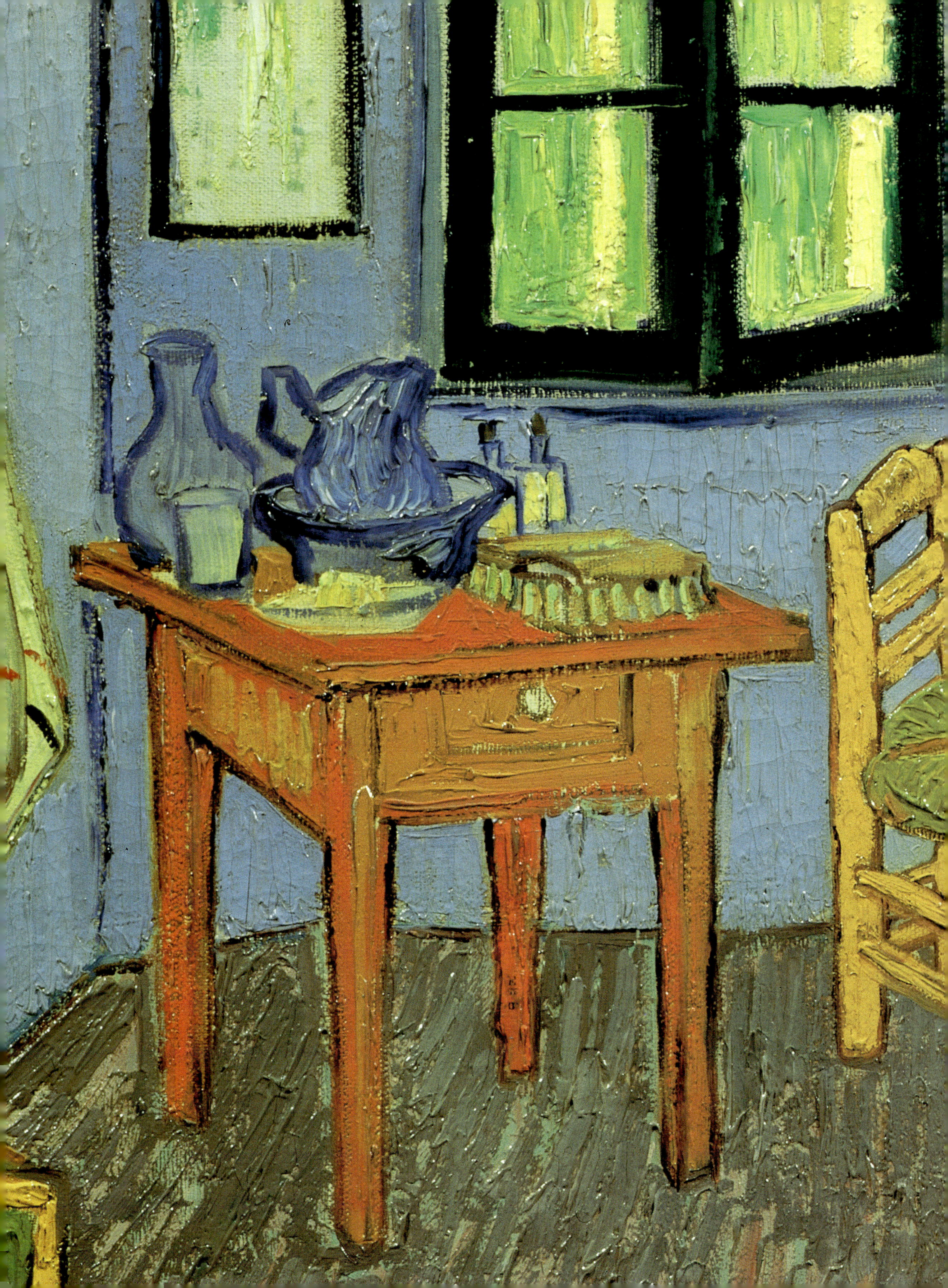

PAUL GAUGUIN LIVED WITH VINCENT for two months in 1888, and their first painting excursion was to the Alyscamps—the ancient Roman burial place on the south side of Arles. Gauguin liked Vincent's rendition of the avenue of sarcophagi, the guardian poplar trees shedding their leaves, and the orange earth. Gaugin had recently done a painting with red earth, which perhaps was among the ones he brought for Vincent to see. Gauguin's red was symbolic while Vincent's orange represented a carpet of autumn leaves. Both men had dedicated themselves to art later in life and were self-trained in painting, and both of them began to explore expressive and symbolic uses of color at about the same time. An egoist, Gauguin probably took the role of the teacher as they experimented together. Vincent would gladly have served as acolyte and pupil.

The Alyscamps (Elysian fields) dates from the period when Arles was one of the wealthiest cities of the Roman Empire. A number of outstanding ruins survived, but Vincent painted only this one. Perhaps the choice was Gauguin's. An embankment allowed Vincent to paint the promenade and sarcophagi from above, casting the figures against an orange and yellow background. They seem to float in the color-charged environment for they cast no shadows. The man in the tailcoat is old, Vincent wrote, and the woman is "as fat and round as a ball." The embankment on the right side of the scene, the black outlines of the lilac-colored trees, the edge of the road, and the horizon line in the upper left corner all crisscross, confusing but not destroying the sense of a foreground, middle ground, and background.

LES ALYSCAMPS, FALLING AUTUMN LEAVES
ARLES, NOVEMBER 1888
OIL ON CANVAS, 28 3/4 X 36 1/4 INCHES
KRÖLLER-MÜLLER MUSEUM, OTTERLO, THE NETHERLANDS

➢

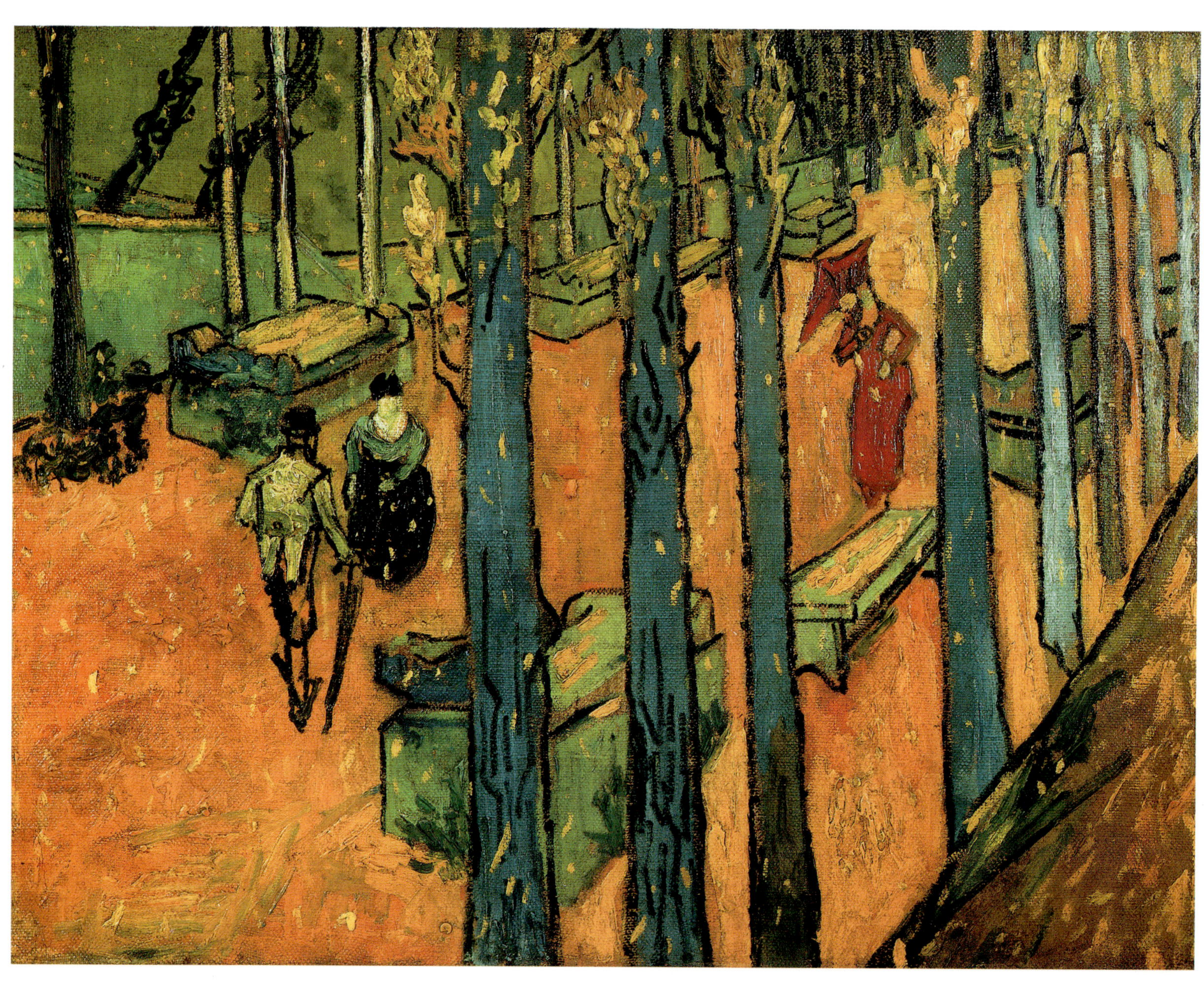

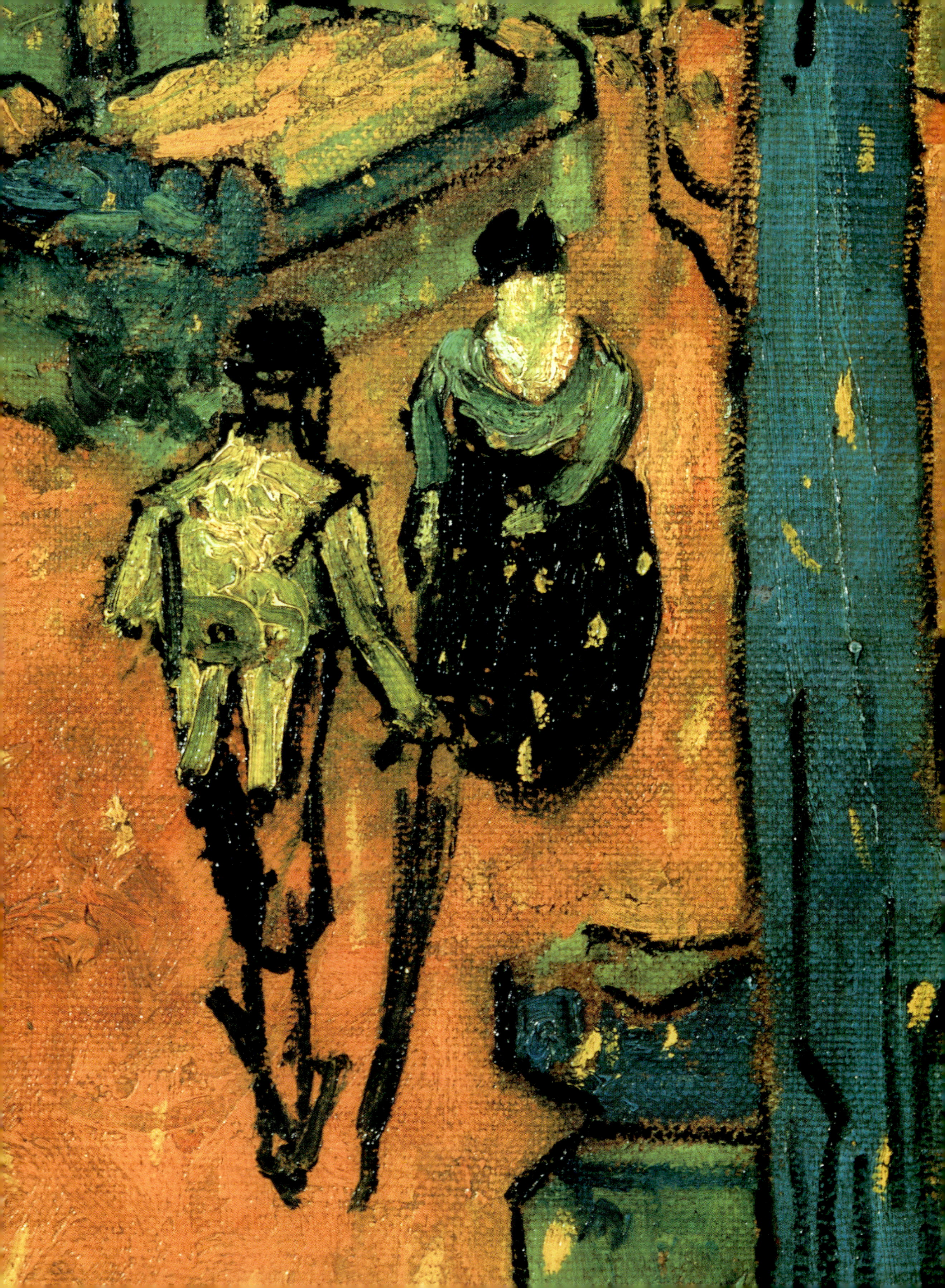

NEAR MONTMAJOUR, THE DESTINATION of fifty of his treks, Vincent fell upon a vineyard turned fiery red by the first frost of the season. The yellow sunlight, purple earth, and red foliage prompted him to paint it. While he worked on his canvas, more than a dozen laborers picked ripe grapes from the vines. They darted from vine to vine before the precious crop might be lost to an even colder chill than the last one. The vines had been held for frosting, a method that yields an exceptionally sweet dessert wine, but that also risks losing a harvest if the first winter blast is too severe.

Trees on the horizon leaning toward the harvest, the yellow sky, and the wet road define the shape of the vineyard as a cornucopia—a sign of richness and plenty. The workers are not affected by such a symbol; they are the same poor peasants Vincent knew in the potato fields. Their faces are hidden, details of their clothing are abbreviated, and their postures suggest backbreaking labor. Outlines around each of them seem to keep Vincent's fast-moving brush from blending them into the red of the vineyard. Representing their work in but a few strokes of the brush was Vincent's goal. At the start of his painting career, he wrote, "I should be desperate if my figures were correct....[M]y great longing is to learn to make those very incorrectnesses...those deviations, remodelings, changes in reality, so that they may become...truer than the literal truth."

THE RED VINEYARD
ARLES, NOVEMBER 1888
OIL ON CANVAS, 29 1/2 X 36 1/2 INCHES
PUSHKIN MUSEUM OF FINE ARTS, MOSCOW, RUSSIA/
ART RESOURCE, NEW YORK

➢

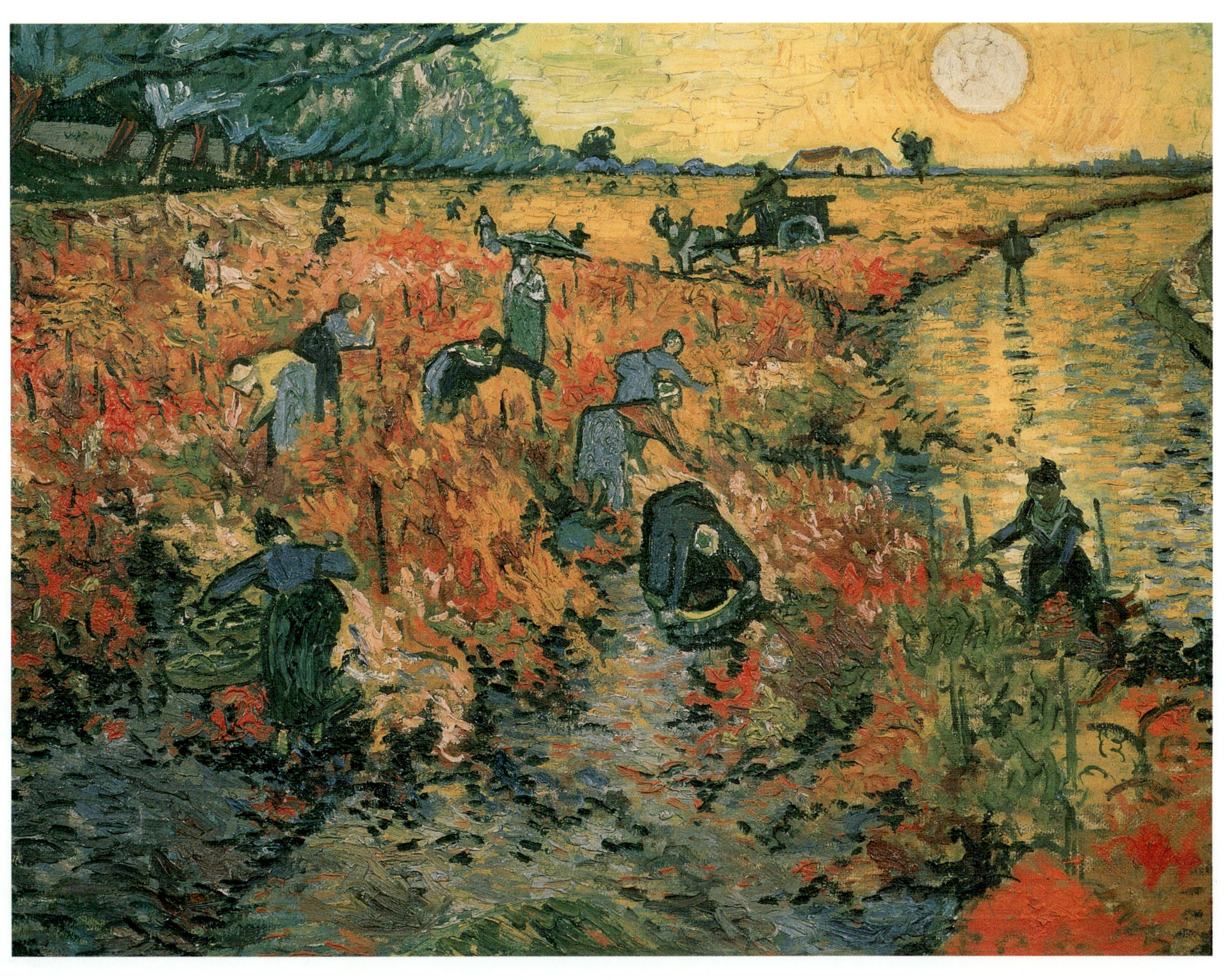

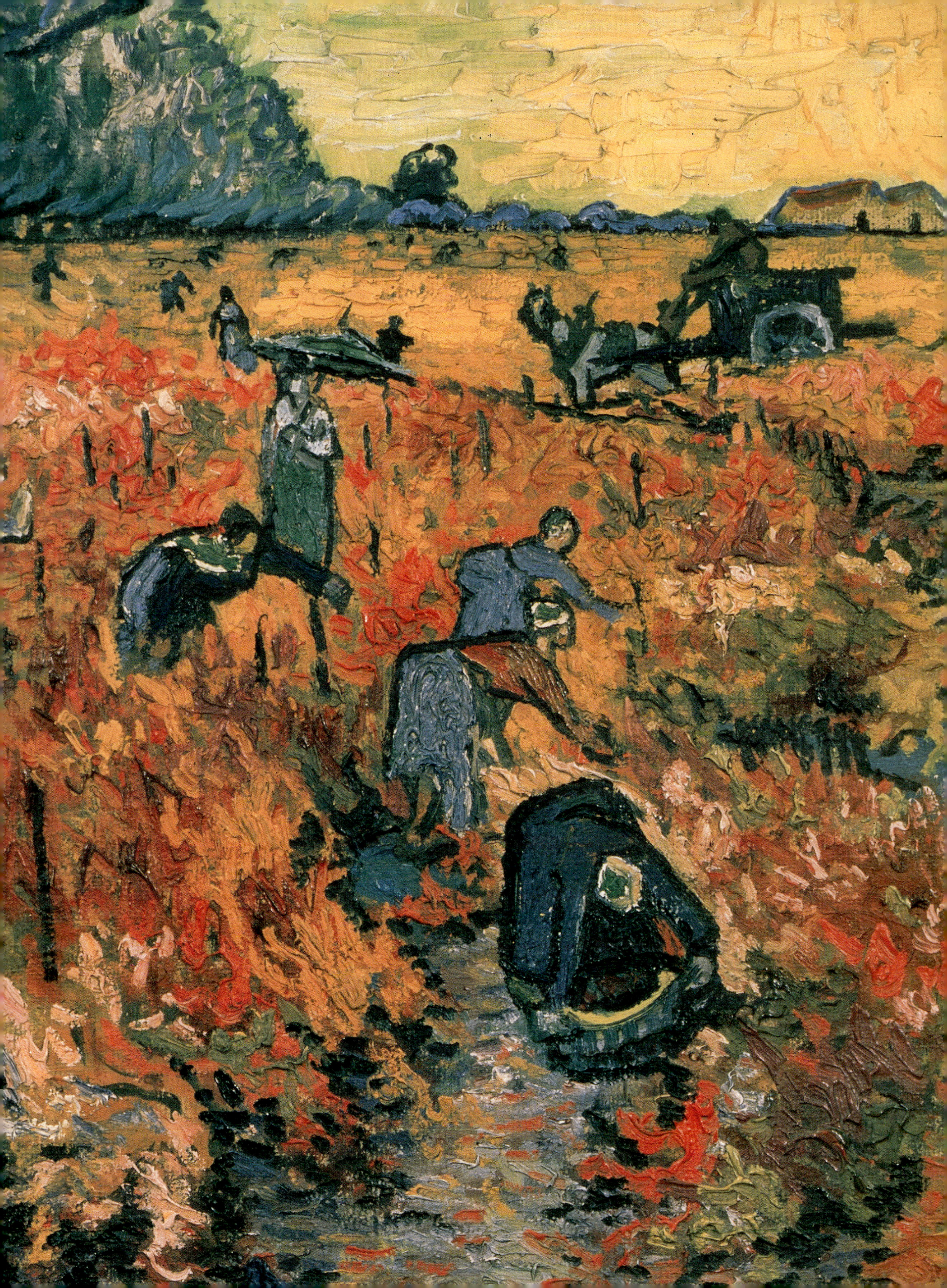

MANY OF GAUGUIN'S IDEAS RUBBED off on Vincent for he revered the overpowering painter. Never before had he thought of abandoning the facts of the visual world for those of memory, but here he determinedly rendered a garden as it might be seen in a dream, stranger than in reality.

In a long letter to Wilhelmien, the sister he called Wil, Vincent said that the picture is of the garden at Etten, a town where their father once worked as a minister. "Let us suppose that the two ladies out for a walk are you and our mother; let us even suppose that there is not the least, absolutely not the least vulgar and fatuous resemblance—yet the deliberate choice of the color, the somber violet with the blotch of violent citron yellow of the dahlias, suggests Mother's personality to me.... I don't know whether you can understand that one may make a poem only by arranging colors, in the same way that one can say comforting things in music."

The left side of the painting seems like an apparition, with patterns choking out all the air. Had the women not been anchored by the bright red lining of the umbrella carried by the younger one, they might have drifted from the canvas. The composition is brought back to earth by the gardener. She represents reality, but the path and beds beyond her are shaped and colored to echo the massing of the strange strollers.

MEMORY OF THE GARDEN AT ETTEN
ARLES, NOVEMBER 1888
OIL ON CANVAS, 29 X 36 1/2 INCHES
THE HERMITAGE, ST. PETERSBURG, RUSSIA/ART RESOURCE, NEW YORK

➢

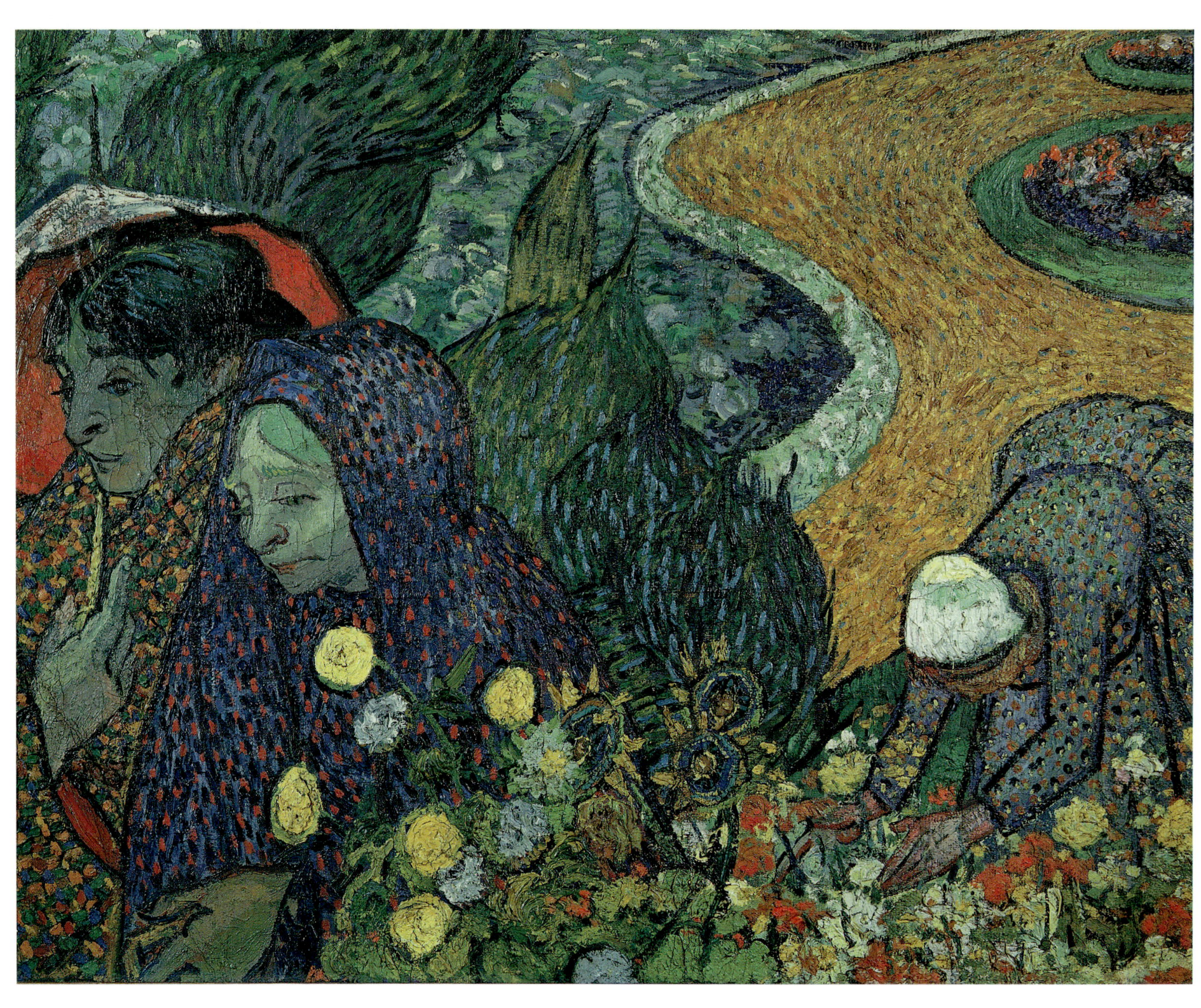

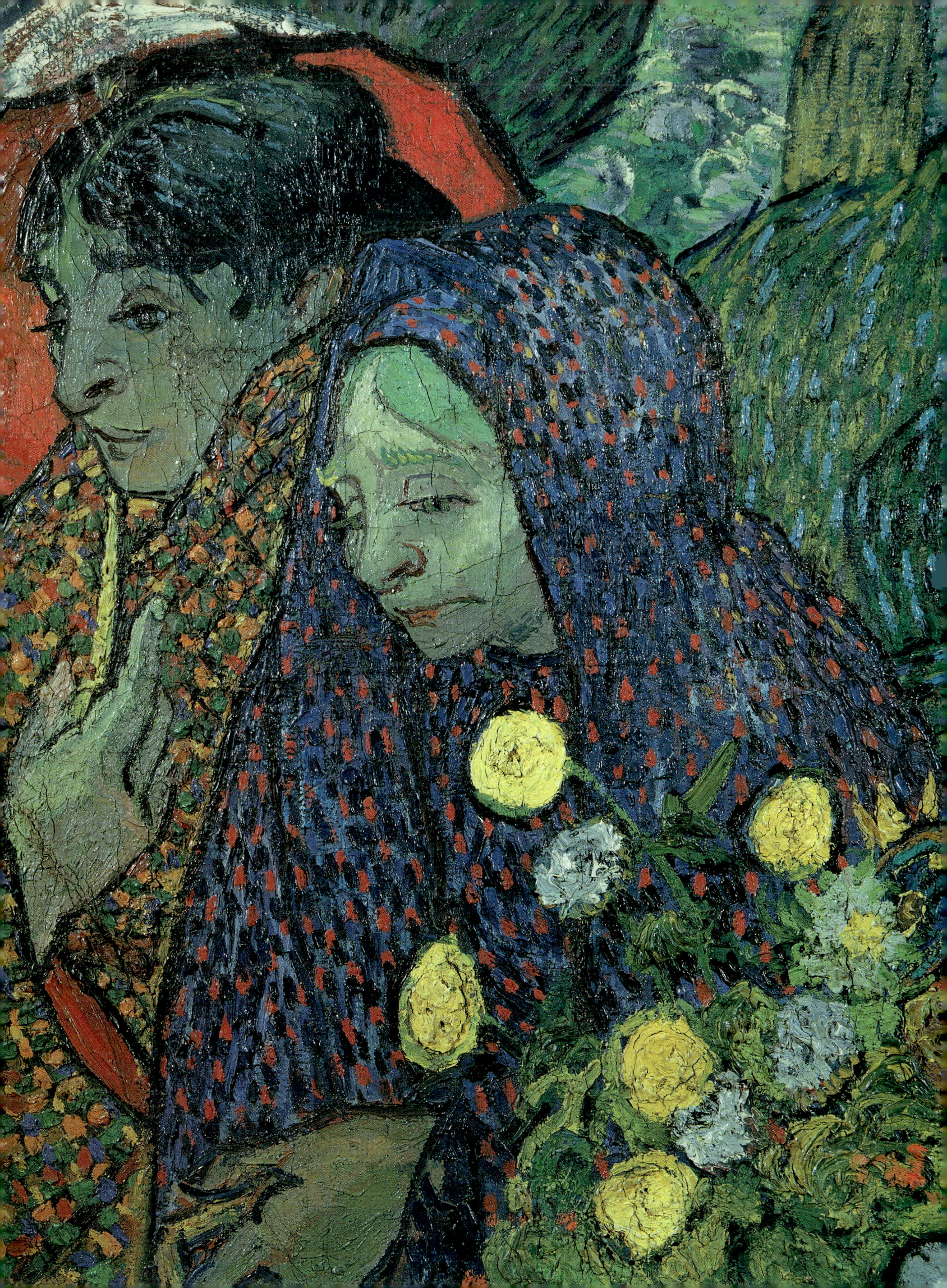

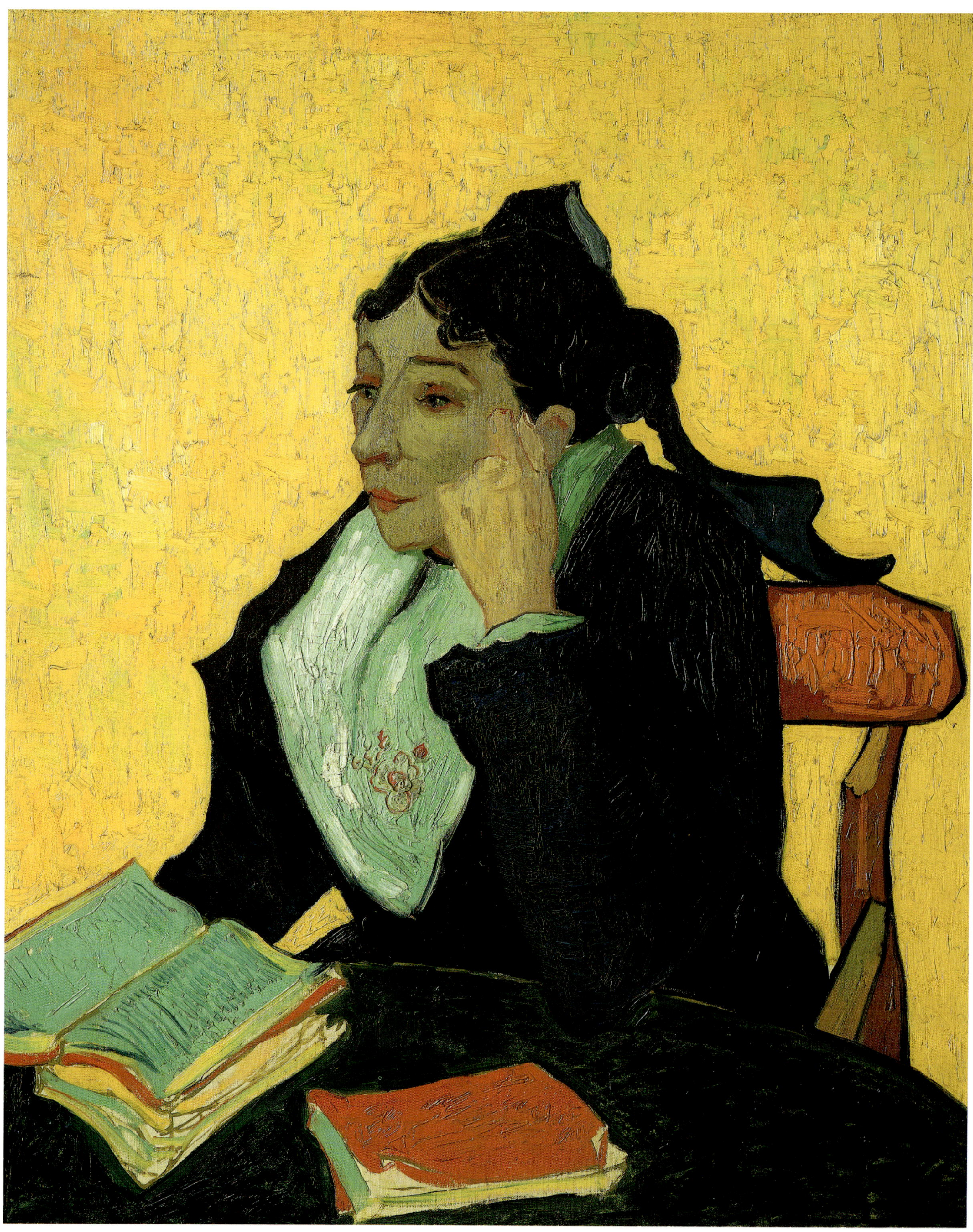

MADAME GINOUX AND HER HUSBAND ran the station café where Vincent ate many of his meals and was once a boarder in an upstairs room. It was the very night café that Vincent had painted with red walls and a green ceiling. Madame Ginoux became Vincent's friend and accepted his invitation to wear the local folk costume and pose for him and Gauguin at the yellow house. Vincent liked to encounter his portrait subjects face on, sometimes talking to them as he worked, but Gauguin stole his usual position. The profile of the woman's black sleeves and headdress were Vincent's. The curves and peaks he saw inspired him to echo them in the pages of the books on the table.

Gauguin made a drawing of Madame Ginoux while Vincent "slashed on" paint to complete this canvas in less than an hour. "That's what I'm good at", he once bragged to his brother, "doing a fellow roughly in one sitting." Vincent's virtuosity brought remarkable results, but the purpose of speed in this case may have been to free Madame Ginoux from a long posing session, for Vincent knew that she suffered a nervous condition. Later, Vincent completed four canvases based on the Gauguin drawing. In them, the two volumes appear to be new and their titles can be seen. They are *Uncle Tom's Cabin* by Harriet Beecher Stowe and *A Christmas Carol* by Charles Dickens, books of an earlier time that remained popular in Europe and that represented some of Vincent's favorite reading. Another of Vincent's versions of L'Arlésienne substitutes an unfurled parasol for the books, showing that well-chosen props and costumes can change the character of a portrait.

L'ARLÉSIENNE: MADAME GINOUX WITH BOOKS
ARLES, NOVEMBER 1888 OR MAY 1889
OIL ON CANVAS, 35 1/2 X 28 1/4 INCHES
THE METROPOLITAN MUSEUM OF ART, NEW YORK
BEQUEST OF SAM A. LEWISOHN, 1951 (51.112.3)

≺

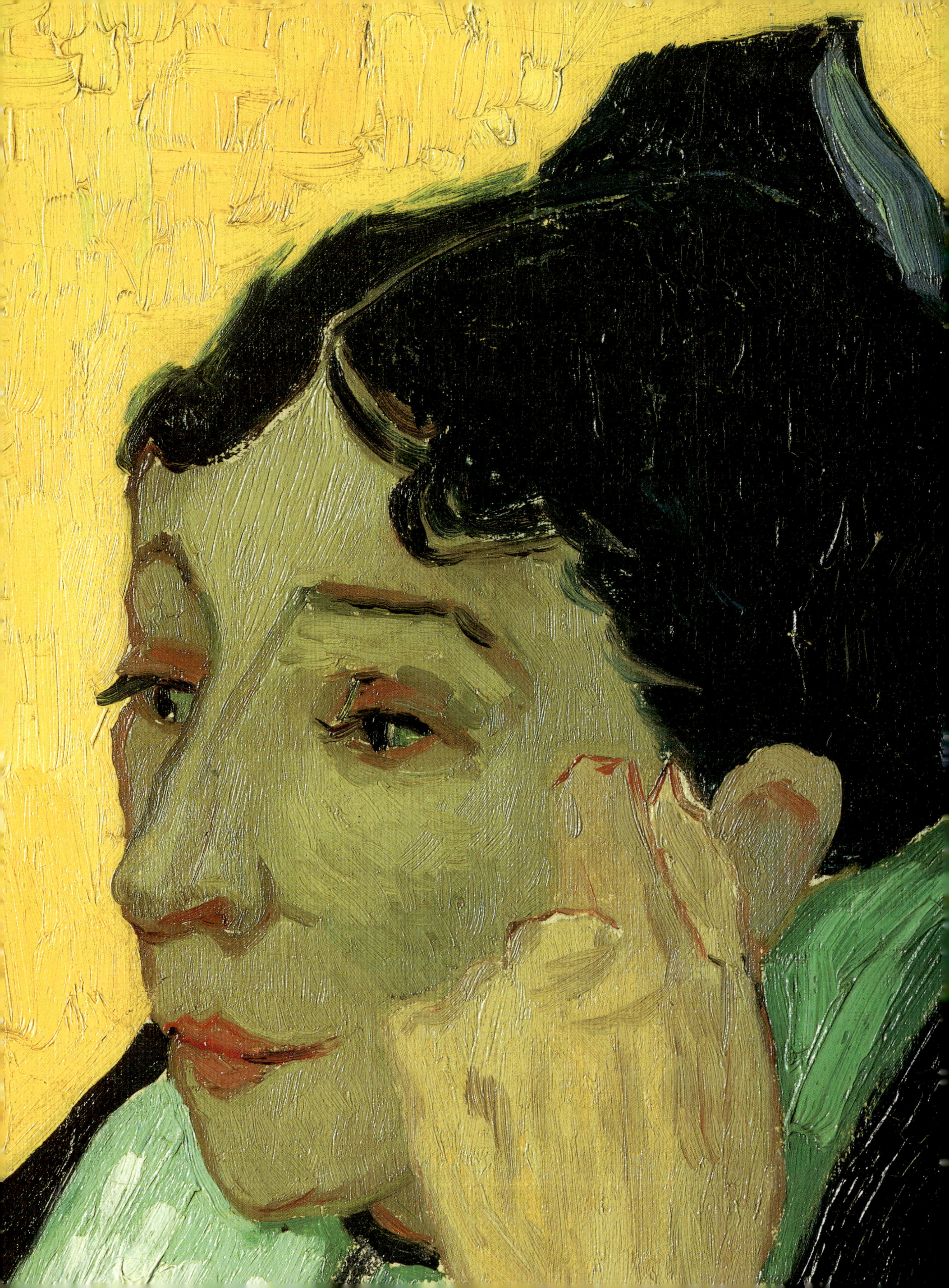

When Vincent was a student away from home, he wept at the sight of an empty chair his father had sat in while visiting him. In his mind, empty chairs symbolized absence and death. Yet he described his painting of his own chair briefly and dispassionately in two of his letters, mentioning the pouch of tobacco and pipe on the empty chair and the incidence of daytime. Theo soon received it among a shipment of paintings and told his brother that he preferred it to all the others.

Behind the plain chair, a wood crate full of sprouting onions is pushed against the wall. Vincent showed but a corner of it on which he carefully painted the letters of his first name to look as though they were applied to the crate itself. As usual, he did not sign his last name, van Gogh. After one of many spats with his family, he told Theo that he had renounced the name. He had another story for everyone else. They were told, "Van Gogh is such an impossible name...the whole world can pronounce the name Vincent correctly." The use of his first name with onions might seem a poorly chosen personal emblem save that the onions have burst forth with life.

VINCENT'S CHAIR WITH HIS PIPE
Arles, December 1888
Oil on canvas, 36 x 29 inches
National Gallery, London/Art Resource, New York

➢

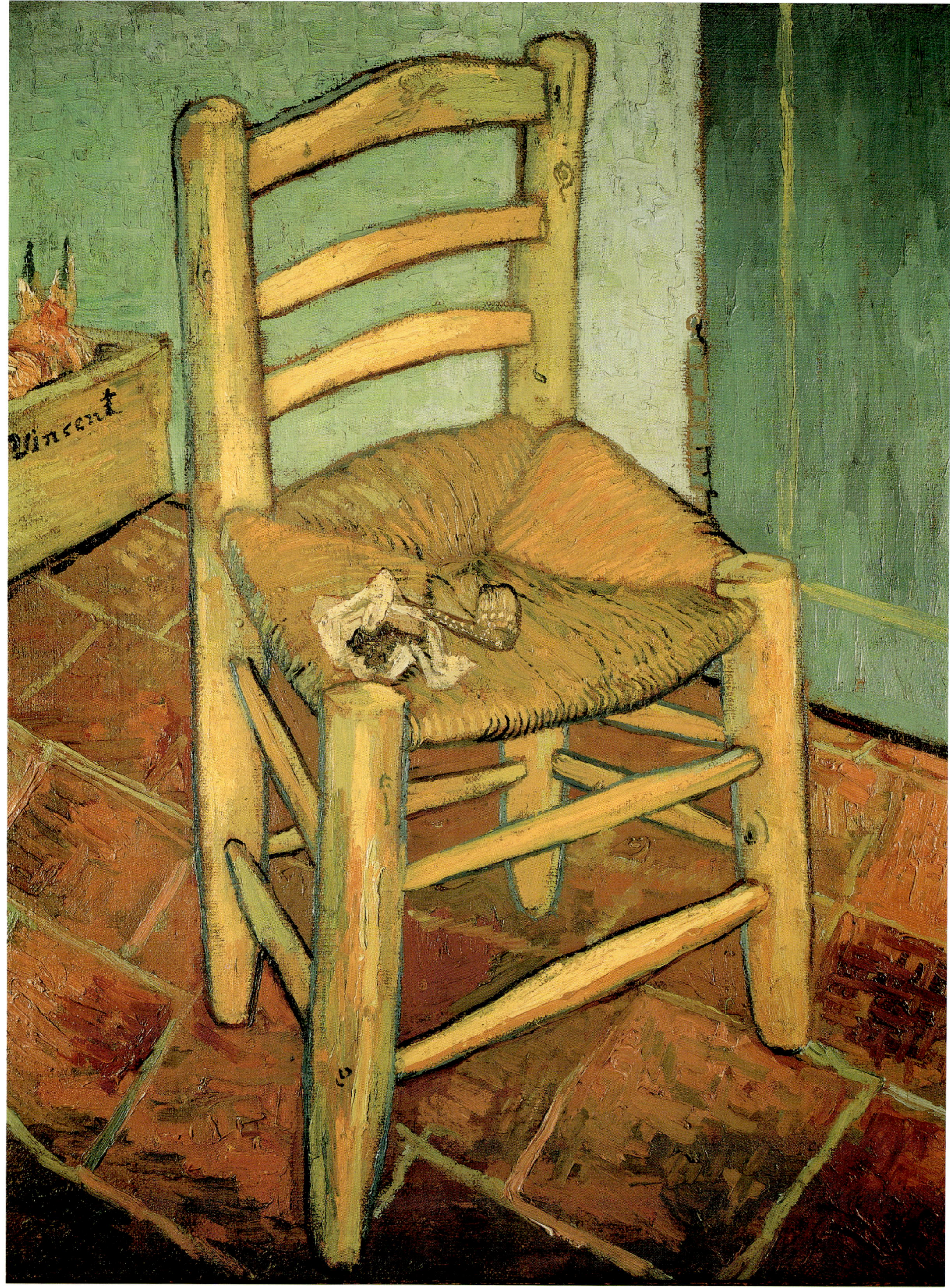
Vincent

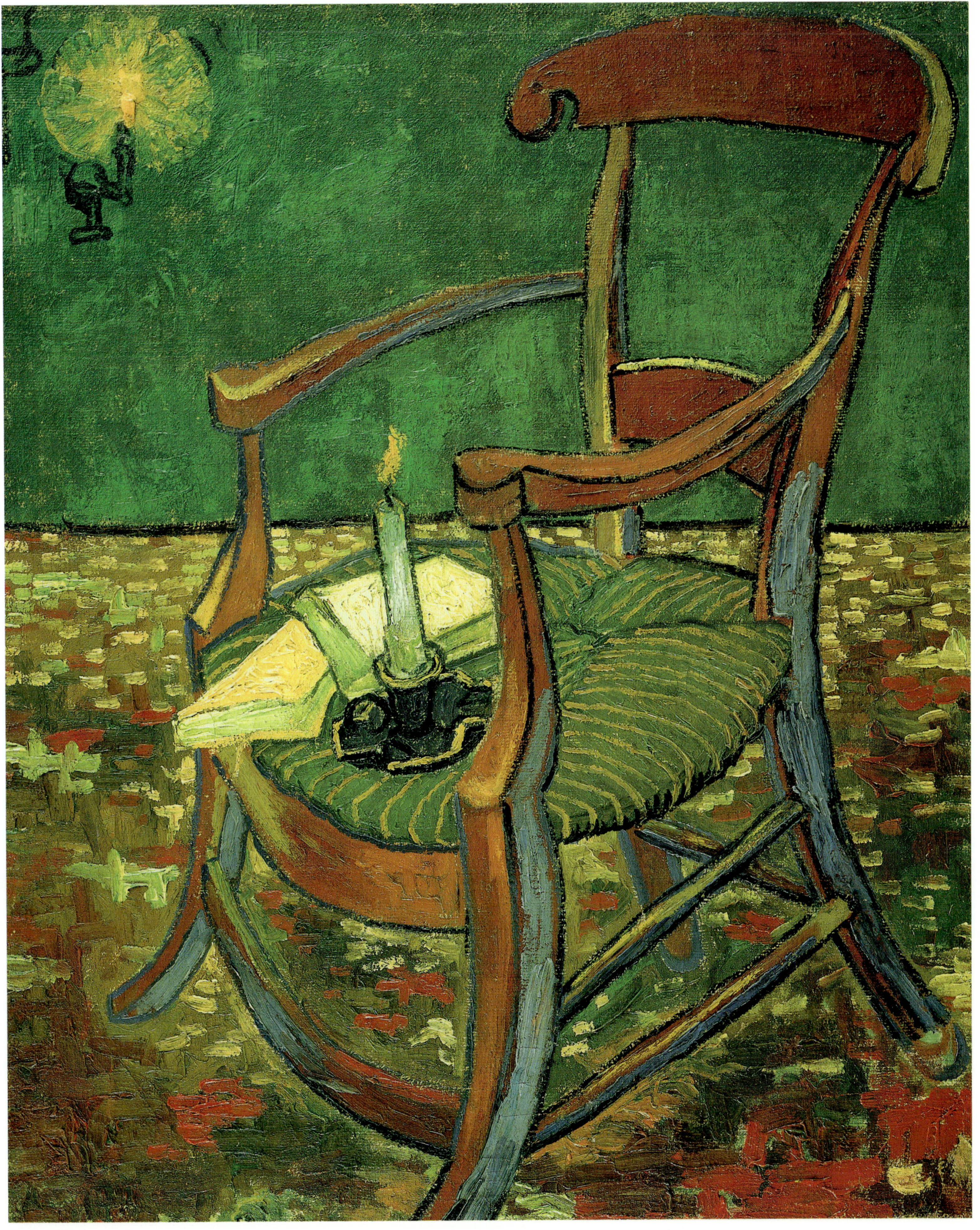

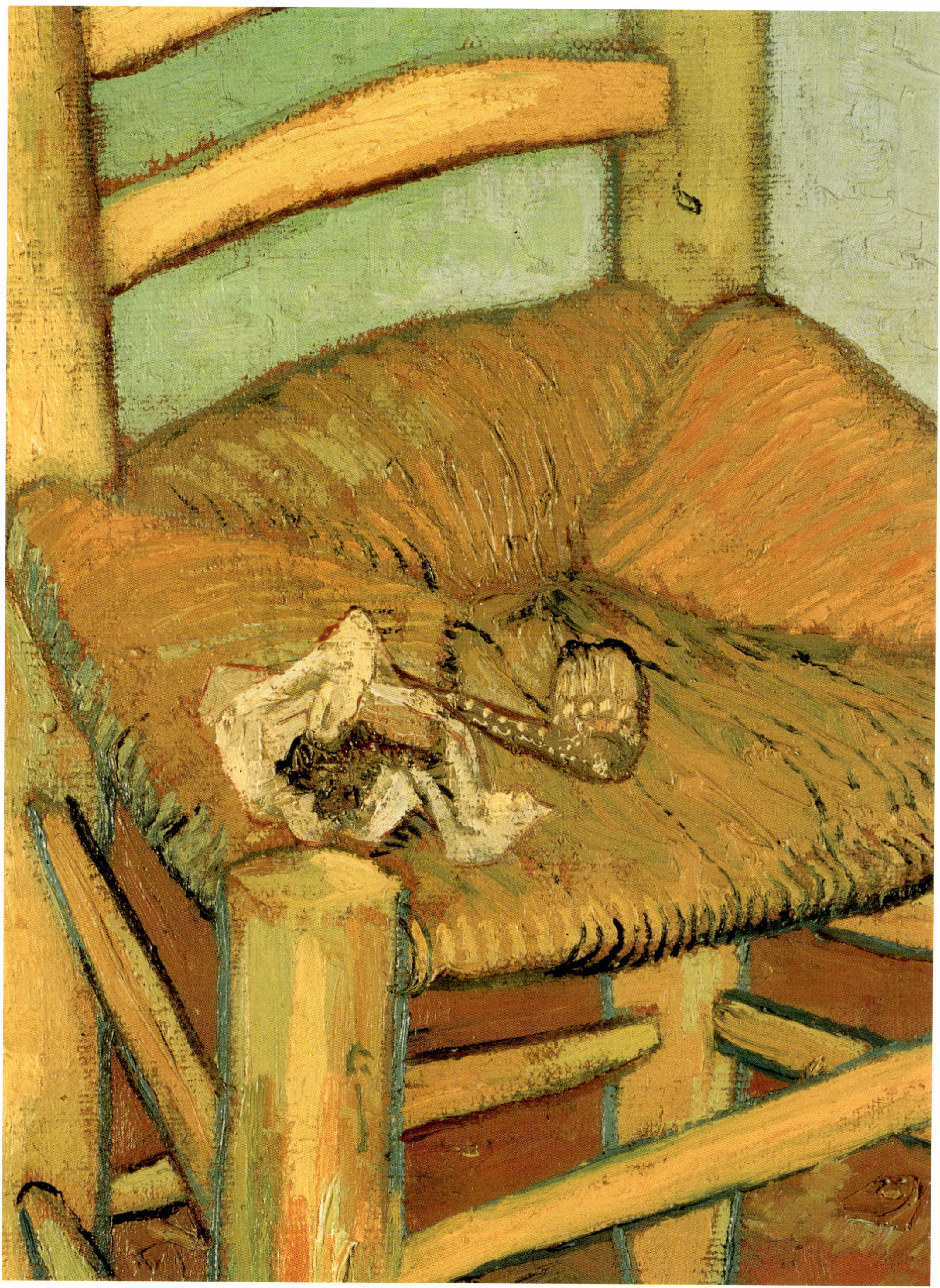

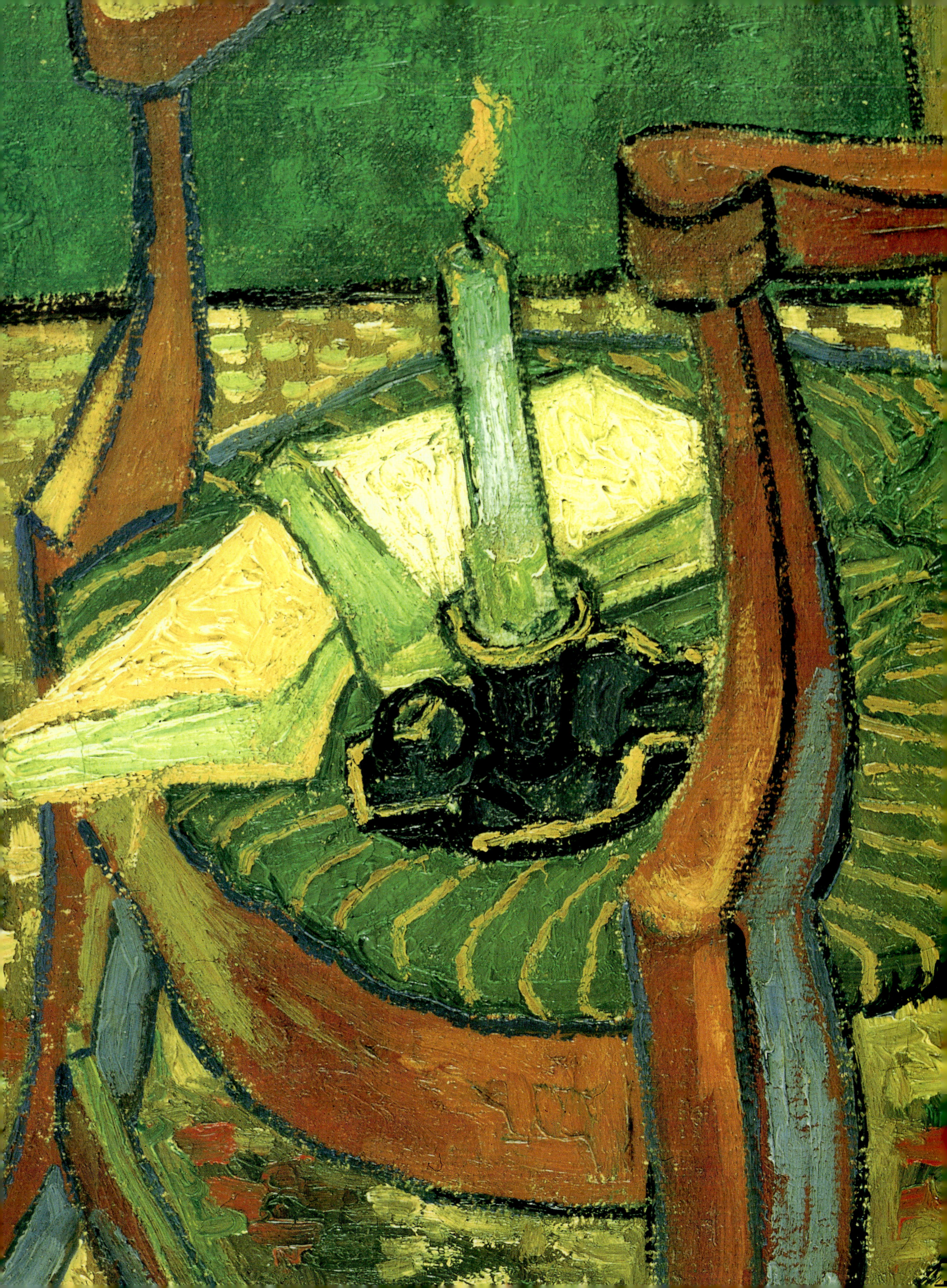

By the end of his sojourn with van Gogh, Gauguin wrote, "I feel a complete stranger in Arles.... Vincent and I rarely agree on much, least of all where painting is concerned....I say to him, 'You're right, boss,' for the sake of a quiet life." Though Gauguin painted Vincent at work, there is no portrait of Gauguin by Vincent, save for this moody rendition of Gauguin's armchair. Seen at night from a standing position, the chair seems to have sprung from the patterned carpet. The plain green wall and the green straw seat clash with lavender shadows across the chair's splayed legs, delicate joints, and curved rails. Vincent purchased the piece of furniture with Gauguin in mind. Two novels and a lighted candle are there "in the absent one's place," according to Vincent, while a fluttering gas light seems to be a beacon to lead Gauguin back.

PAUL GAUGUIN'S ARMCHAIR
Arles, December 1888
Oil on canvas, 35 3/4 x 28 1/4 inches
Van Gogh Museum (Vincent van Gogh Foundation)
Amsterdam, the Netherlands

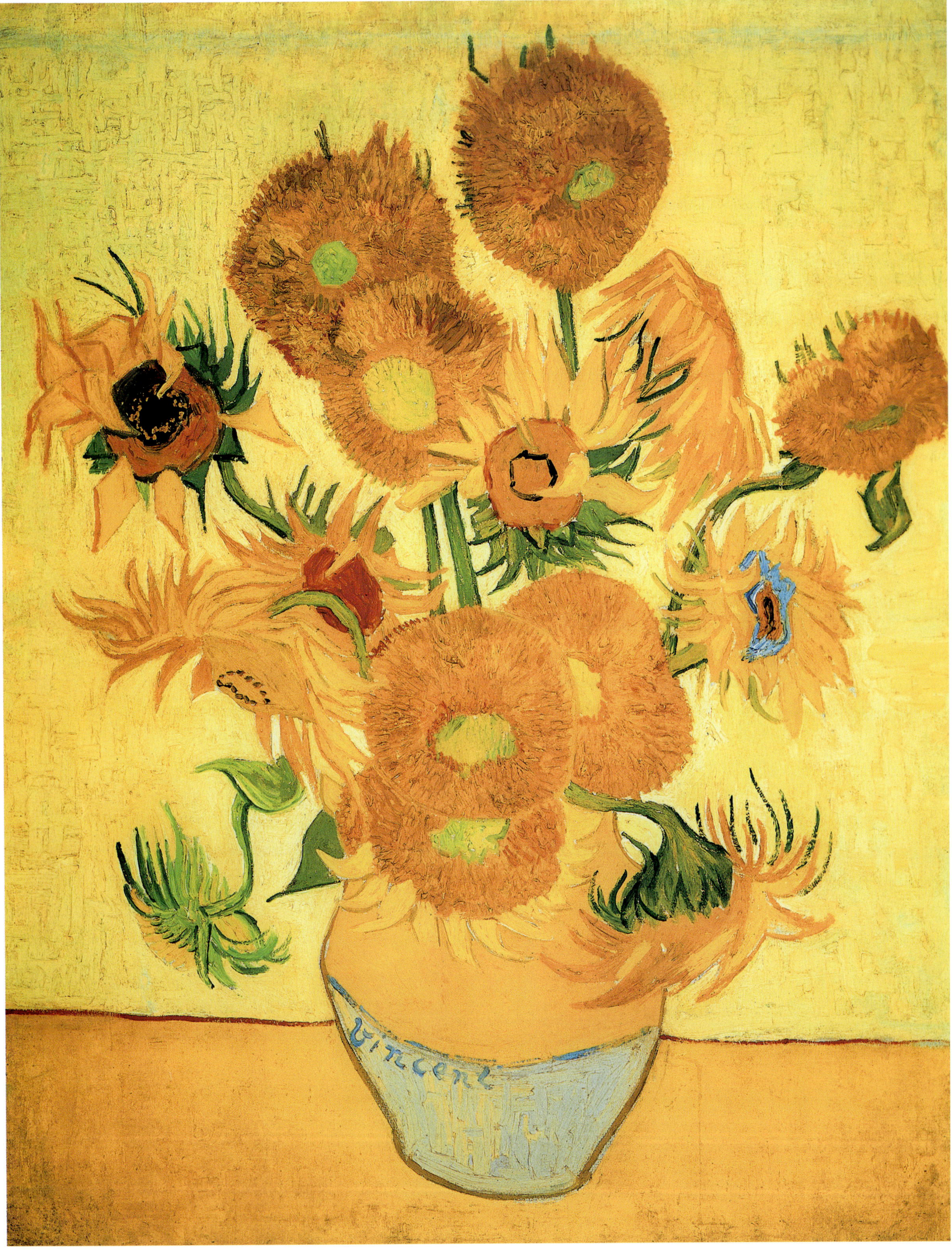
Vincent

VINCENT DECIDED TO DECORATE THE walls of the yellow house with paintings of sunflowers, which edged the nearby railroad tracks where Vincent harvested them early every morning. He worked fast to paint the blooms before they wilted. They would be just as in nature, "chrome yellows will blaze forth on various backgrounds—blue, from the palest malachite green to royal blue.…Effects like those of stained glass windows in a Gothic church," he announced to an artist friend. A number of the paintings were in place when Gauguin arrived, and a portrait by Gaugin shows Vincent working on yet another sunflower canvas. Vincent offered one to Gauguin as a gift when he left Arles, but he took two with him—a brash sign of his regard for Vincent's work.

Vincent's health had been deteriorating for months until a breakdown caused him to be hospitalized. "One could have created life at less cost than creating art," he had written to Theo a few months earlier. He had described himself as "spent, ill, a broken pitcher, by so much more am I an artist—a creative artist". As soon as he was back in the yellow house, he painted replacements for the paintings Gauguin had taken. In this one, fourteen flowers crane to find the sun. The symmetry of the composition is violated by the irregular placement of flowers and the intrusion of the background color into the oval shape of the bouquet. Vincent's earlier idea of a background of blue gave way to the quieter contrast of pale yellow—the color of his house. The sunflower paintings, created to make the yellow house a cheerful place to visit, are emblems of Vincent's hospitality to other artists.

STILL LIFE: VASE WITH FOURTEEN SUNFLOWERS
ARLES, JANUARY 1889
OIL ON CANVAS, 37 1/2 X 28 3/4 INCHES
VAN GOGH MUSEUM (VINCENT VAN GOGH FOUNDATION)
AMSTERDAM, THE NETHERLANDS

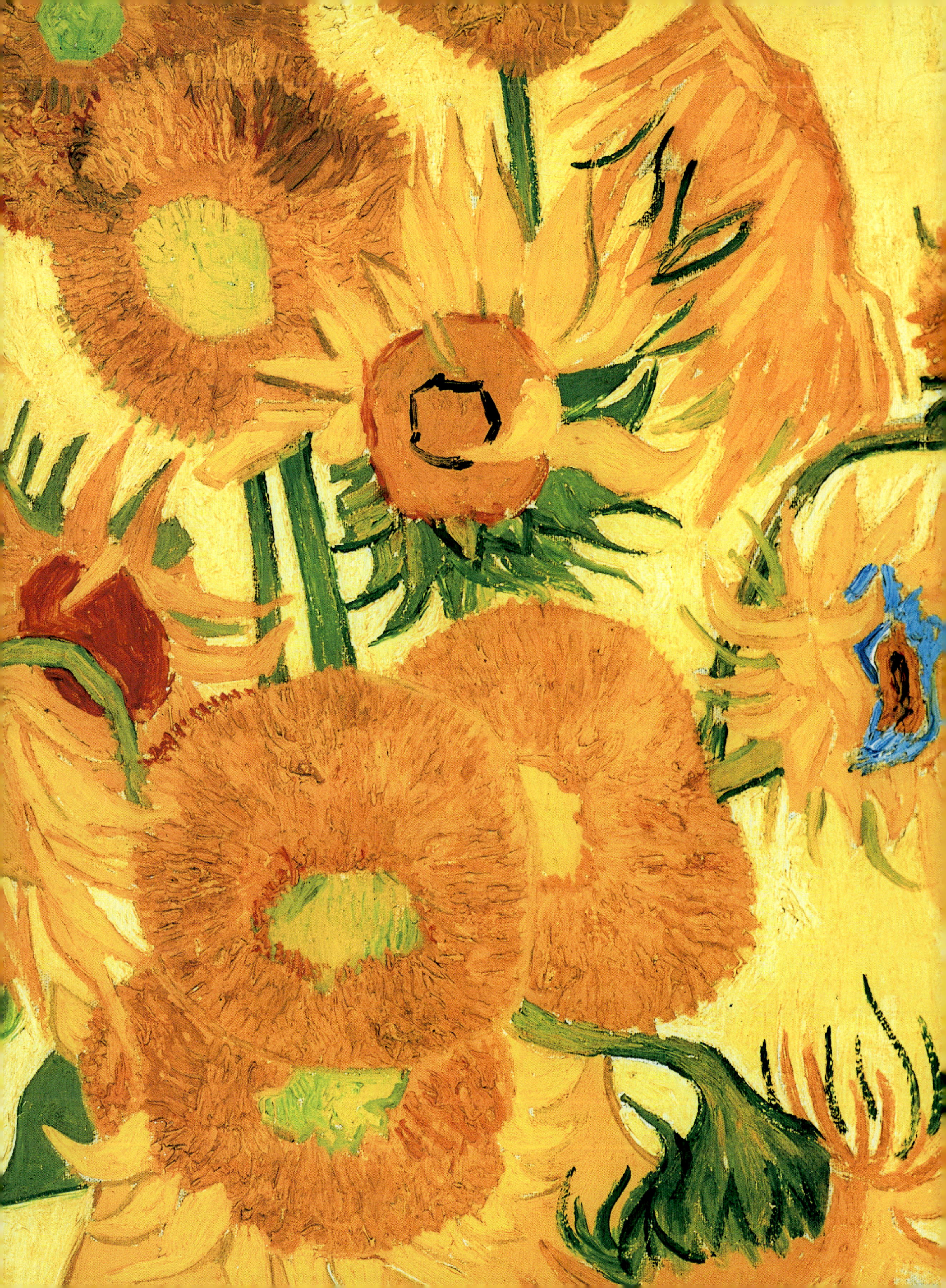

VINCENT BECAME FRIENDLY WITH HIS postman, Joseph Roulin, and painted at least twenty-two portraits of him, his children, and his wife. He dubbed this portrait of Madame Roulin *La Berceuse,* the French word for a woman who rocks an infant (the cord she loosely holds is attached to a cradle on the floor). Vincent's breakdown occurred during the time that he was painting Madame Roulin, and he got back to the project soon after he was released from the hospital. Five versions of the painting exist; Vincent called them "absolutely identical replicas," but they were not. Madame Roulin "had a good eye and took the best," he conceded. He gave a canvas to Gauguin, one to another artist friend, and one to Theo.

Vincent suggested that his brother flank *La Berceuse* with two canvases of the sunflowers, like a triptych—"then the yellow and orange tones of the head will gain in brilliance by the proximity of the yellow wings." The emerald green of the mother's skirt and wallpaper against the red floor causes the same result. These lively colors and an animated wallpaper design are mitigated by Madame's bulk and sobriety. Her hands betray an existence of hard housework and her face seems sorrowed by life.

LA BERCEUSE (MME. AUGUSTINE ROULIN)
ARLES, FEBRUARY 1889
OIL ON CANVAS, 36 1/4 X 28 1/4 INCHES
MUSEUM OF FINE ARTS, BOSTON
BEQUEST OF JOHN T. SPAULDING

➢

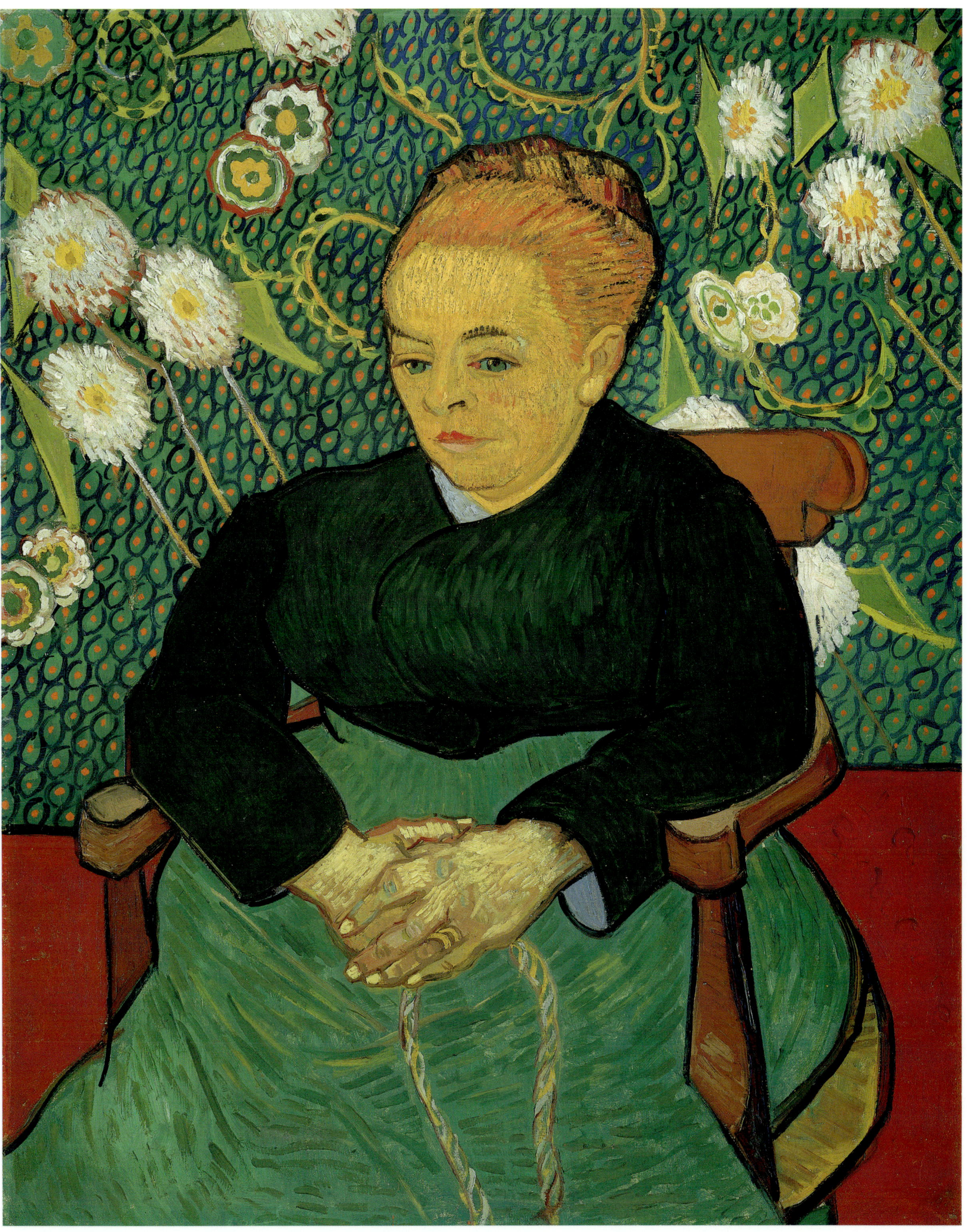

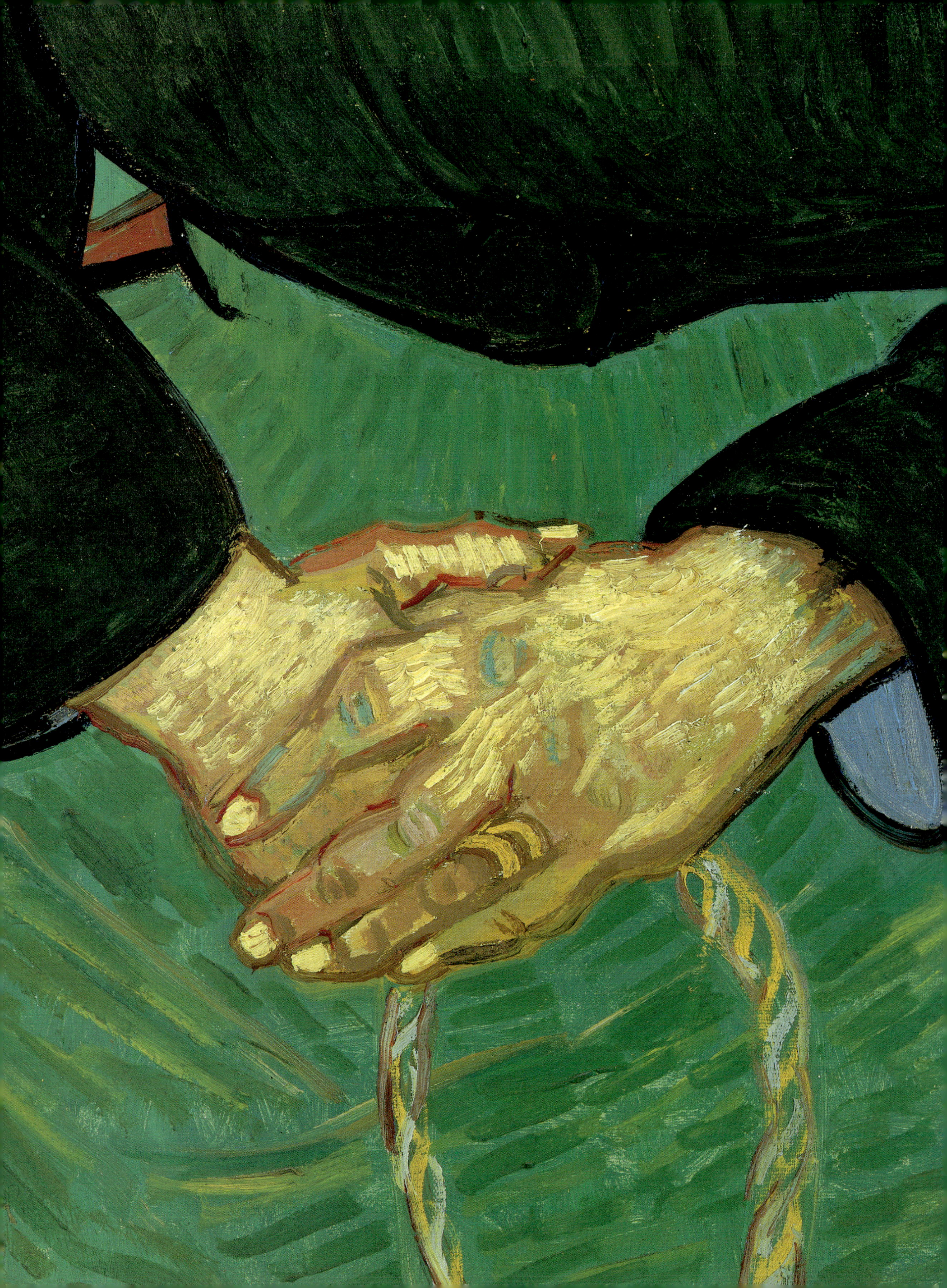

Père Tanguy's shop had been Vincent's most reliable outlet for exhibiting his work. His old friend always seemed ready to hang one of Vincent's paintings in his show window. Then a group of French artists included Vincent in their Salon des Artistes Indépendants in 1888, 1889, and 1890, and a Belgian group of avant-garde artists called Les Vingt (The Twenty) invited him to be a "guest artist" along with Cézanne and others in their exhibition of 1890. One of the paintings he wanted to send to Brussels was already in Père Tanguy's window but was released by him. Theo van Gogh described it as "a view of the countryside in spring with poplars that run across the canvas in such a way that one can see neither the bottoms nor the tops of the trees."

Vincent called himself "a beast," who cannot reproduce "the eternal beauty of things," the very beauty that often entranced him. "In my pictures I render it as something ugly and coarse." The artist was writing from the perspective of a Dutch preacher's son, conventional and shy of the new. The Vincent who painted this scene was another man—a modern artist who saw beauty in gnarled, butchered trees sprouting fresh, raw growth. Conditioned by Japanese prints and his love of spring, Vincent heroically tipped up the earth to show more of its fecundity. By doing so, he also created two horizontal lines to counter the vertical screen of the poplars—the ragged black border of the foreground grass rendered in abstract patterns, and the horizon line incorporating the buildings of Arles.

ORCHARD IN BLOSSOM WITH VIEW OF ARLES
Arles, April 1889
Oil on canvas, 28 1/4 x 36 1/4 inches
Neue Pinakothek, Munich/Art Resource, New York

➢

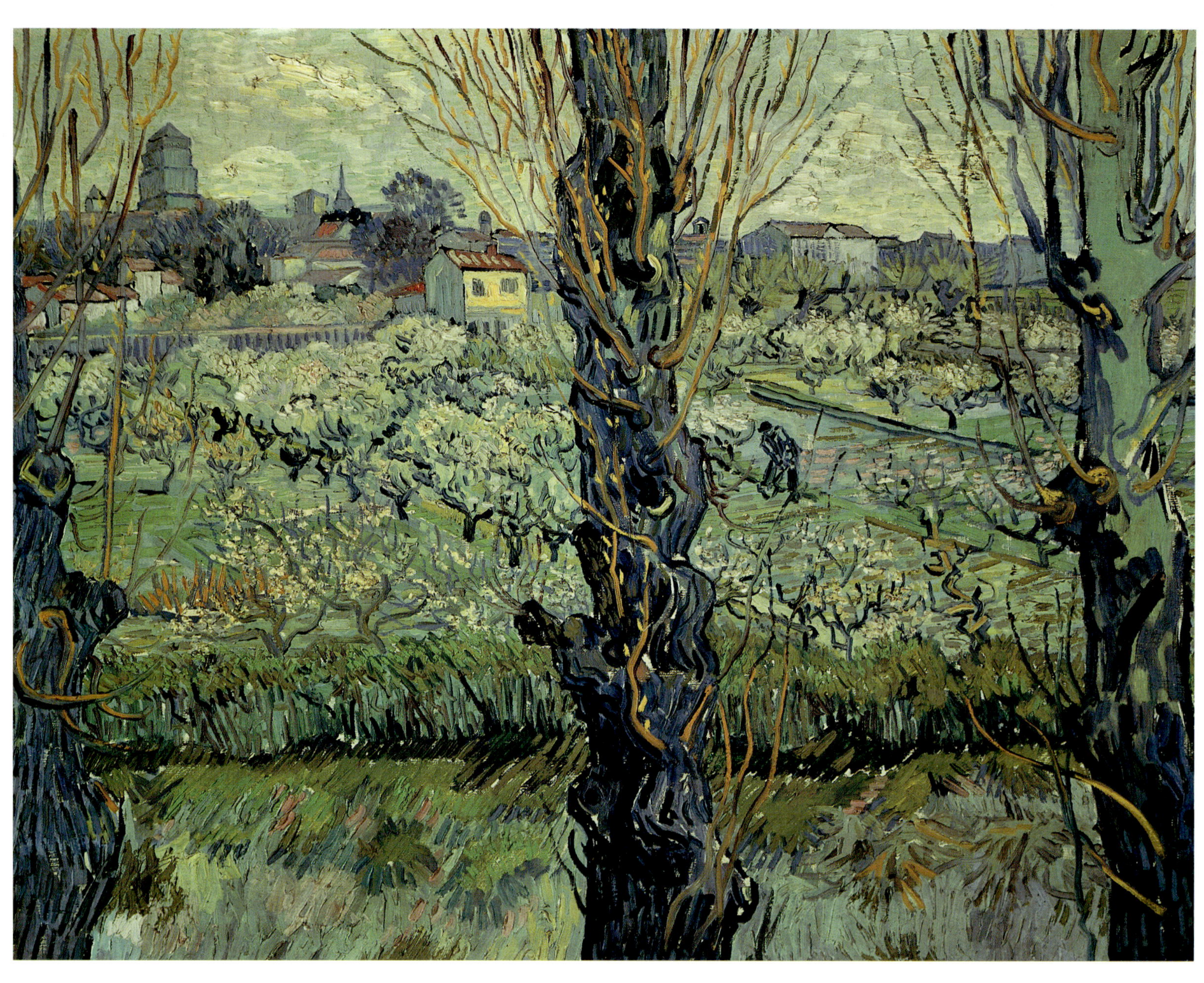

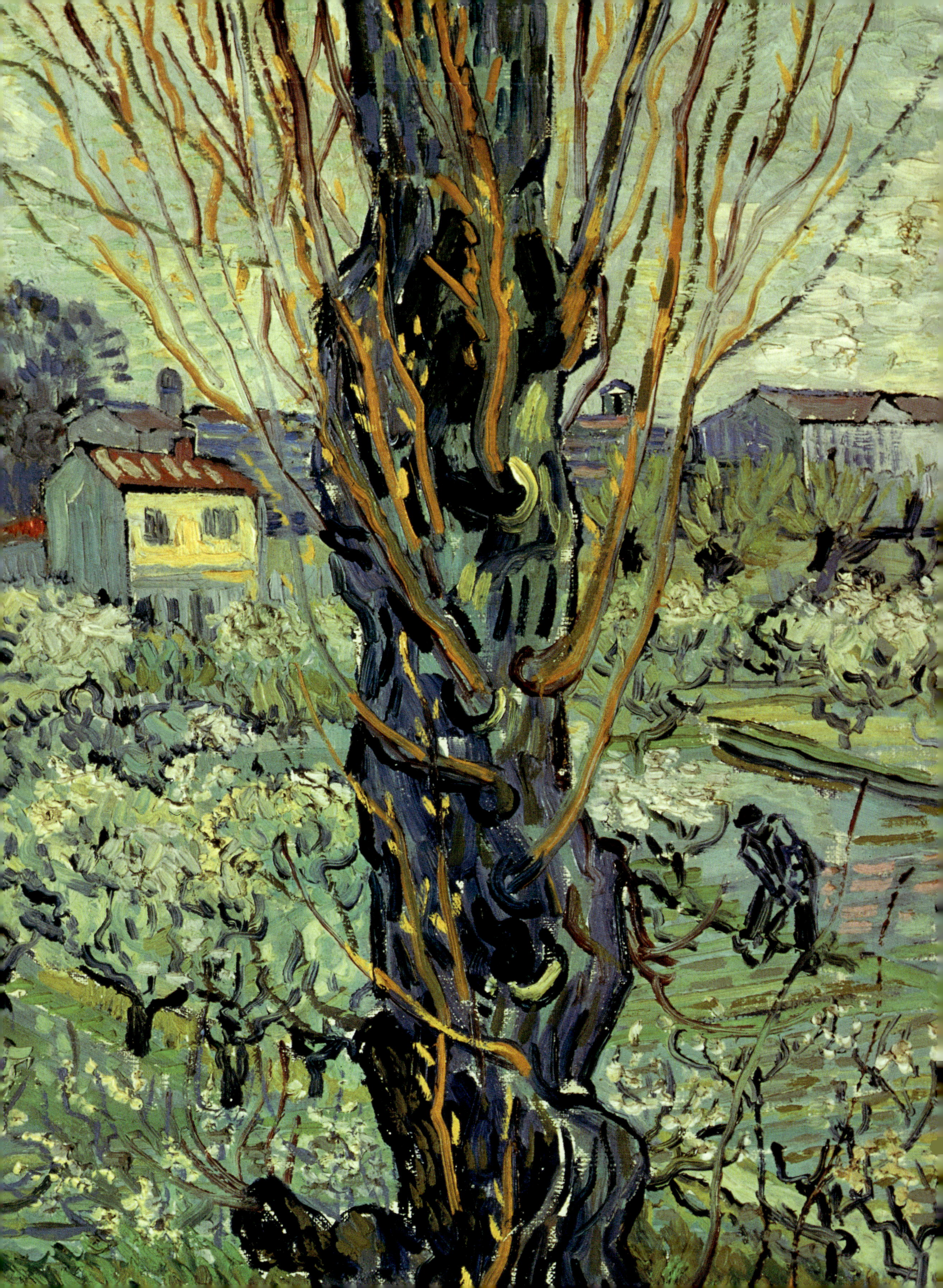

INSOMNIA, HALLUCINATIONS, AND delusions tore at Vincent's mind and body, and on May 8, 1889, he committed himself to Saint-Paul-de-Mausole, a mental asylum at Saint-Rémy-de-Provence, about twelve miles from Arles. For a full year, the place was to be Vincent's asylum, monastery, and studio all in one. Though seriously ill, he only stopped painting for a short while when his colors were taken from him to keep him from ingesting them, a bad habit he engaged in when he felt he could paint faster by using his fingers instead of brushes.

Vincent drew detailed lines to represent grass, tree trunks, branches, and leaves. He softly blended greens, oranges, yellows, and reds to create an intimate space in a corner of the asylum garden where a bench waits at the end of a path. At first the scene appears to be peaceful, but the bright, flat green of the field beyond the trees is a strident note. It says "Go" to a sudden wind and shows the agitation of the leaves straining against it. The grass bends and branches whip toward the asylum wall, though winds never stopped Vincent from painting.

THE GARDEN OF SAINT-PAUL HOSPITAL
Saint-Rémy, May 1889
Oil on canvas, 37 1/2 x 29 3/4 inches
Kröller-Müller Museum, Otterlo, the Netherlands

➢

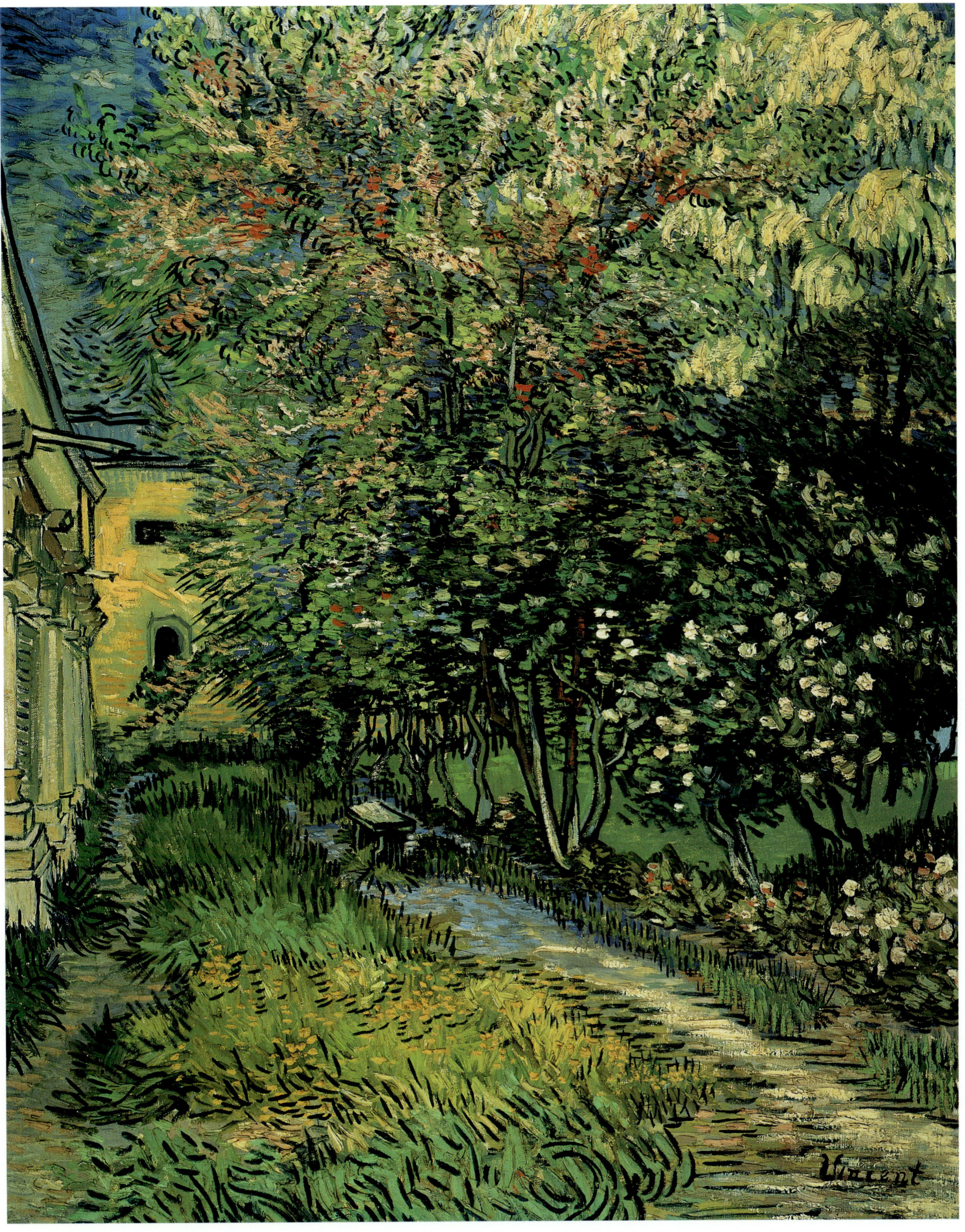
Vincent

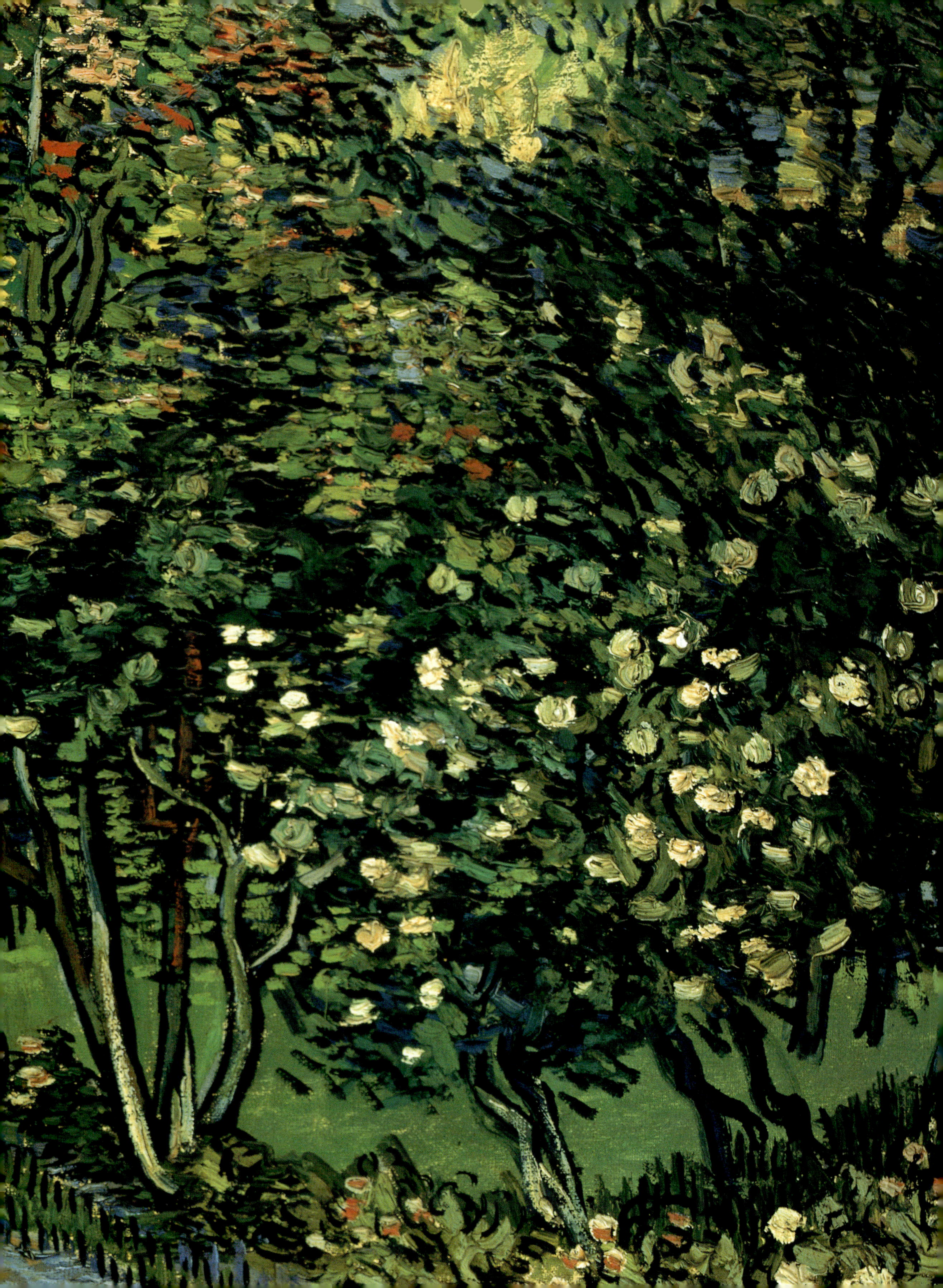

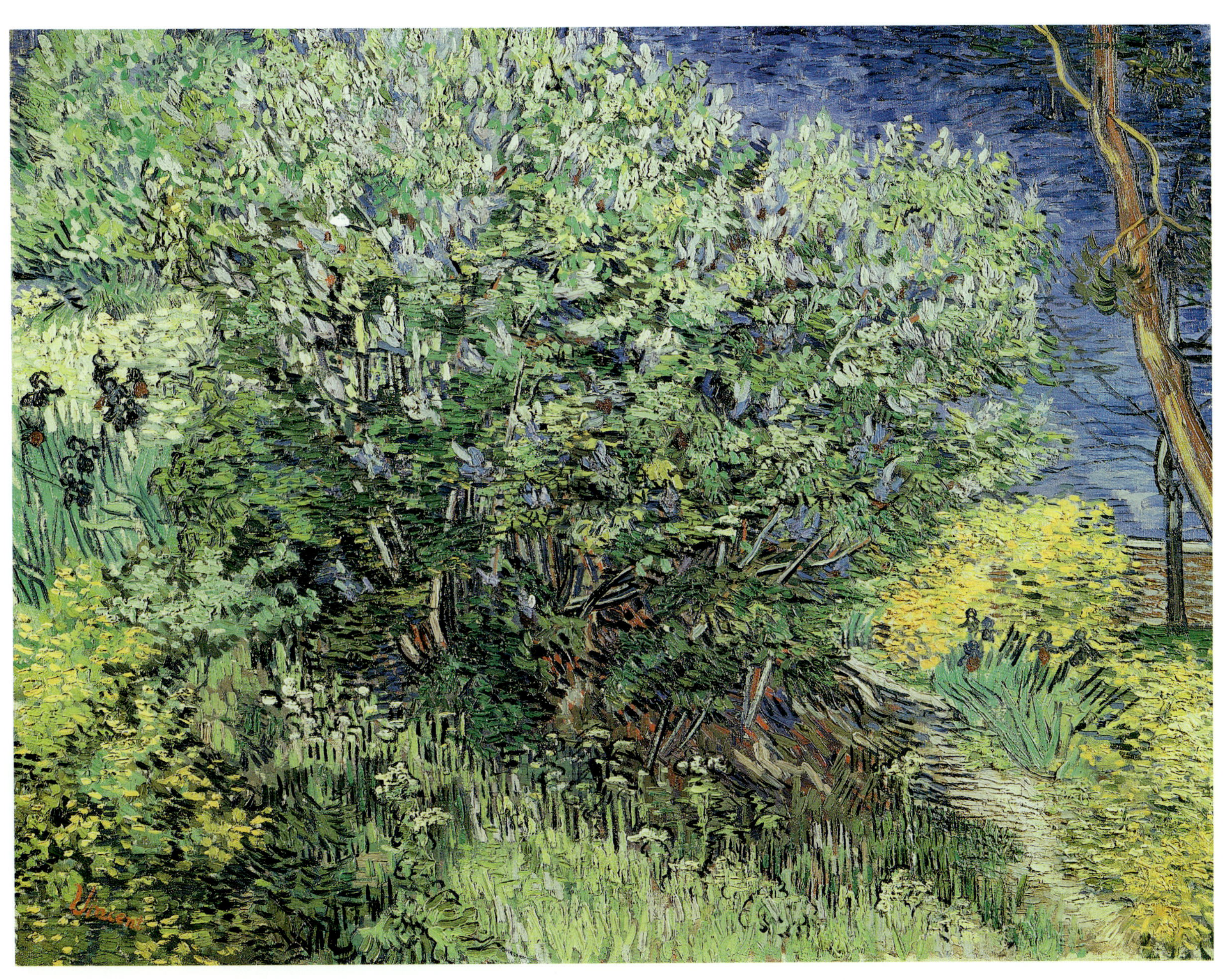

DURING HIS FIRST MONTHS AT THE asylum, Vincent painted in the hospital hallways and cloister, within the walled grounds, and while looking out the windows of his two simple rooms. As he learned this territory, he discovered an old lilac bush that stood in the way of a path that led to the asylum wall. Vincent drew and painted the tangled mass of the flowering bush and indicated hints of spring all around it. A purple sky intensifies the flecks of yellow scattered throughout the painting.

When Vincent decided to enter the asylum, he told Theo, *I have tried to make up my mind to begin again, but at the moment it's not possible…so let's try it three months to begin with, and afterwards we shall see.* Fortunately for him, spring came early at Saint-Rémy.

LILACS
SAINT-RÉMY, MAY 1889
OIL ON CANVAS, 28 3/4 X 36 1/4 INCHES
THE HERMITAGE, ST. PETERSBURG, RUSSIA/ART RESOURCE, NEW YORK

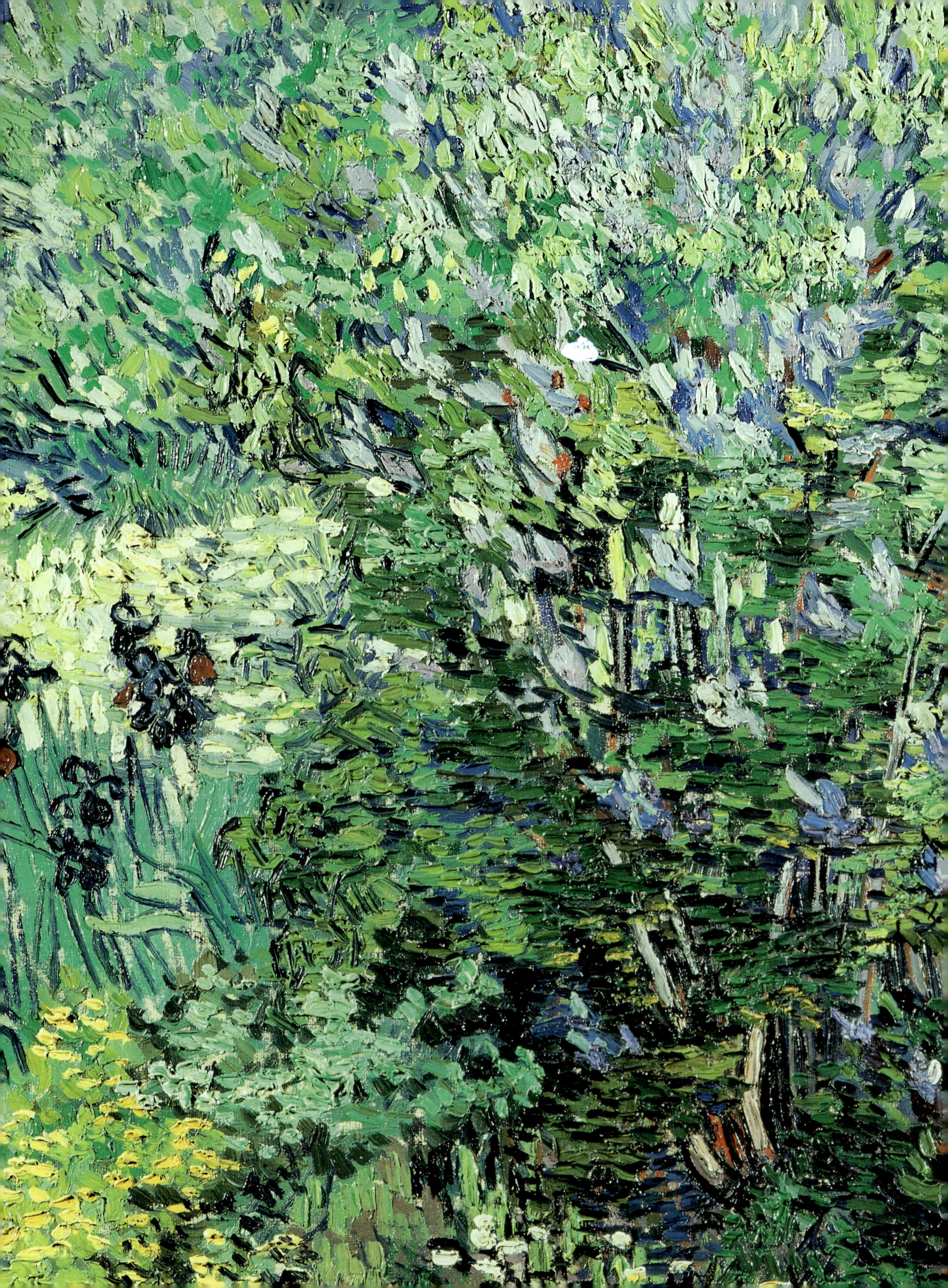

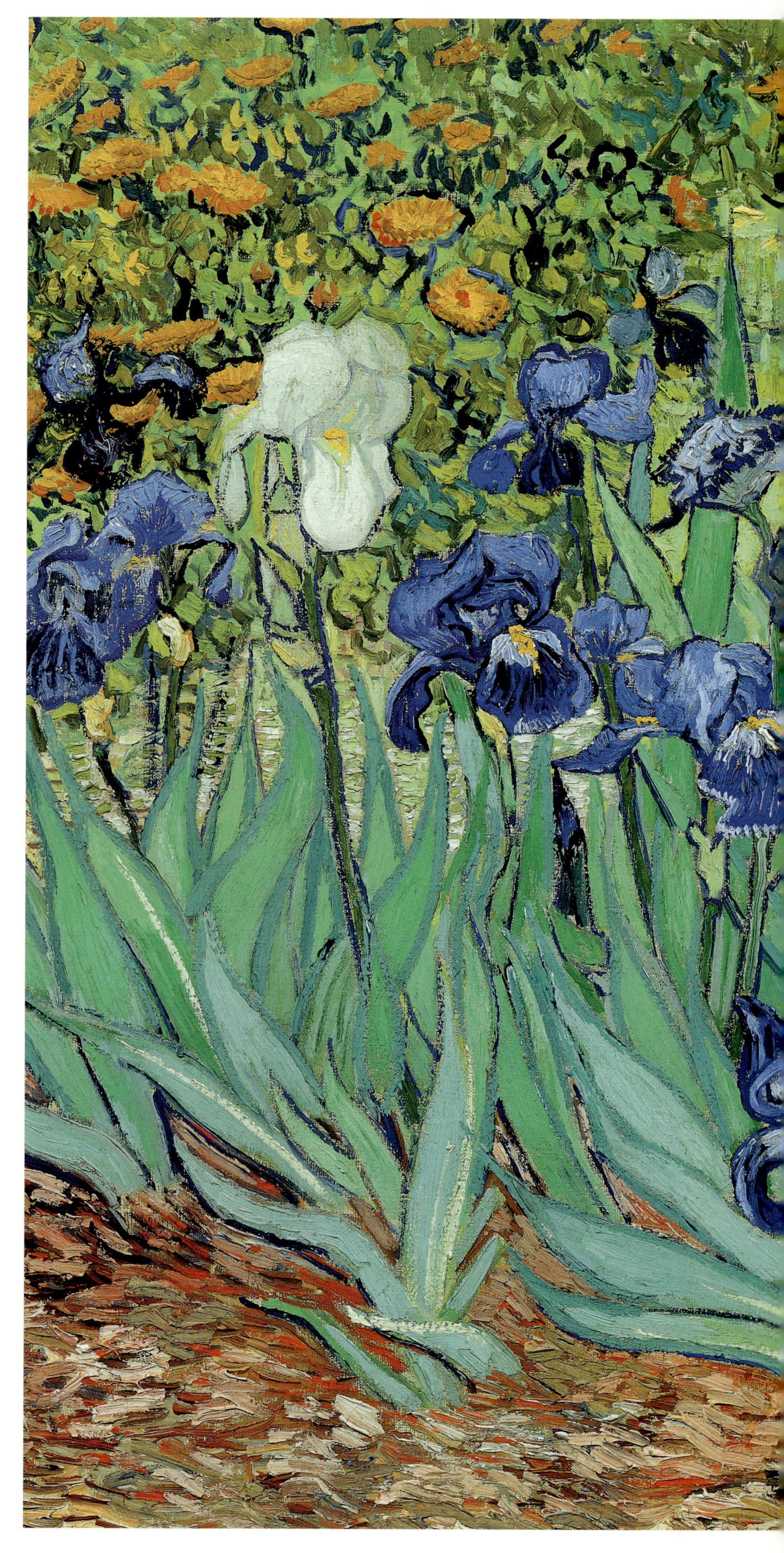

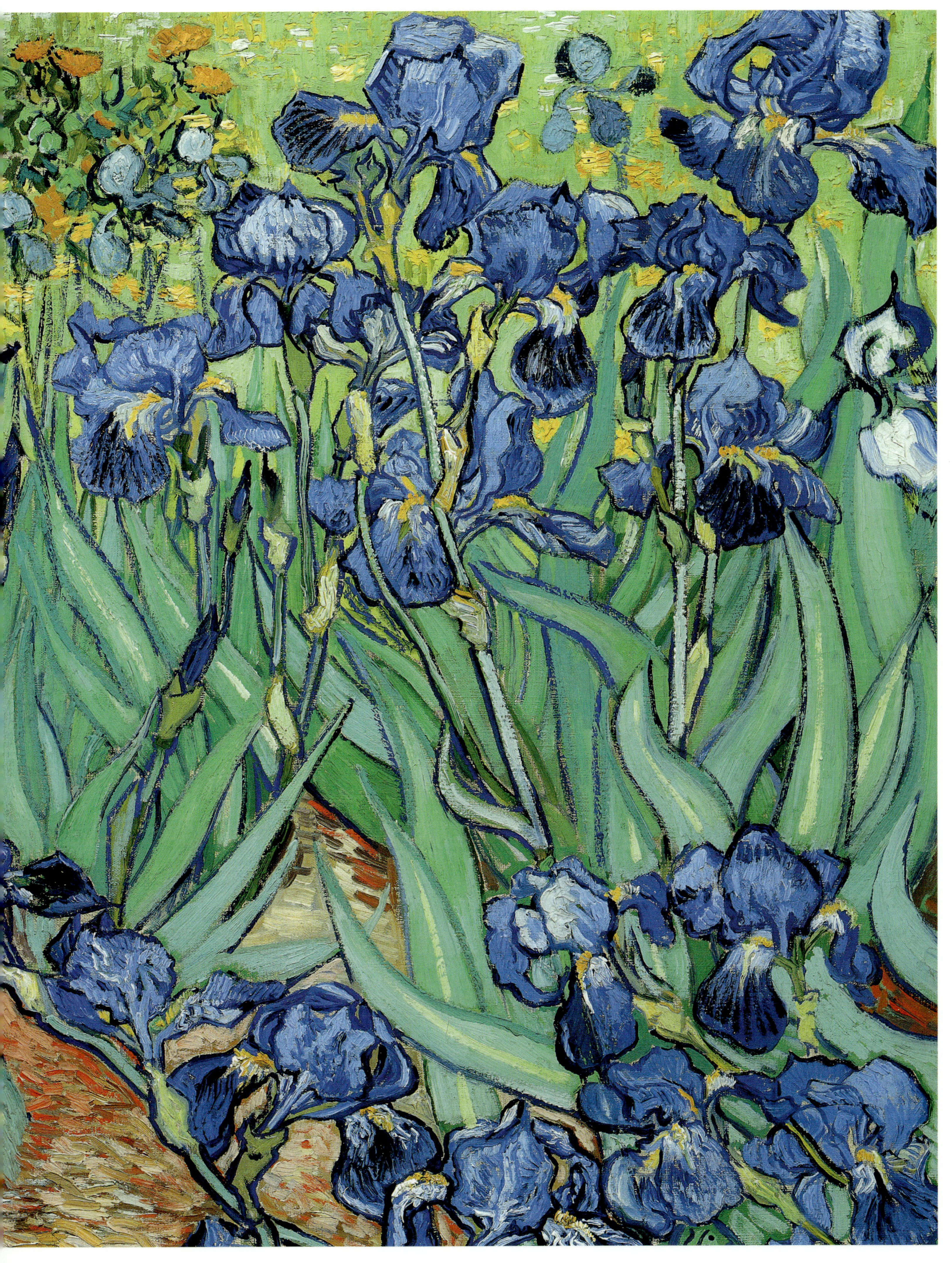

A BED OF HEAVY-HEADED BEARDED iris struggle to stand erect in the asylum garden. Leaves fold over leaves—bending, twisting, and getting in the way of the flowers as they reach for light. Purple blossoms at the bottom corner of the canvas stretch across the earth as though to get a better look at the odd flower in their midst. Springing from orange earth with bowing leaves at its base is a white iris. The pure flower is the center of attention even though it is not near the center of the painting. Vincent showed *Irises* in the Indépendants' exhibition in Paris, and his brother dryly remarked, "It is one of your good things."

IRISES
SAINT-RÉMY, MAY 1889
OIL ON CANVAS, 28 X 36 3/4 INCHES
THE J. PAUL GETTY MUSEUM, LOS ANGELES

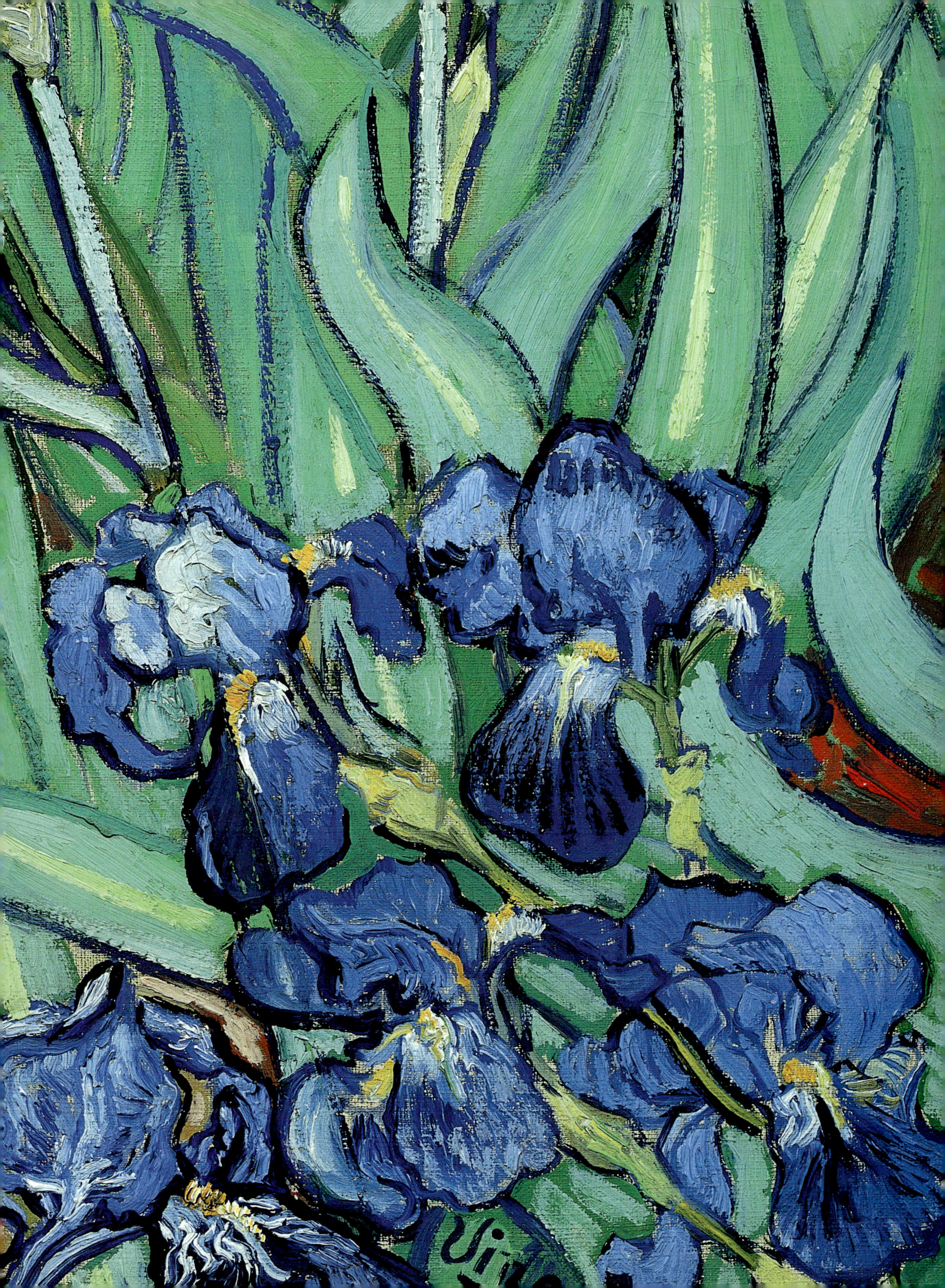

VINCENT WAS A PAYING GUEST AT THE asylum, courtesy of his brother Theo. His only obligations were to perform some menial tasks each day and to abide by his treatment; otherwise, he was free to come and go. It took a while before he dared venture into the unfamiliar landscape of olive groves, cypress trees, and the sparsely vegetated slopes of the rough foothills of the Alpilles mountains. Against a sky of fast-moving white arabesques, he created a congregation of cypresses growing from a verdant field, reaching up with twisting, flame-like tendrils—some of them beyond the top of the canvas. Anything bizarre in the originality of the sky and trees is balanced by the presence in the scene of a very ordinary farmhouse and two proper young ladies, who walk together at the base of a tumble of orange, red, and green. Their small size against the cypresses provides a measure of the immensity of nature in Vincent's mind and eyes.

CYPRESSES WITH TWO FEMALE FIGURES
SAINT-RÉMY, JUNE 1889
OIL ON CANVAS, 36 1/4 X 28 3/4 INCHES
KRÖLLER-MÜLLER MUSEUM, OTTERLO, THE NETHERLANDS

➢

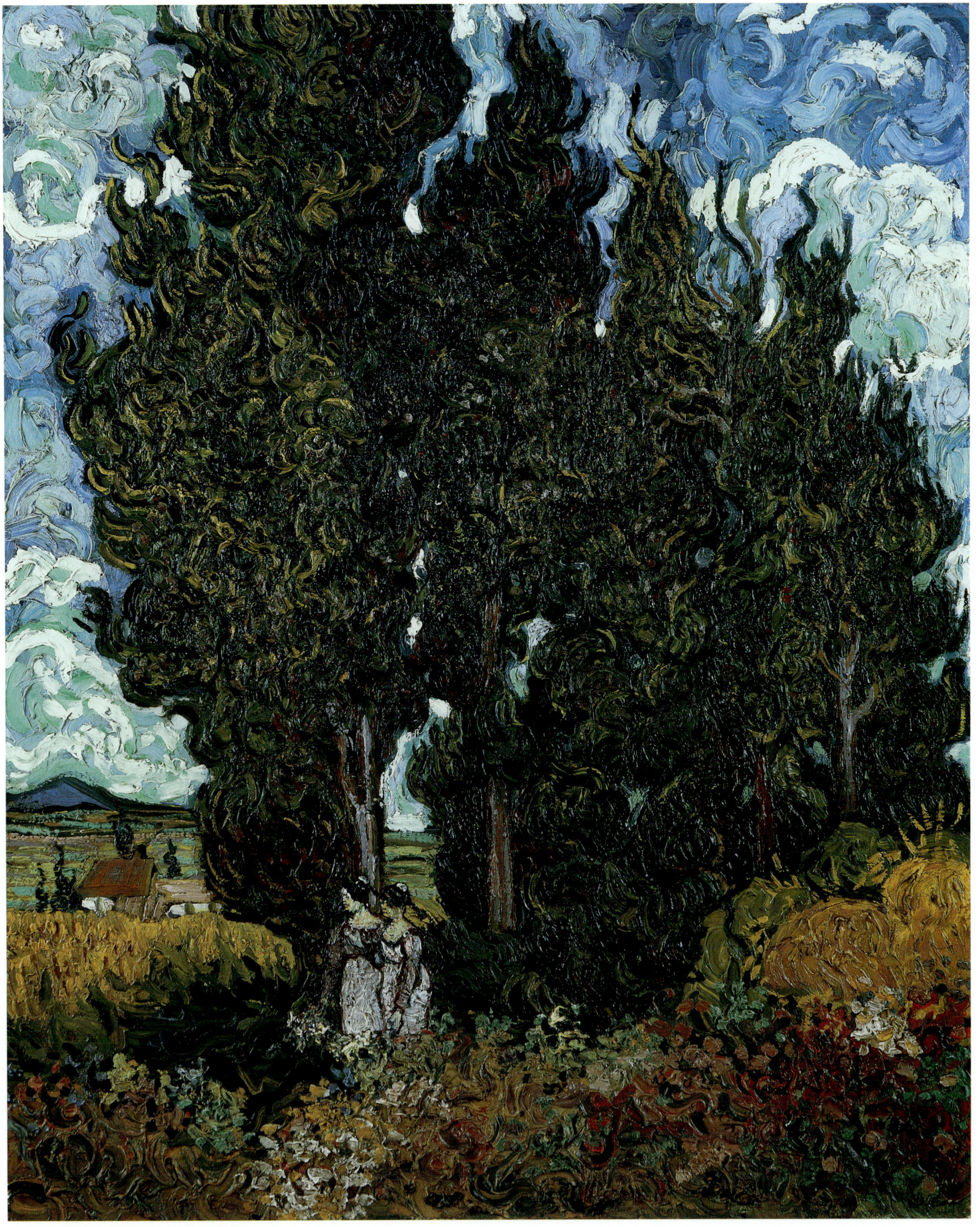

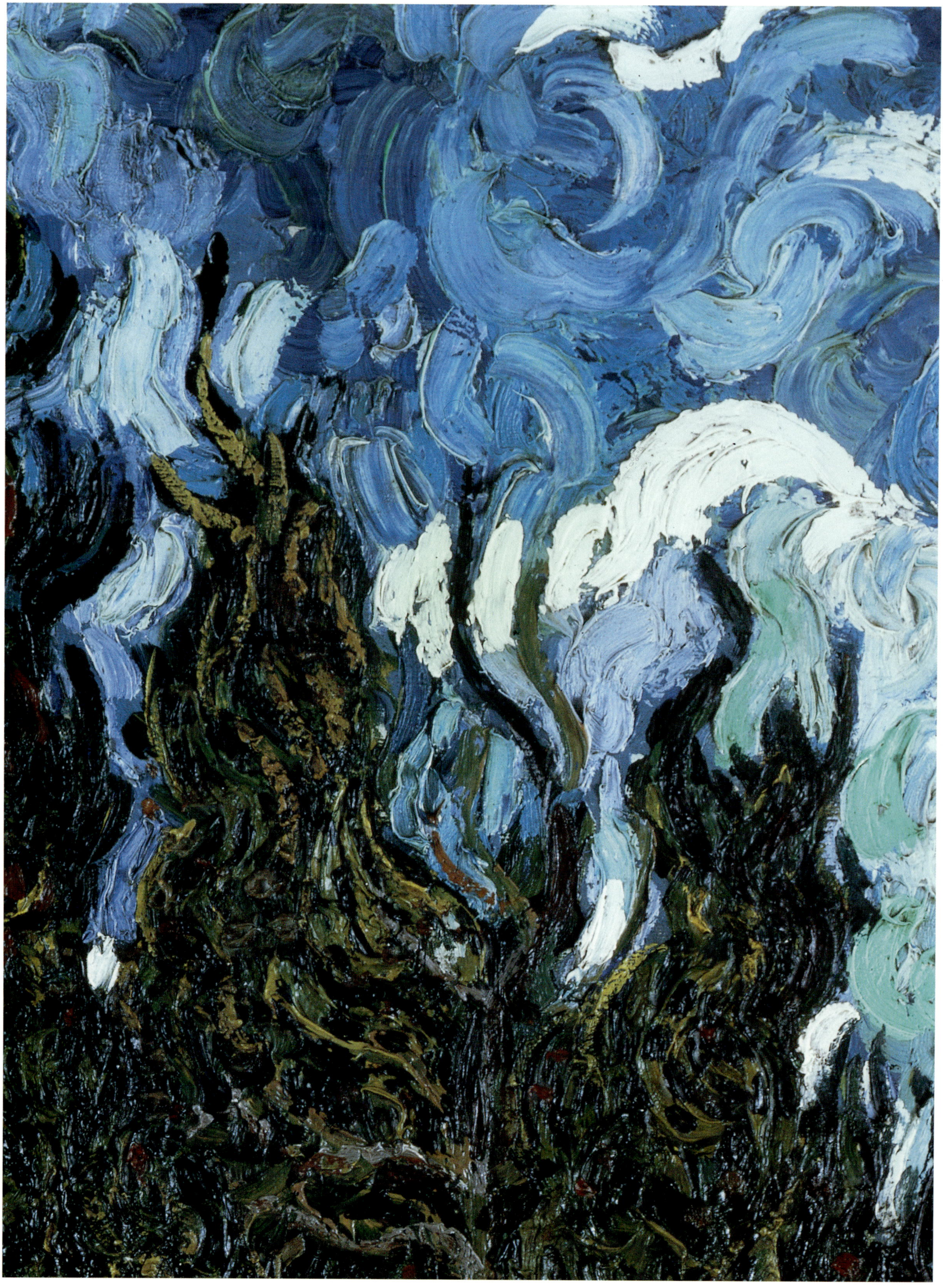

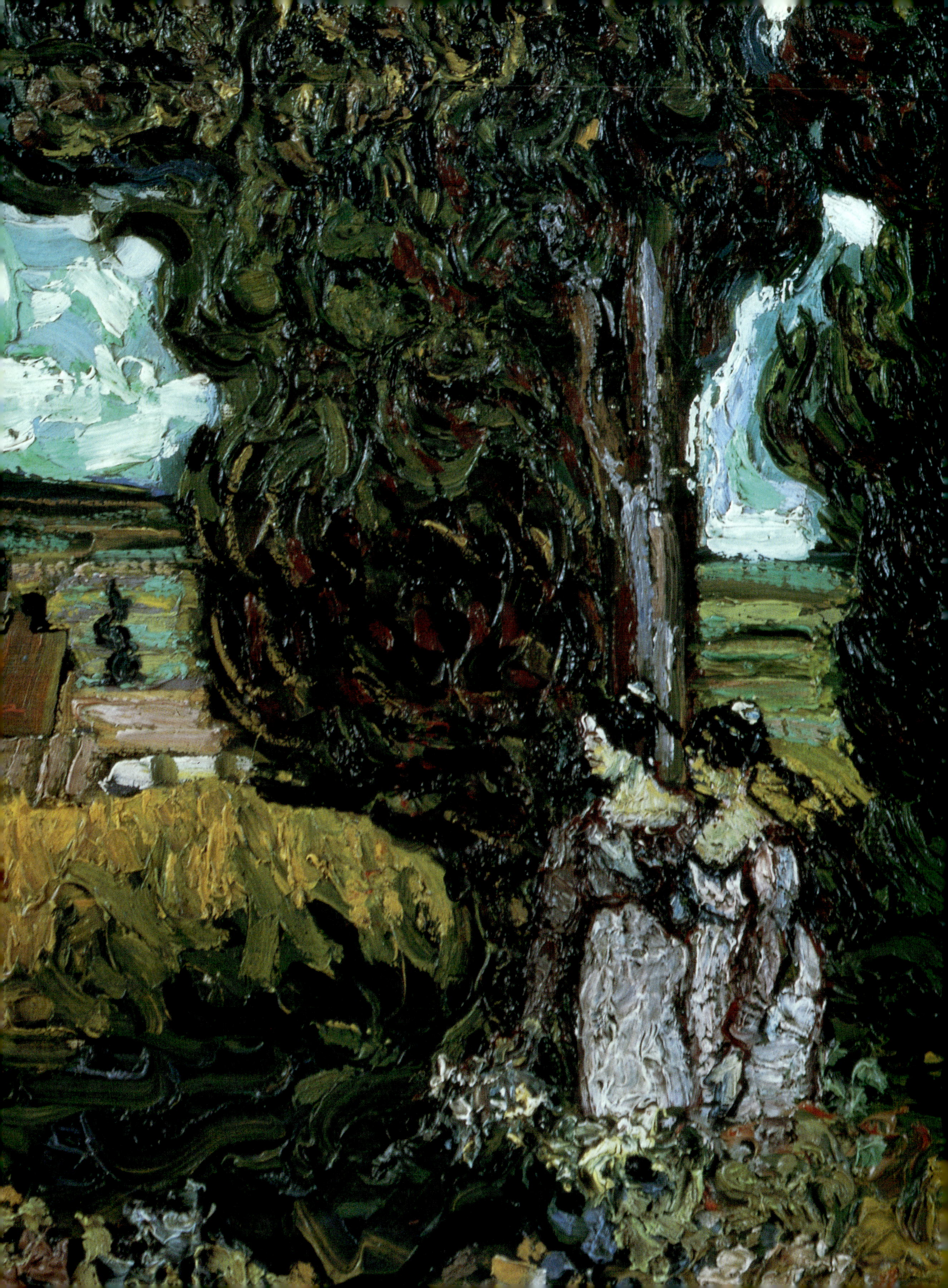

When Gauguin was with him, Vincent said he received "courage to imagine things and certainly things from the imagination take on a more mysterious character," but when he painted alone he preferred to base his art on actuality. A change came after he suffered a vivid hallucination and painted what he had seen in this dramatic revelation.

Magnified stars and swirling nebulae careen through a menacing firmament in which the moon and the sun are one. The luminous power of this strange sky is mated with nature below through the reach of a cypress tree. Undulating hills cooperate with the heavenly race while a town on the edge of an olive grove stands as witness. Lights are turned on, and in the midst of the dwellings is a darkened church.

The landscape is that of Provence, though the church seems a memory of those his father served in Zundert, Etten, or Nuenen in the Netherlands. The village is emphasized through the use of architectural details Vincent created out of basic geometric shapes. To link the village with the uproar in the sky, he elongated the church steeple. An ordinary steeple would not have reached the horizon, but Vincent stretched his steeple until it pierced the heavens. Just as the towering cypress tree shows earth's participation in the momentous event above, the steeple might stand for man's aspirations. Vincent had a sentimental attachment to stars from his youth; he said that when he felt a need for religion, he went out at night and painted them. This scene gave him no choice.

STARRY NIGHT
Saint-Rémy, June 1889
Oil on canvas, 28 3/4 x 36 1/4 inches
The Museum of Modern Art, New York
Acquired through the Lillie P. Bliss Bequest

➢

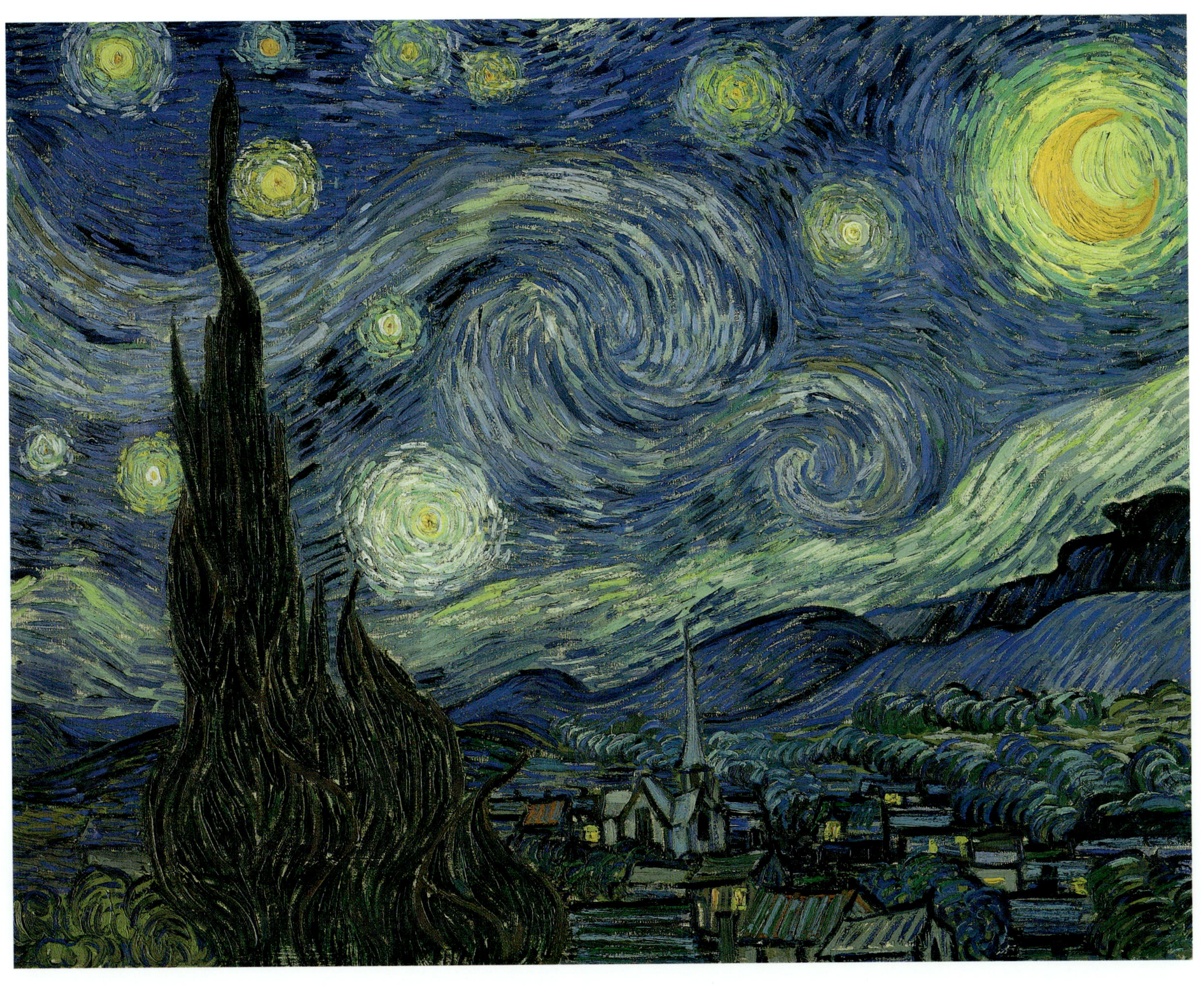

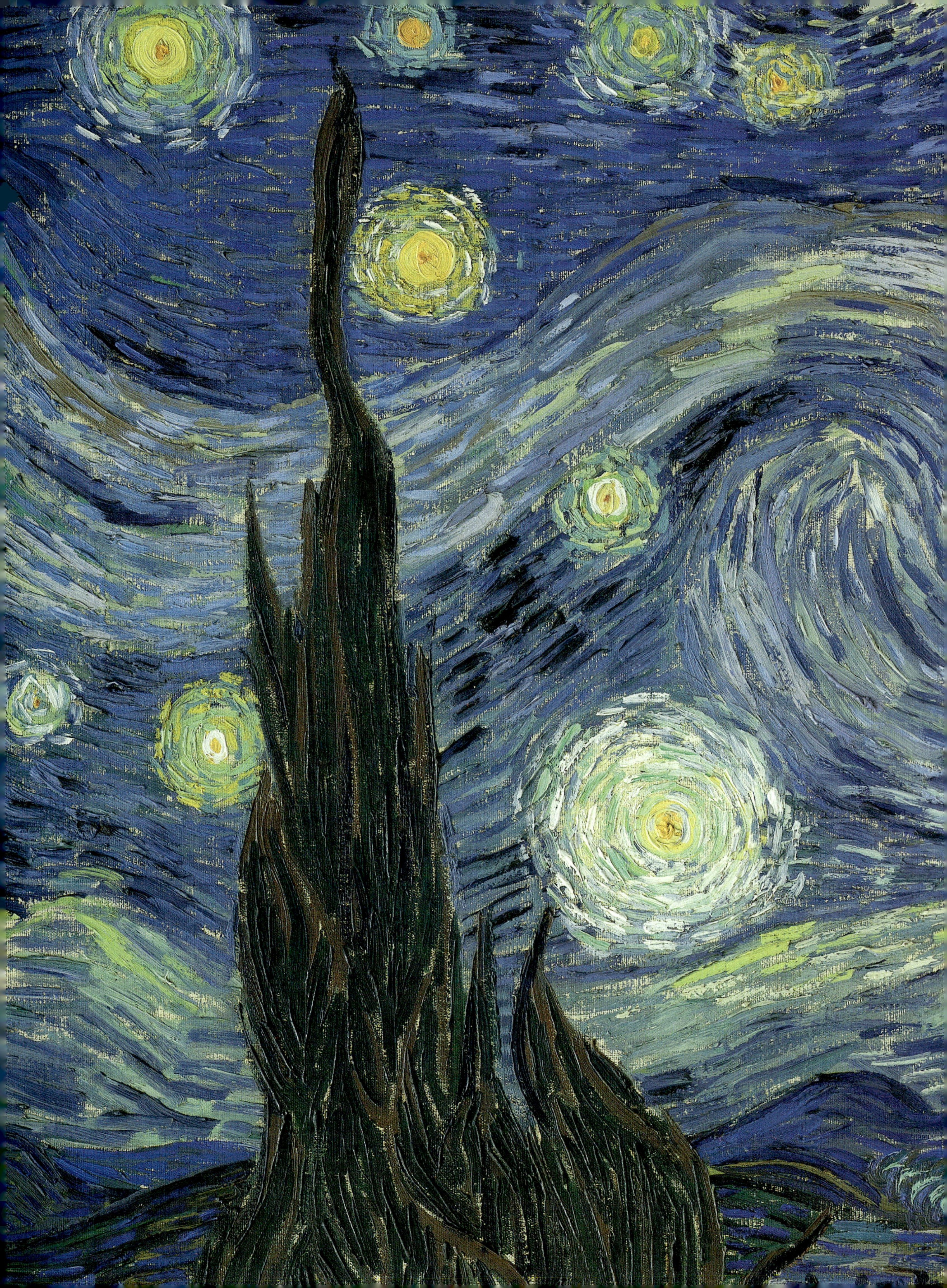

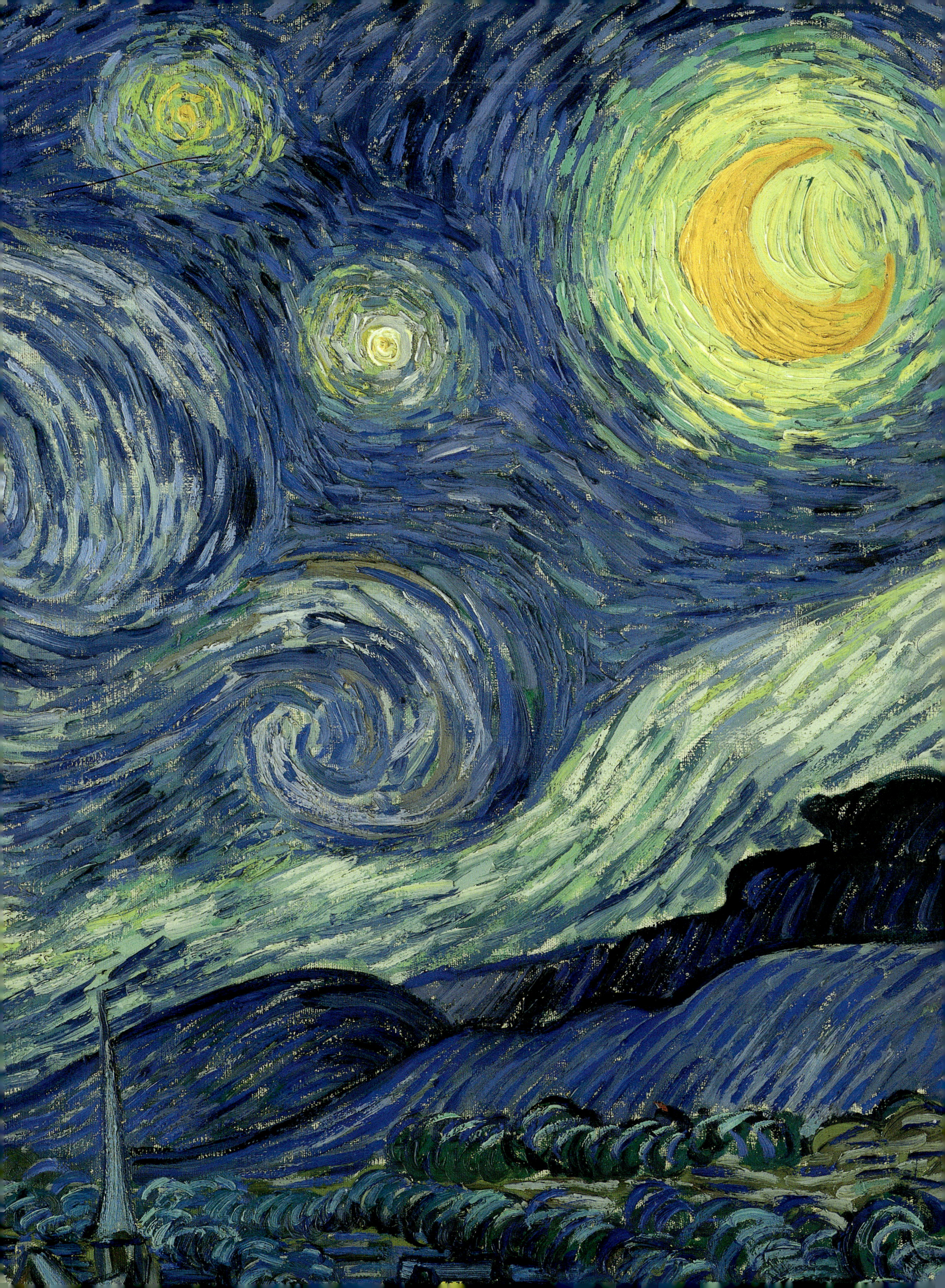

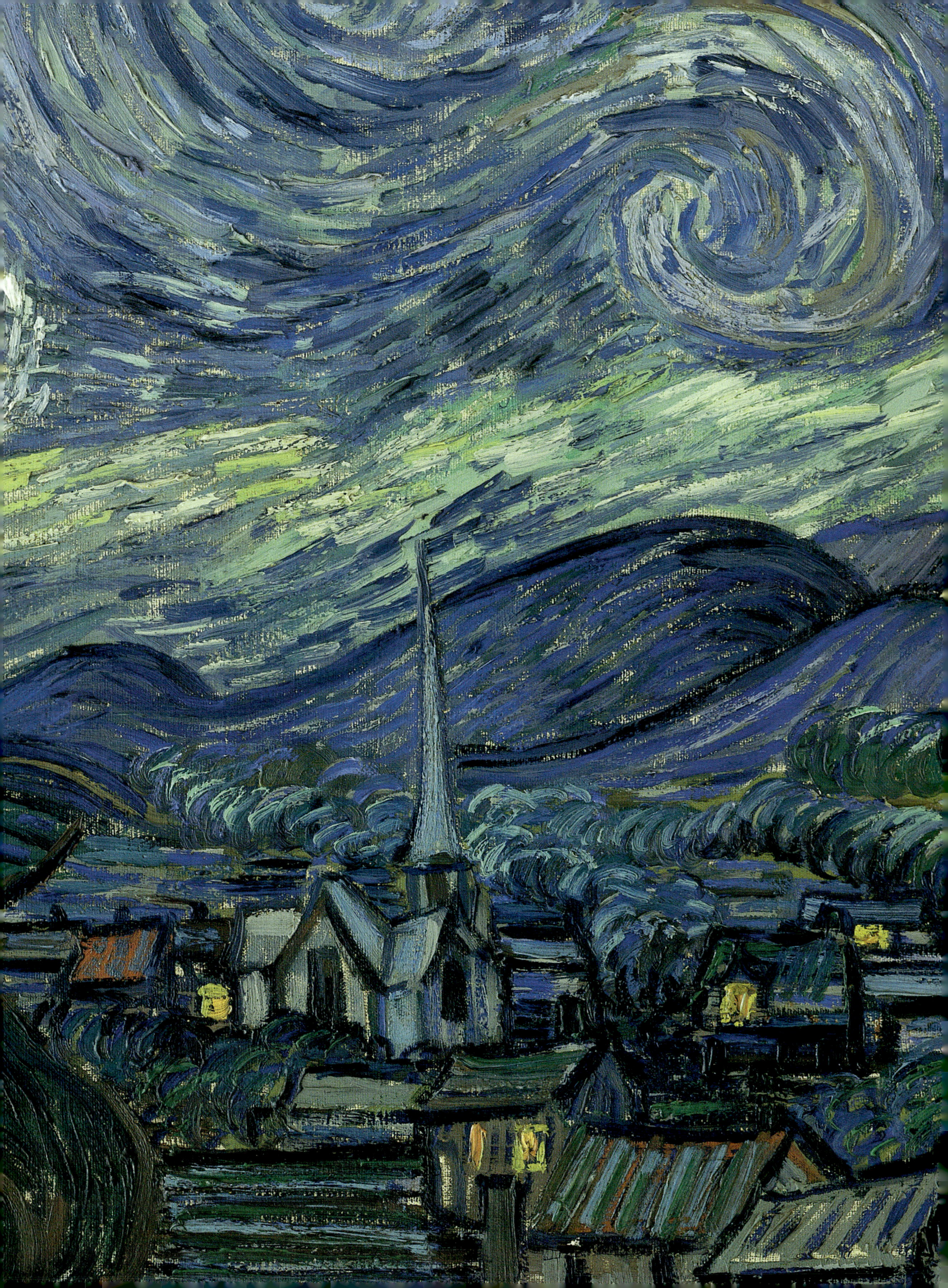

FROM HIS STUDIO WINDOW IN THE "rest home," as he described the asylum, Vincent saw this enclosed field and the rugged slopes of the mountain foothills. This landscape became the convenient subject of many of his paintings. In all of them, a wall cuts through the composition. Here it brings the eye to the scribbles and colliding lines that describe, in Vincent's words, a harsh study of "clods of earth...rough fields and rocks, with a thistle and dried grass in a corner." On top of blended neutral tones, Vincent's brush made short dash-like marks and choppy lines in a manner closer to drawing than painting. They flow in contrary formations toward the farmer, "a little fellow, violet and yellow...dragging a truss of straw."

In contrast, small plots of land beyond the wall are carefully plowed and planted. The violet color of the hills invades some of them and bright green suggests verdure. There seems to be unlimited space under the slice of "green-blue sky with a little white and violet cloud." Other paintings of the same scene by Vincent make clear what this one does not—that the lone farmer's labor will be rewarded with a rich harvest of wheat.

ENCLOSED WHEAT FIELD WITH PEASANT
Saint-Rémy, October 1889
Oil on canvas, 28 3/4 x 36 1/4 inches
Indianapolis Museum of Art
Gift of Mrs. James W. Fesler in memory of
Daniel W. and Elizabeth C. Marmon

➢

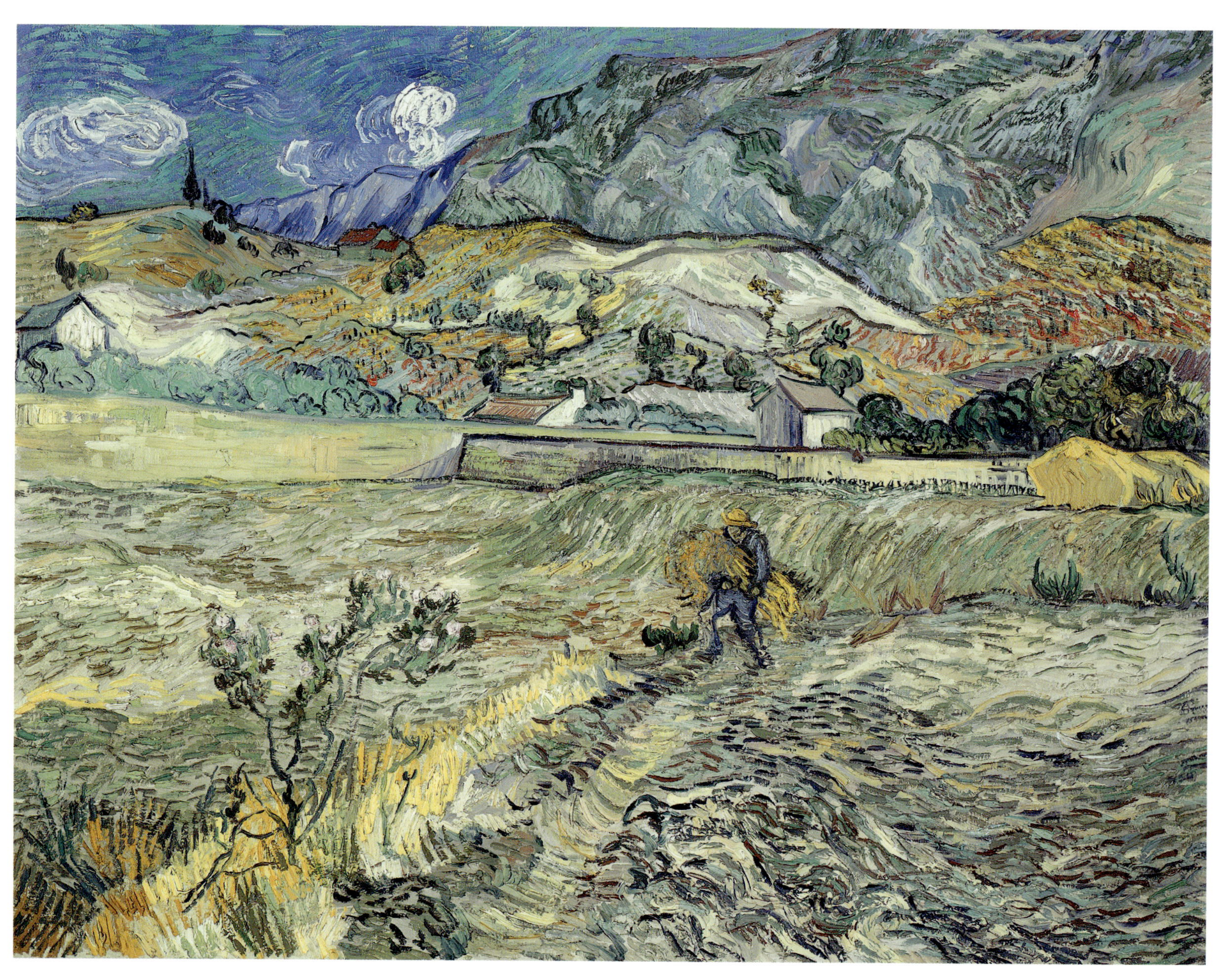

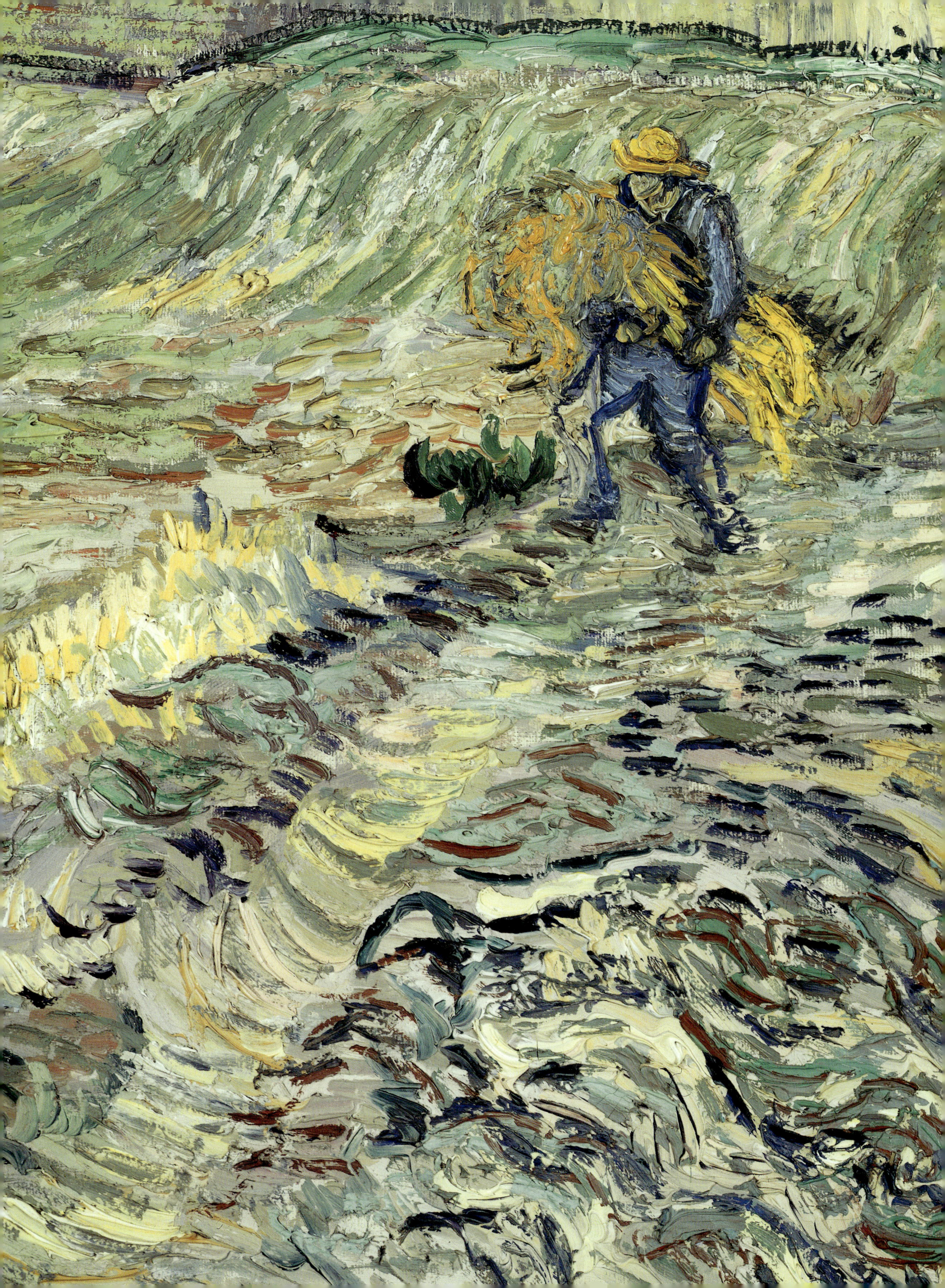

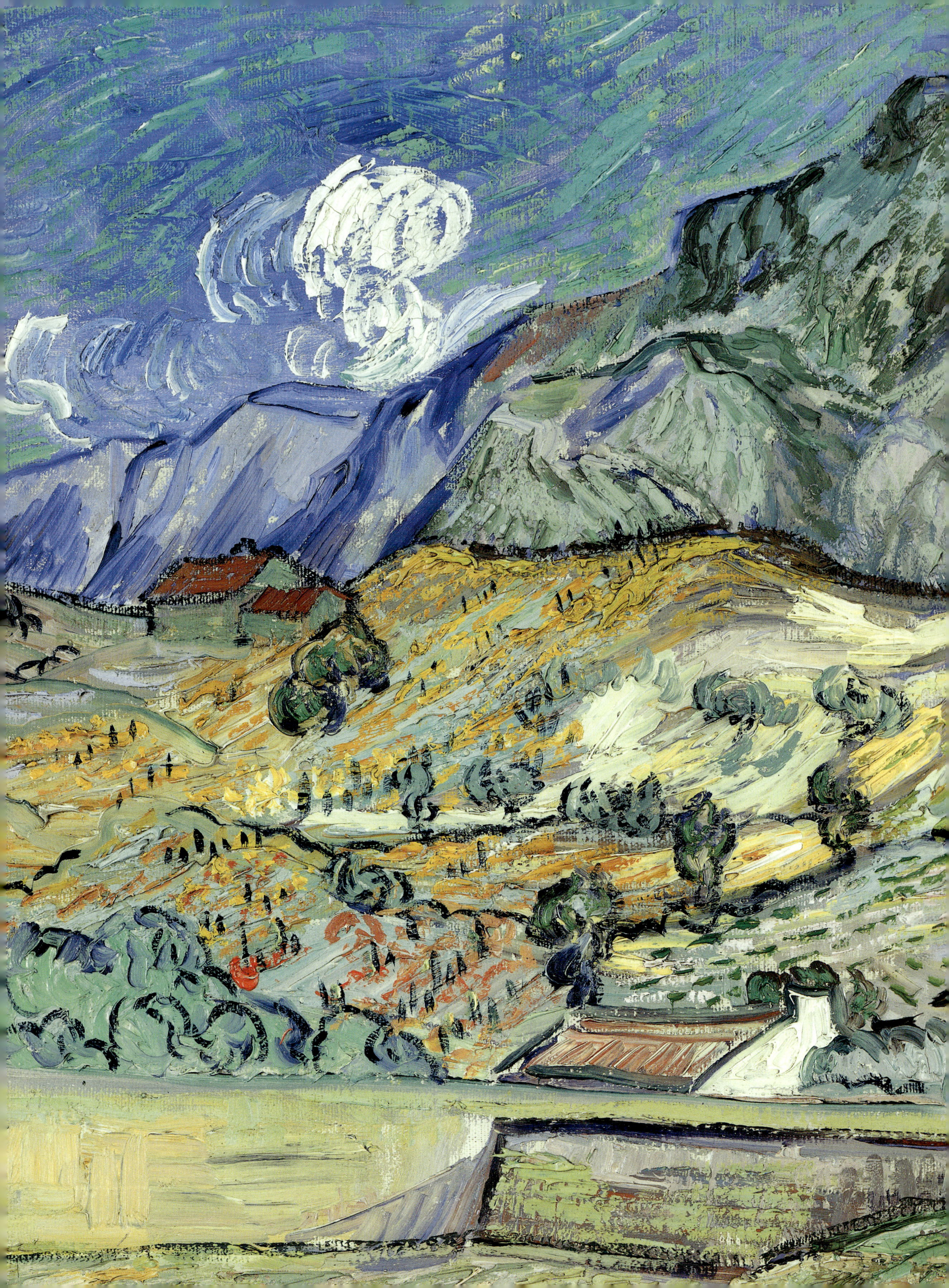

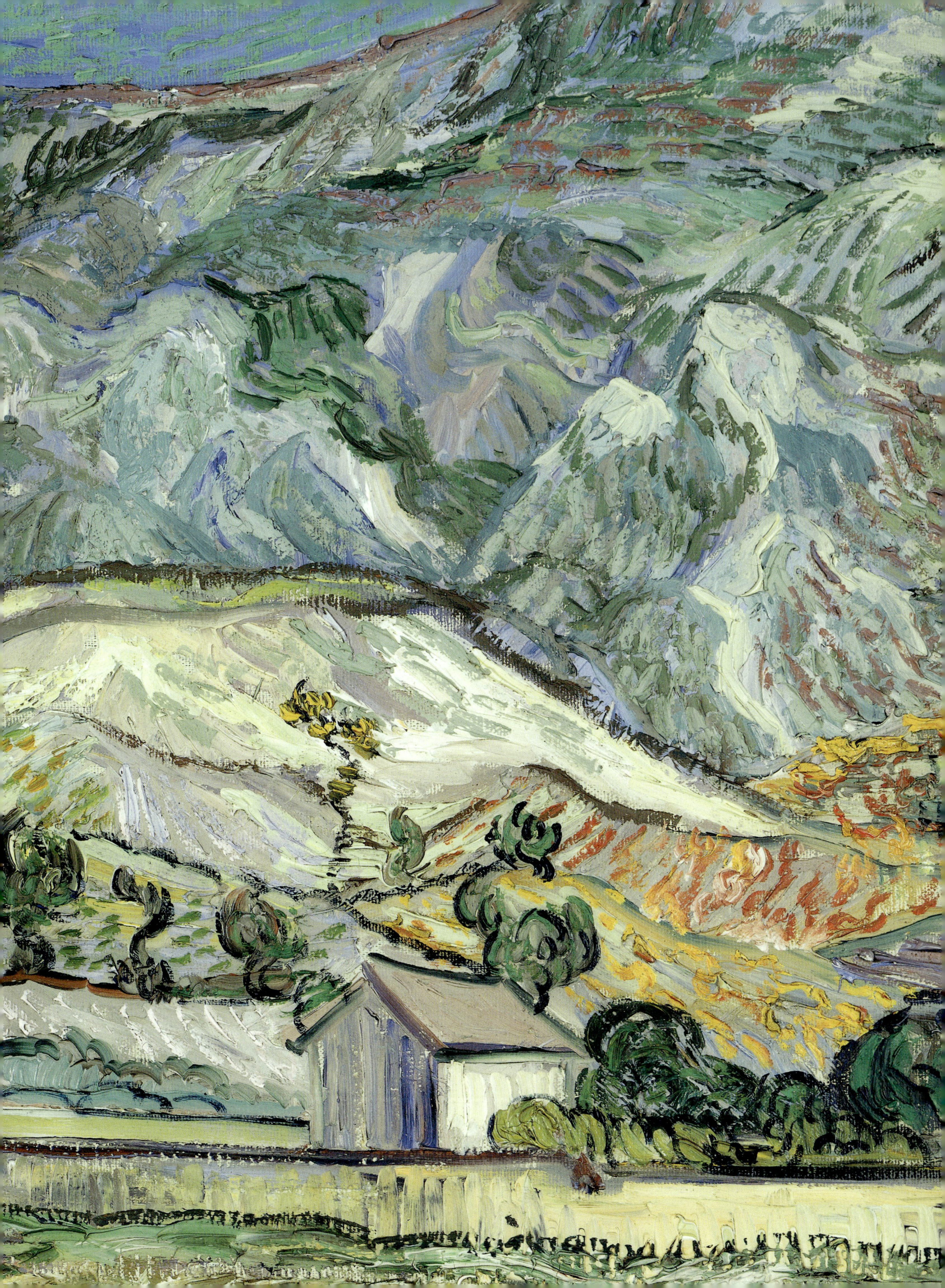

VINCENT'S UNDERSTATED DESCRIPTION of this painting was, "Two yellowing poplars against a background of mountains." Using his terse inventory style, he said nothing more. Descriptions sent to Theo were meant to let him know what pictures would be arriving at his gallery or which ones were to be set aside for exhibitions. It is not unusual that colors are not described correctly; Vincent probably reworked the paintings after he wrote about them. Here, the yellow has turned into orange.

A mountainous path winds along the edge of a drop to a narrow valley below. The precipice is delineated by tufts of grass, upright planks, and cut stones. Two tall poplar trees cling to the slope, their violet shadows spilling across the rise on the other side. They mask much of the dramatic landscape and they seem to be the phenomena that are energizing the earth from which they grow. Their torch-like shapes spit flames as they stretch to the highest point in the painting, lifting the earth with them and exciting lightning above. Though the scene seems inhospitable, Vincent placed a house between the poplar trees on the slope that leads to the mountaintop.

TWO POPLARS ON A ROAD THROUGH THE HILLS
SAINT-RÉMY, OCTOBER 1889
OIL ON CANVAS, 24 X 18 INCHES
THE CLEVELAND MUSEUM OF ART
BEQUEST OF LEONARD C. HANNA JR. (1958.32)

➢

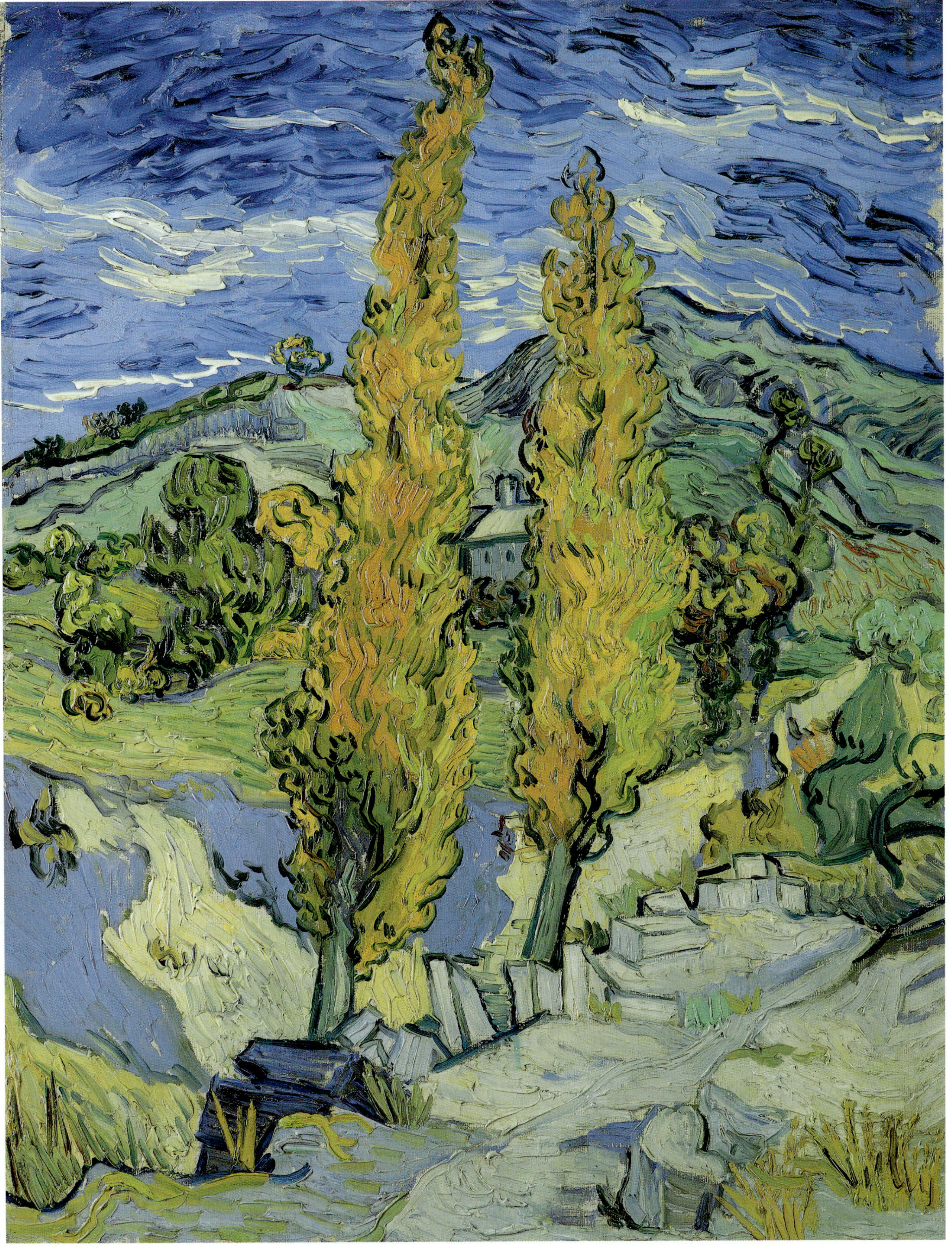

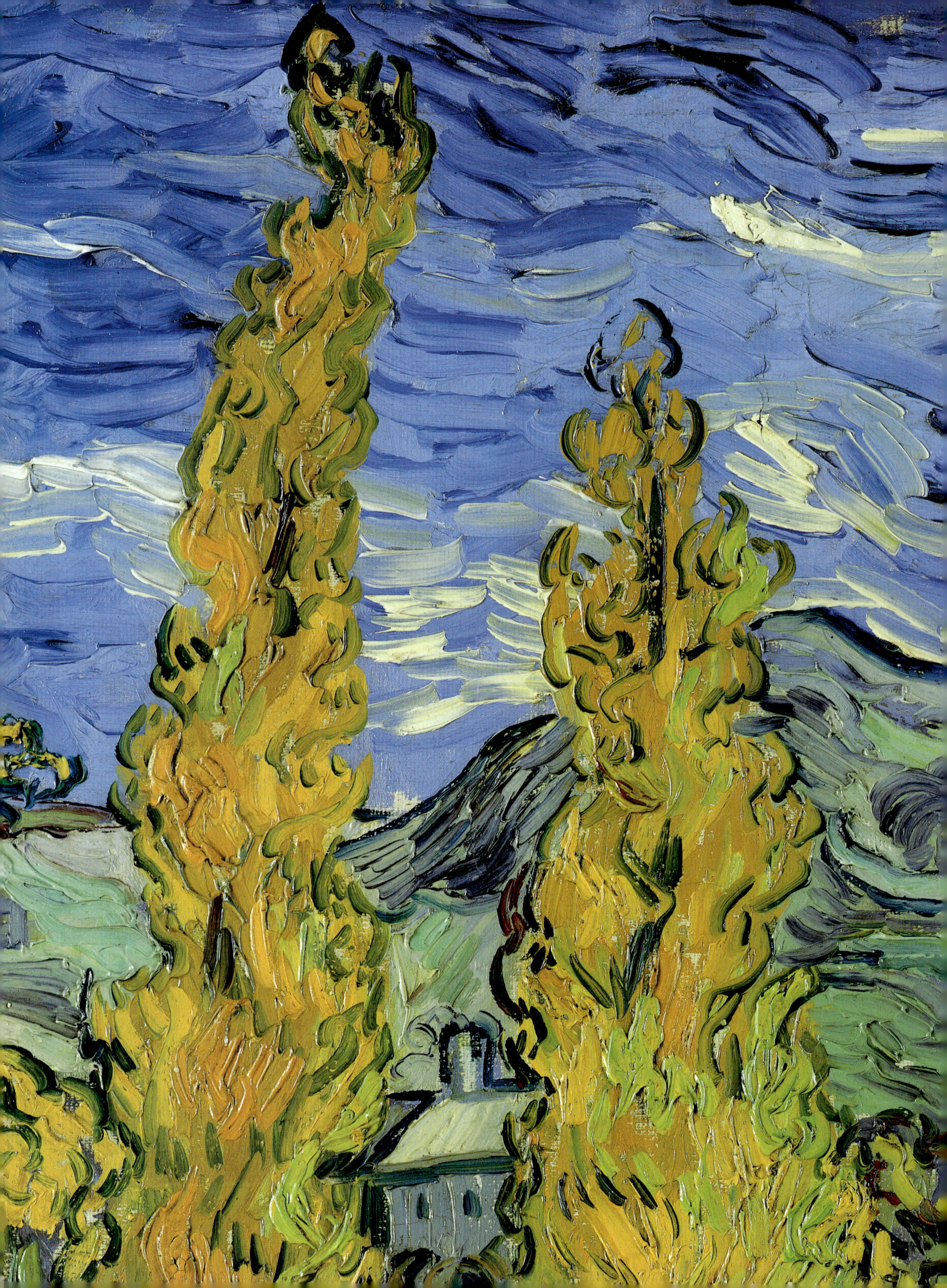

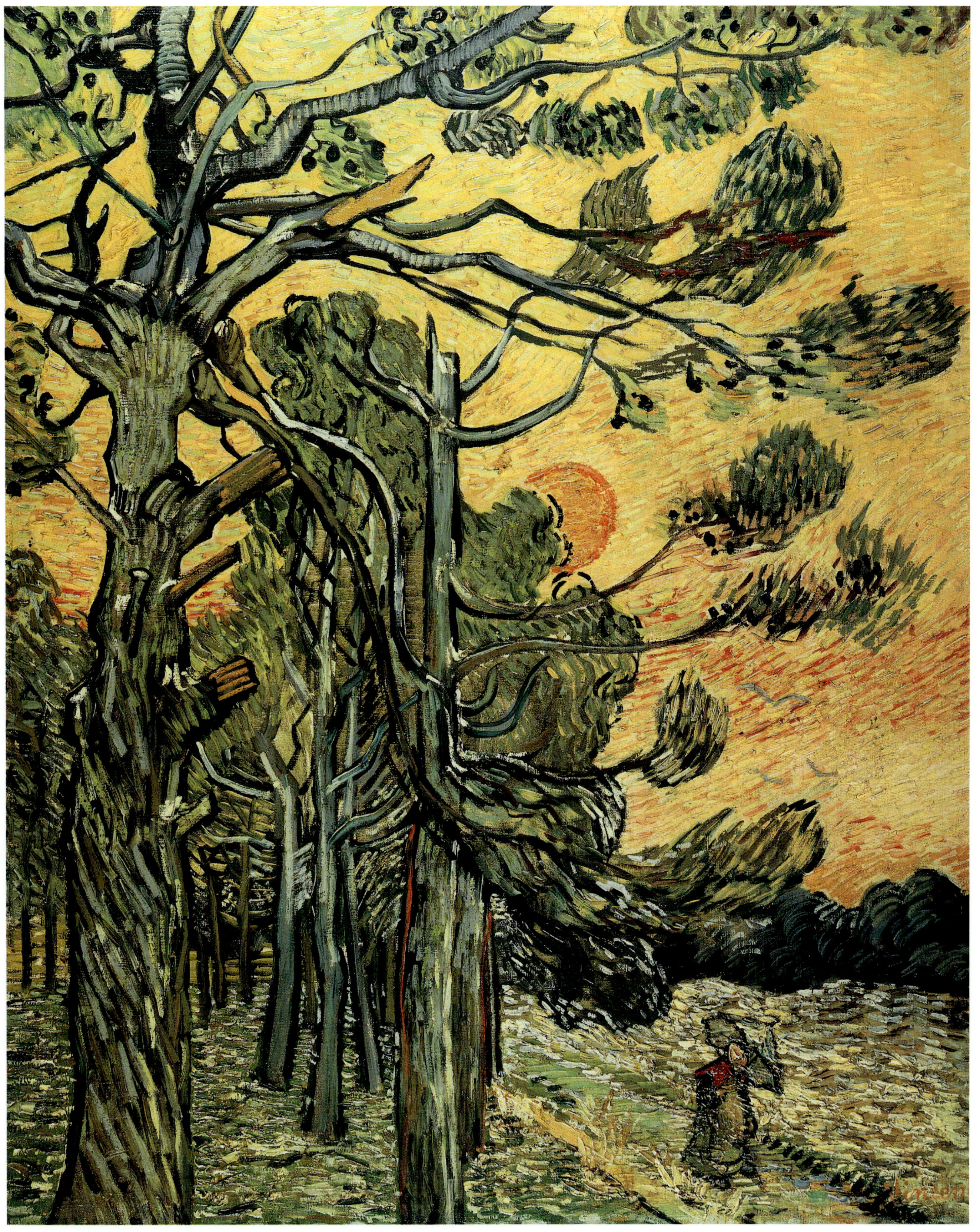

VINCENT OFTEN WORKED ON A NUMBER of canvases at the same time, probably to let the oil paint dry before adding more. He told his sister Wilhelmien that he had twelve in progress at the time he was painting these "tall weather-beaten fir trees against a red, orange, yellow evening sky." In the midst of the letter he said that he "got up in order to put a few brushstrokes" on this, the very canvas he was describing. When he let Theo know about his latest painting, he explained that a mistral was in progress—a squall of dry, cold wind that visits the Rhone valley of France every year. "Toward sunset it generally grows a little calmer, then there are superb sky effects of pale citron, and the mournful pines with their silhouettes standing out in relief against it with exquisite black lace effects."

Dead or lightning-damaged trees are symbolic of death in certain German and American landscape paintings of the nineteenth century. There are no references to such an interpretation in Vincent's letters, but his selection of this grove as a subject suggests a personal identification with weather-beaten trees. Vincent's short, waving lines cover the earth, and the sky is constructed of a dense and glorious mesh of short rising lines. The wounded trees are not mere witnesses to the sunset; they appear to be presiding over the uplifting show of color.

PINE TREES AGAINST A RED SKY WITH SETTING SUN
SAINT-RÉMY, NOVEMBER 1889
OIL ON CANVAS, 36 1/4 X 28 3/4 INCHES
KRÖLLER-MÜLLER MUSEUM, OTTERLO, THE NETHERLANDS

<

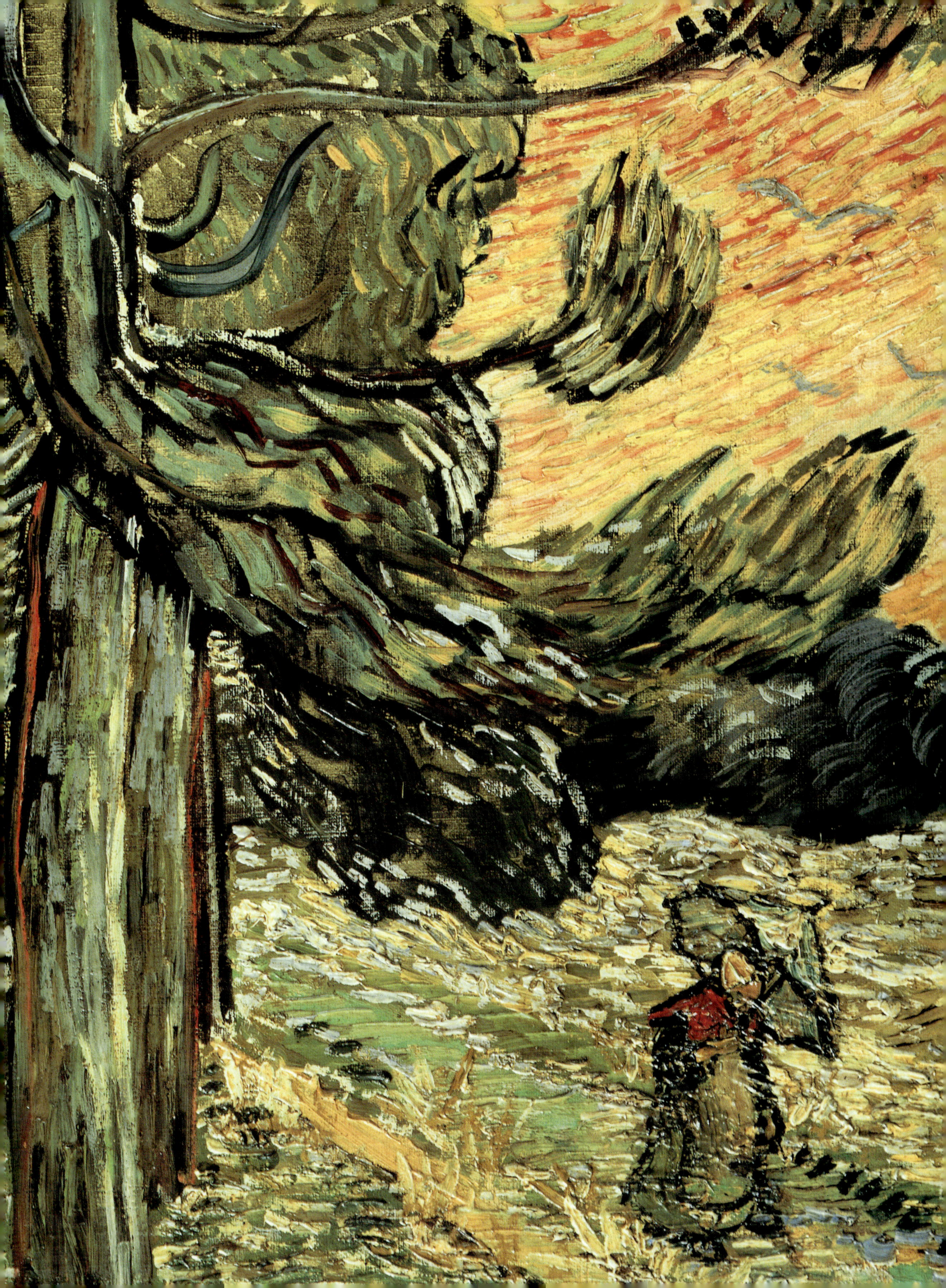

WRITING TO AN ARTIST FRIEND, Vincent described "a canvas which is in front of me at the moment. A view of the park of the asylum where I am staying; on the right a gray terrace and a side wall of the house. Some deflowered rose bushes, on the left a stretch of the park—red ochre—the soil scorched by the sun, covered with fallen pine needles."

Saint-Paul Hospital was built in the twelfth century as the Augustinian monastery of Saint-Paul-de-Mausole. It was quietly located in the shadows of the rugged Alpilles mountains, which appear in a number of Vincent's paintings. During his year there, he lived in one of the old monastic cells and had a second cell for a studio.

The perspective frame that had earlier helped Vincent draw accurate diagonals receding into the distance was forever put aside. He needed no aids to show the length of the building and the dimensions of the terrace. Because he often drew and painted in the garden, he most likely had memorized the shapes and colors of the bowed and bending trees, but—still impressed by the hallucinations of earlier that year—he used his imagination to capture the distant landscape and sky. The jagged mountains are orange and blue mounds, and telegraphic marks skip through the sky to form waving bands of orange, yellow, pink, and blue. The tufts of foliage uplifted by the trees in the garden respond antiphonally to the sensation above—like the chant of a giddy choir of monks.

THE GARDEN OF SAINT-PAUL HOSPITAL
SAINT-RÉMY, NOVEMBER 1889
OIL ON CANVAS, 29 X 36 1/4 INCHES
FOLKWANG MUSEUM, ESSEN, GERMANY/ART RESOURCE, NEW YORK

➢

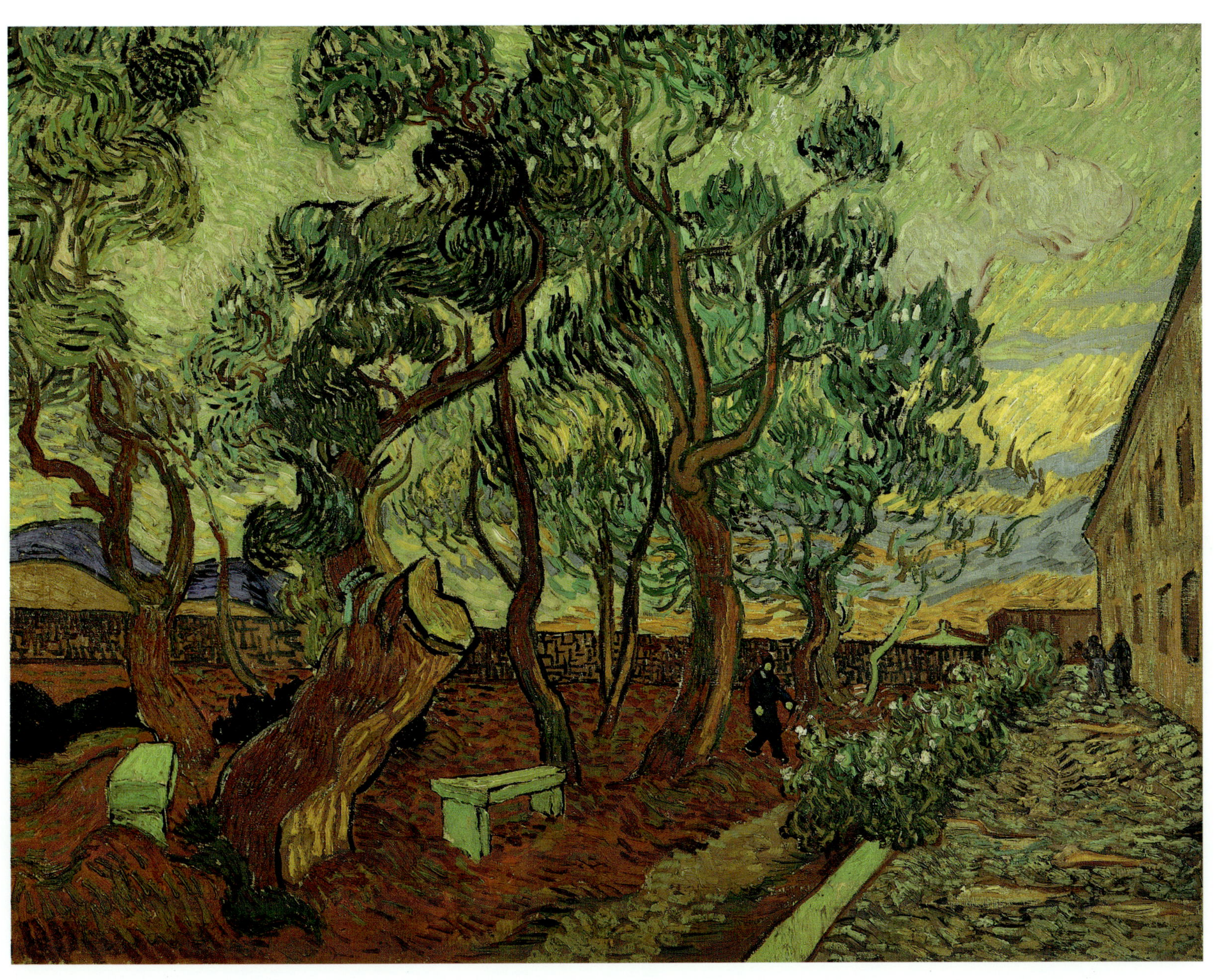

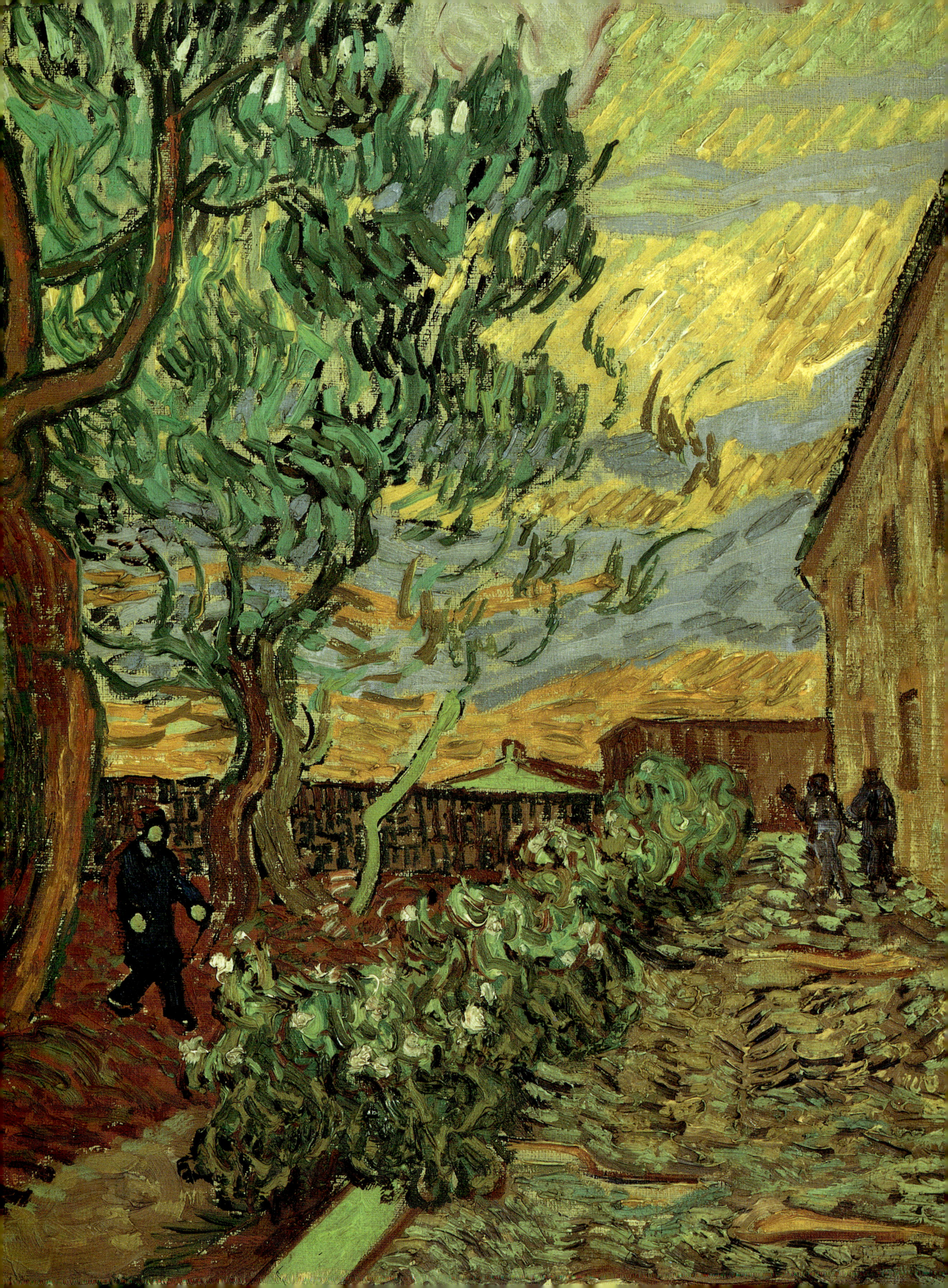

JEAN FRANÇOIS MILLET'S PAINTINGS OF the peasants of modern France gained wide popularity through prints made from them. Vincent copied some in oil paint, saying that they "posed" for him as a subject. He explained that he "started on it accidentally" and found that it was instructive and that "above all it sometimes gives me consolation." In painting this scene, Vincent improvised color by searching for memories of Millet's paintings. "And then my brush goes between my fingers as a bow would on the violin,...absolutely for my own pleasure."

The exhausting work of these field laborers is evident in the huge amounts of wheat they have downed—symbols of the landowner's wealth, not of theirs. They have not used long-handled scythes but sickles, which force them to bend close to the earth with every stroke. The backbreaking tools rest beside them in the shadow of one of the haystacks. The woman curls close to the man and his naked toe reaches for her foot as their rest slips into sleep.

The intimacy of this subject may have attracted Vincent because the pregnancy of his brother Theo's new wife Jo was very much on his mind. Their first child was born on January 31 and was named after the artist.

NOON: REST FROM WORK (AFTER MILLET)
SAINT-RÉMY, JANUARY 1890
OIL ON CANVAS, 28 3/4 X 35 3/4 INCHES
MUSÉE D'ORSAY, PARIS/ART RESOURCE, NEW YORK

➢

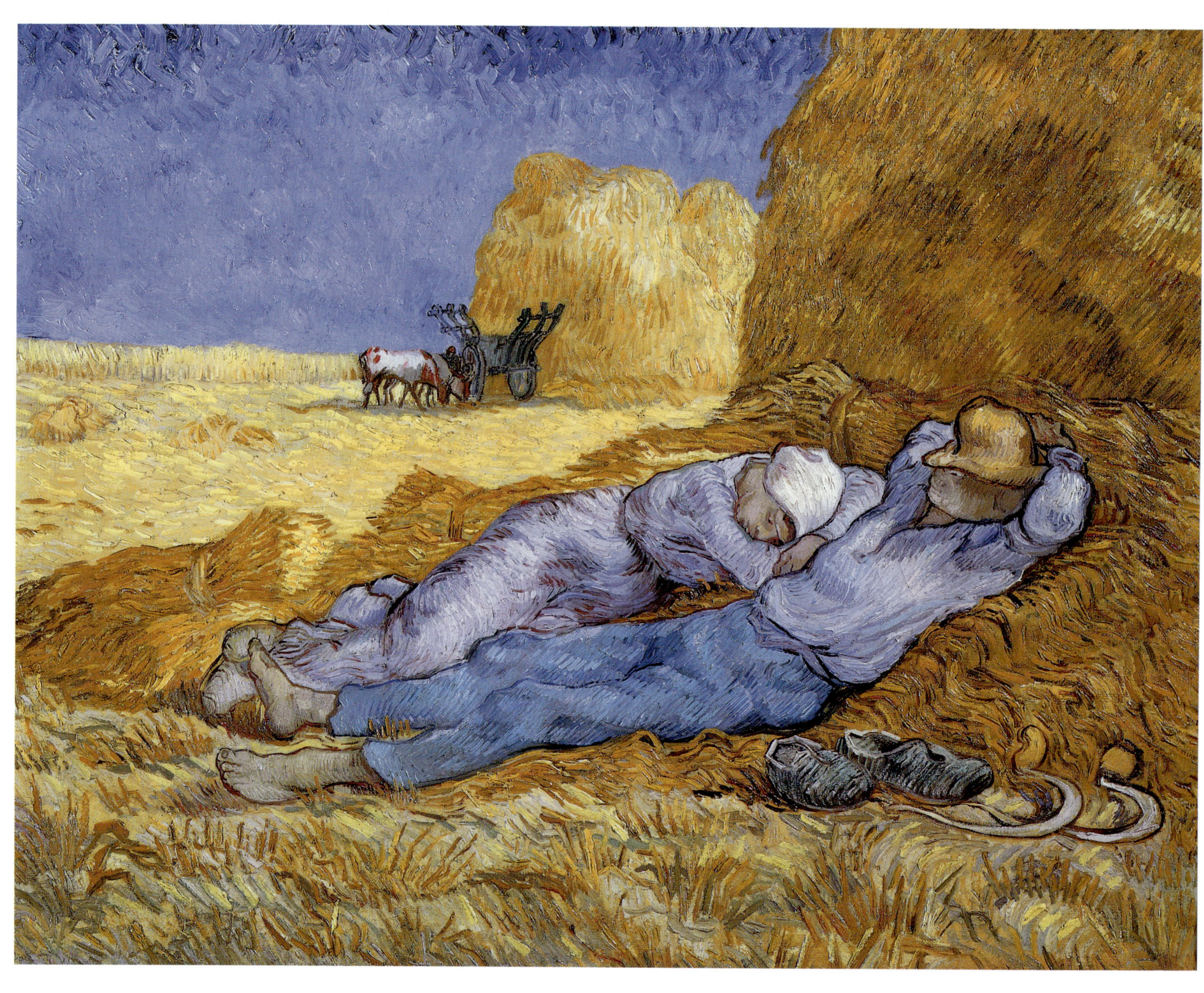

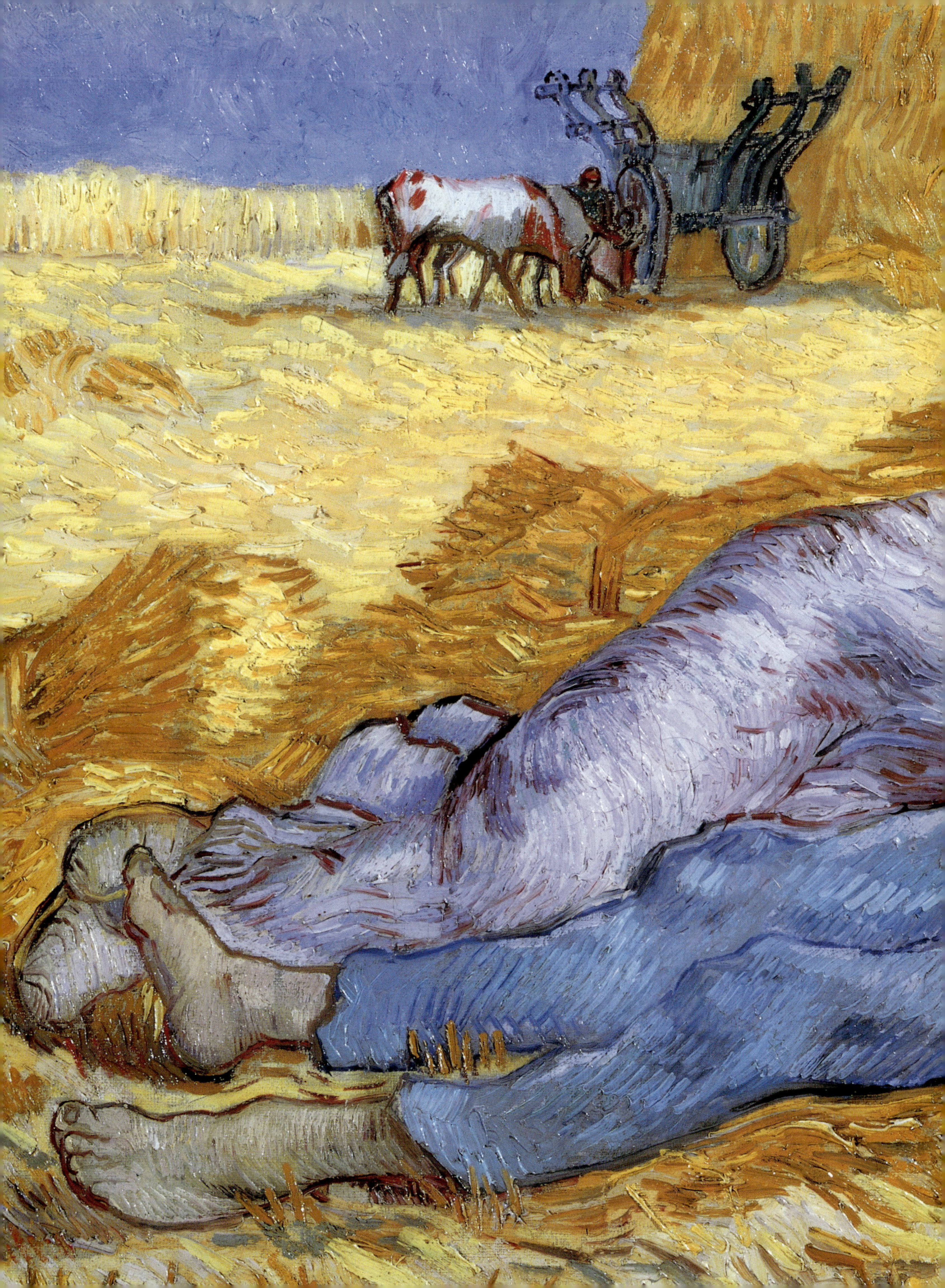

THE UNION OF EARTH AND SKY WAS accomplished in Vincent's paintings of his cloistered year at Saint-Rémy by using the same swirling patterns in trees and foliage as in the firmament. Here he does it by making the sky as verdant as the earth. "He perceived the ties that bound everything in Creation, each to each, and sought ways of giving expression to the connections between great and small in his art."

Green clouds lined in the orange of the setting sun cover a yellow sky that waits to appear. The same orange has touched the shrubs below. Two small figures walk between rows of houses that emit no signs of life.

No explanation is known for this small, miraculous vision. It is one of a number of paintings and drawings that are "Reminiscences of the North." Painted from memory, they show the mossy thatched cottages and flat land that Vincent knew in Brabant when he was young. The sky takes up two thirds of each scene, just as in early seventeenth-century Dutch landscapes. Those paintings, loved by Vincent, were also mainly monochromatic, using earth tones and never even a touch of lively green. At times during his illness, Vincent imagined not only the landscape of his homeland but every room and piece of furniture in the parsonage where he grew up.

COTTAGES AND CYPRESSES: REMINISCENCES OF THE NORTH
SAINT-RÉMY, MARCH–APRIL 1890
OIL ON CANVAS ON PANEL, 11 1/2 X 14 1/2 INCHES
VAN GOGH MUSEUM (VINCENT VAN GOGH FOUNDATION)
AMSTERDAM, THE NETHERLANDS

➣

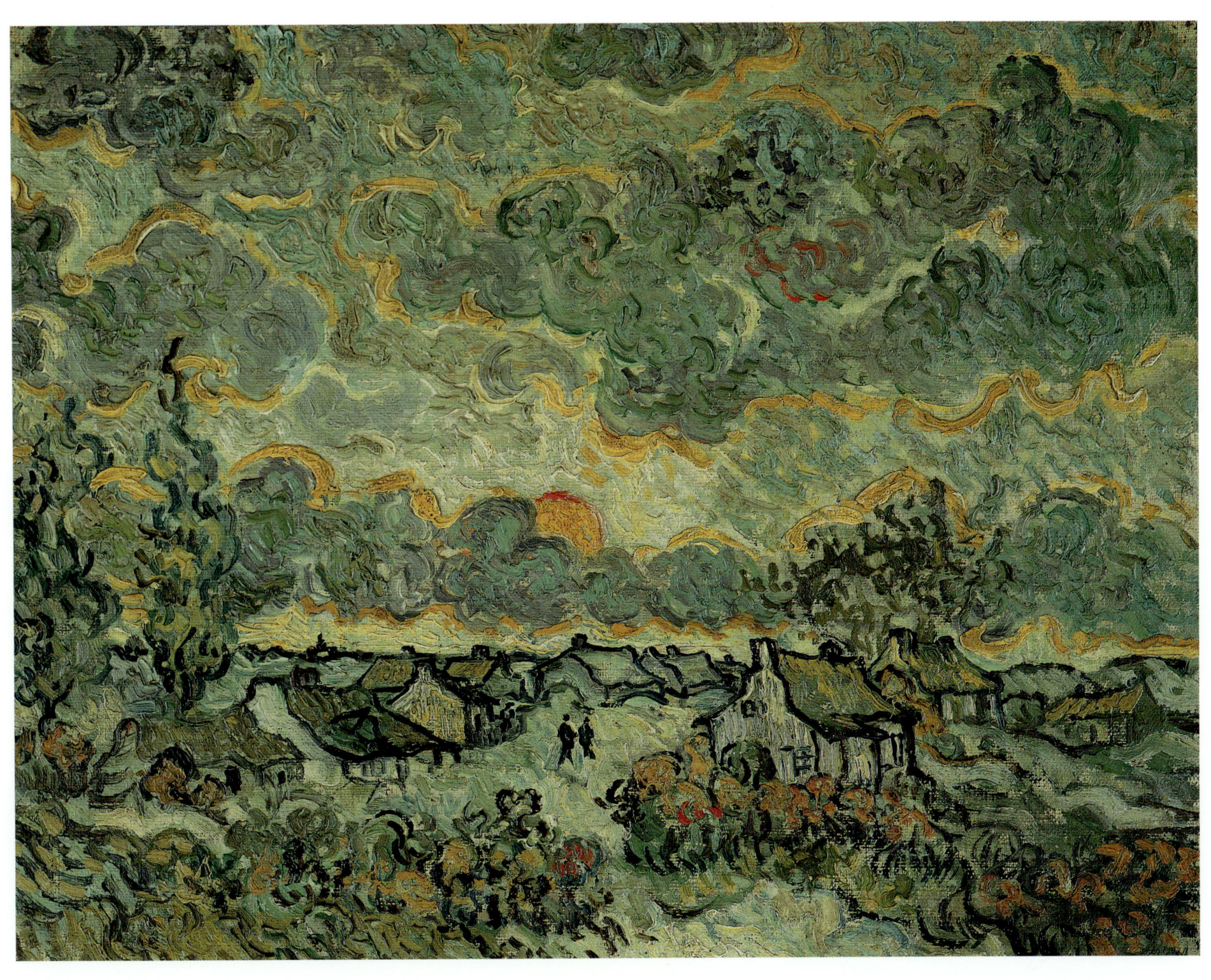

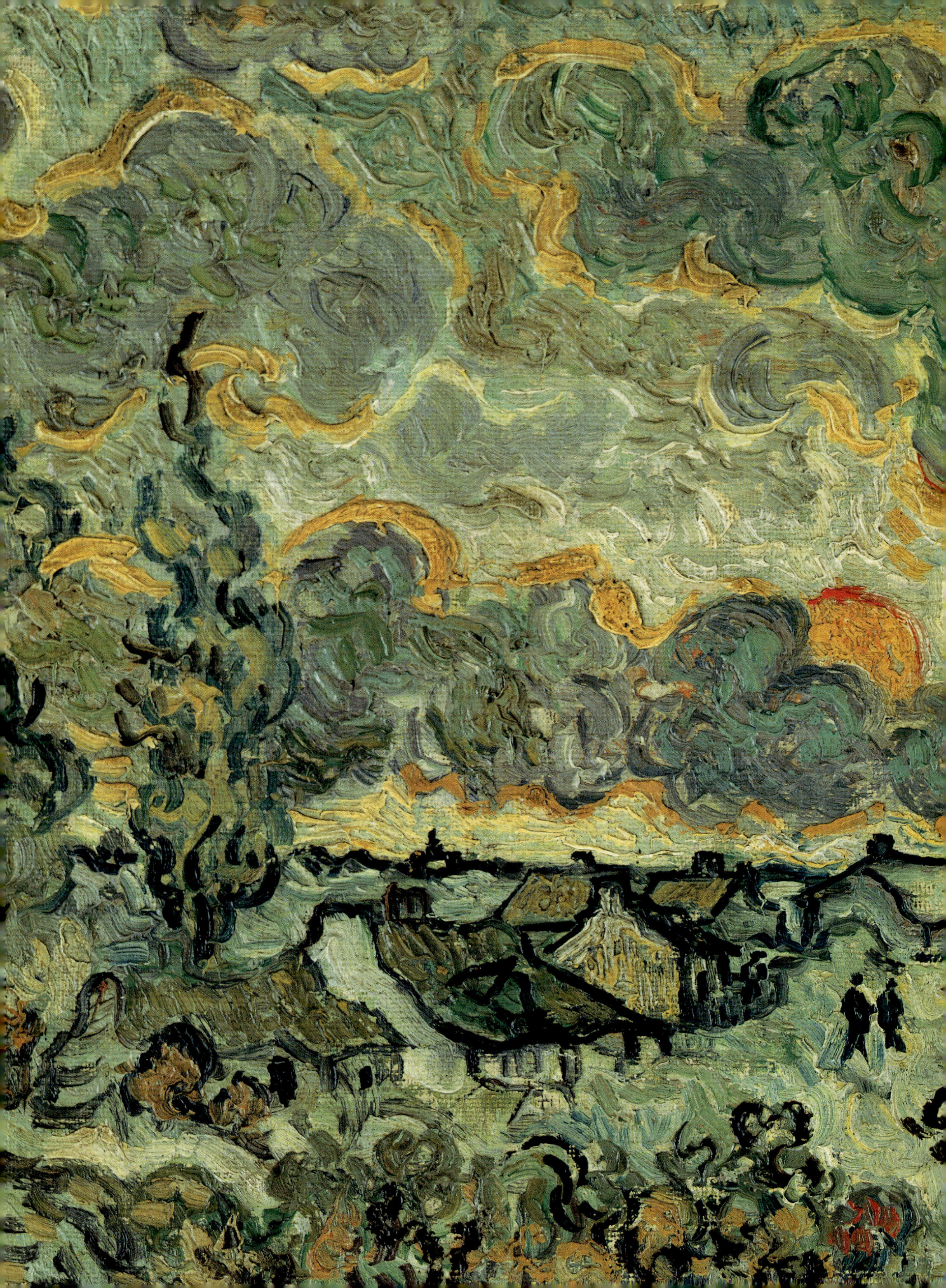

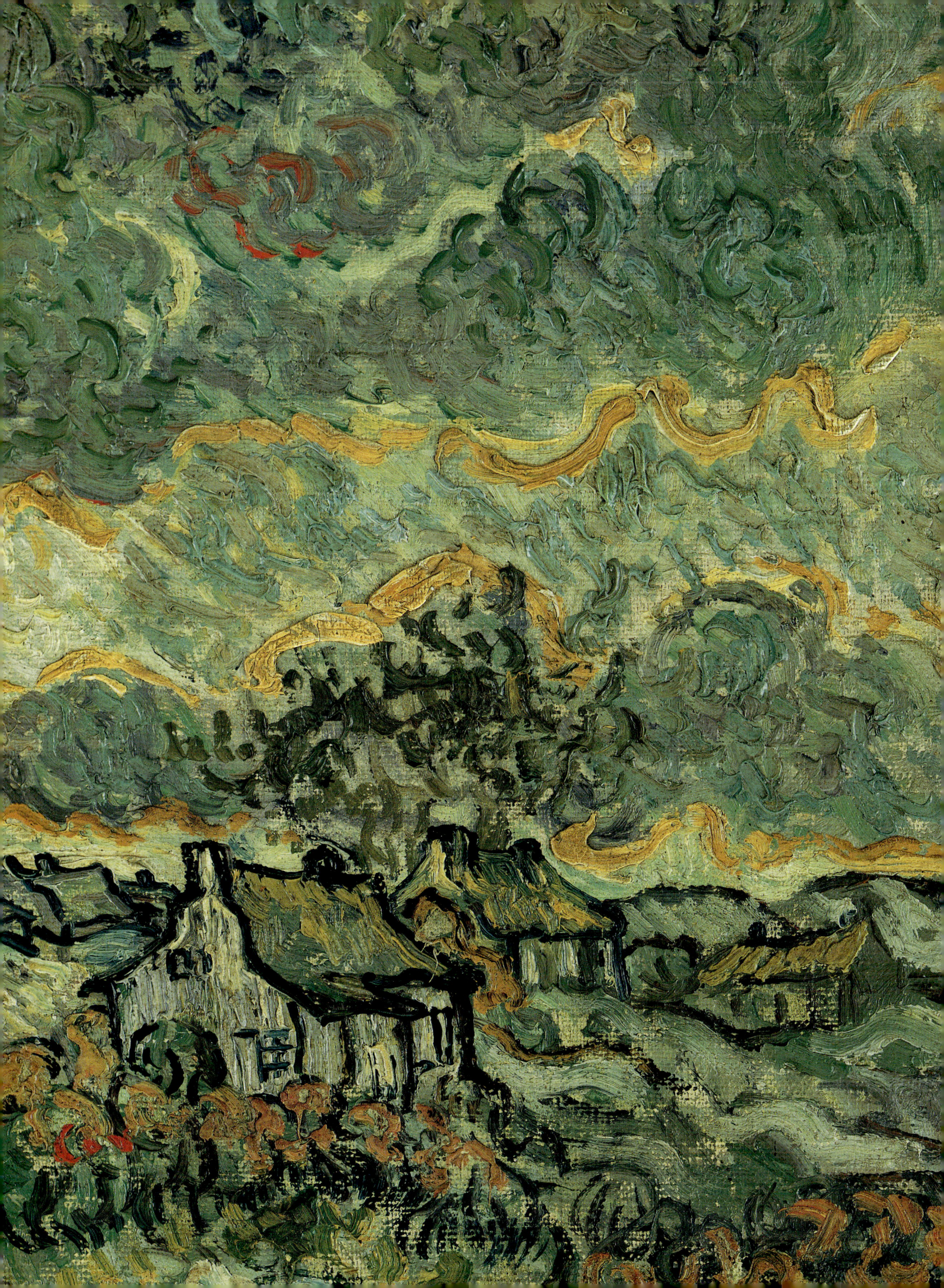

A CORNER OF THE ABBEY GARDEN presented Vincent with the contrasts of trunks of old pine trees, young yellow-green grass, white flowers, dandelions, and the dappled patterns of sunshine coming through a pine bower. He said that he worked on the painting for a few days in the blazing sun and that the result was extremely simple and vigorous.

The tree trunks that occupy one third of the painting have been enlivened by Vincent's fascination with their furrows and knobs and his search for the right "violet-pink" to depict their old bark. Though they lean to the left, the composition moves to the upper right corner of the canvas. In between is a beautiful wavy pattern of grass and flowers that seems to travel with the eye to the intense colors of the sun.

Vincent's modern approach to this scene ties him closely to many historic strains in art. Without his knowledge of Japanese prints, he probably would not have thought of cropping his composition so radically. His grassy patterns resemble the backgrounds of certain tapestries of the late middle ages called millefleurs, and his close-up inspection of nature suggests he was a disciple of Albrecht Dürer, even though the great German artist lived four hundred years earlier.

PINE TREES AND DANDELIONS IN THE GARDEN OF SAINT-PAUL HOSPITAL
Saint-Rémy, April–May 1890
Oil on canvas, 28 1/4 x 35 1/2 inches
Kröller-Müller Museum, Otterlo, the Netherlands

➢

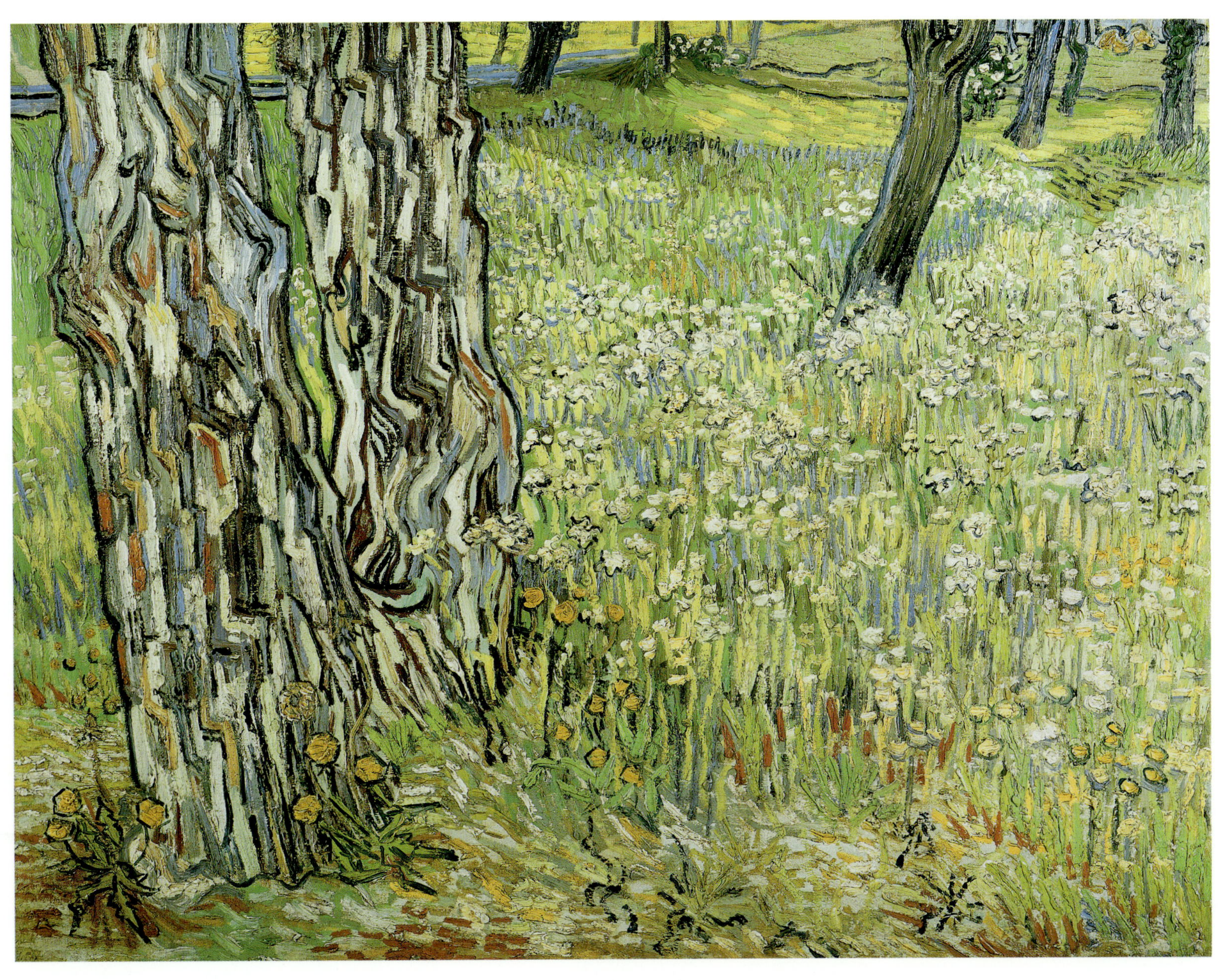

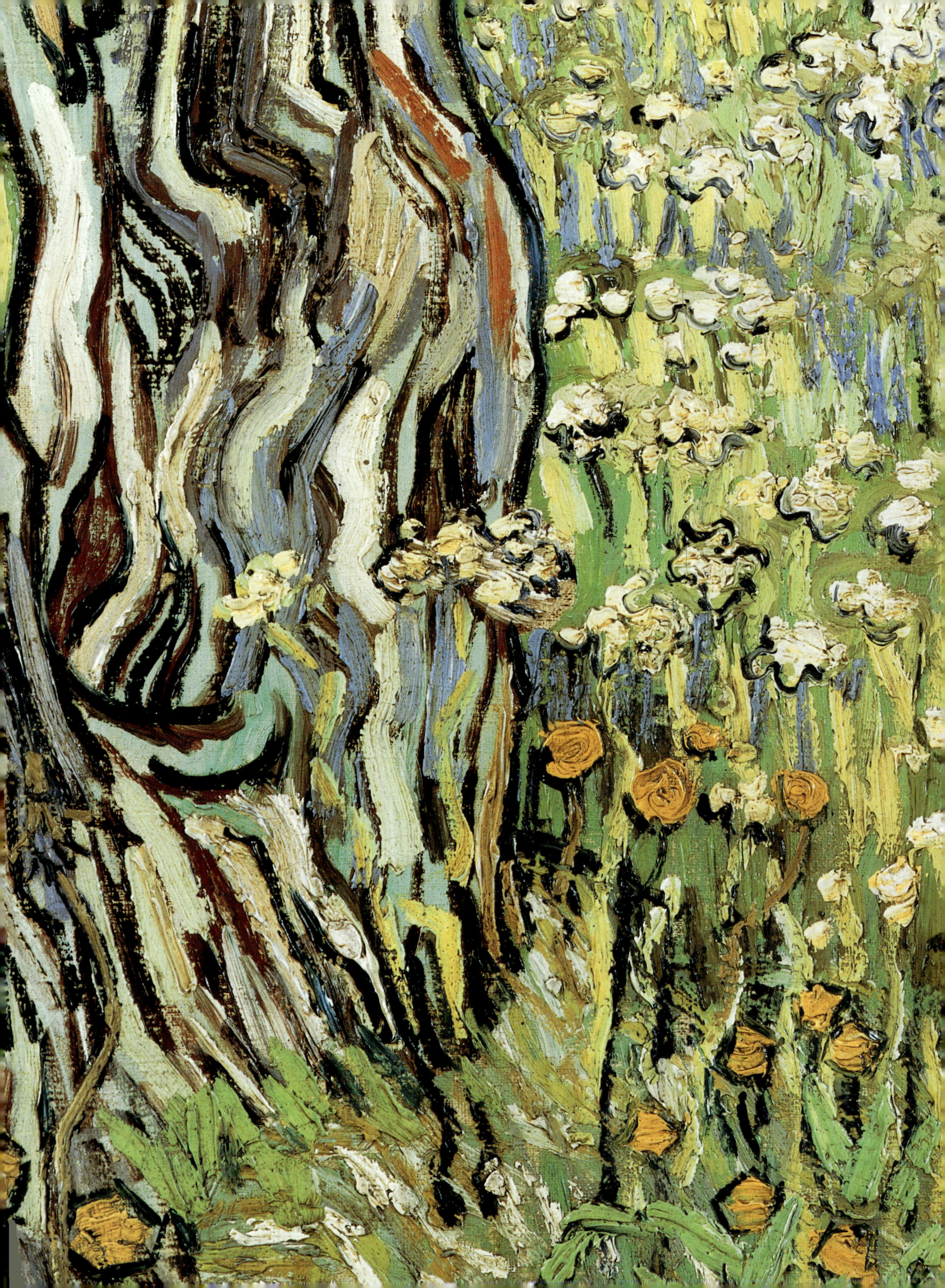

Cypresses were Vincent's "torches of the soul," a way to connect heaven and earth. Here, their quiet majesty contrasts with the awkward reaching in all directions of the olive trees, a duality that could represent the baser and higher instincts of man.

The cypresses are the only witnesses to a sunset that colors a crescent moon, for the couple at the bottom of the canvas is heading away from the remarkable sky. The upraised hand of the plump woman in yellow might indicate a lively conversation or that she has lost her step—or, perhaps, her way. Her redheaded companion looks toward her but they both walk on. The couple is not following a path but passing through an olive grove.

Psychological studies of Vincent's paintings say that couples, or a cypress tree growing from two trunks, seem to represent the kind of pairing that Vincent often desired. On reflective days, however, he was happy to say, "To do good work one must eat well, be well housed, have one's fling from time to time, smoke one's pipe and drink one's coffee in peace." His medieval abbey home provided him with everything—in frugality—except the "fling from time to time," which might suggest the destination of the couple.

LANDSCAPE WITH COUPLE WALKING AND CRESCENT MOON
Saint-Rémy, May 1890
Oil on canvas, 19 1/2 x 18 inches
Museu de Arte, São Paulo, Brazil/Art Resource, New York

➢

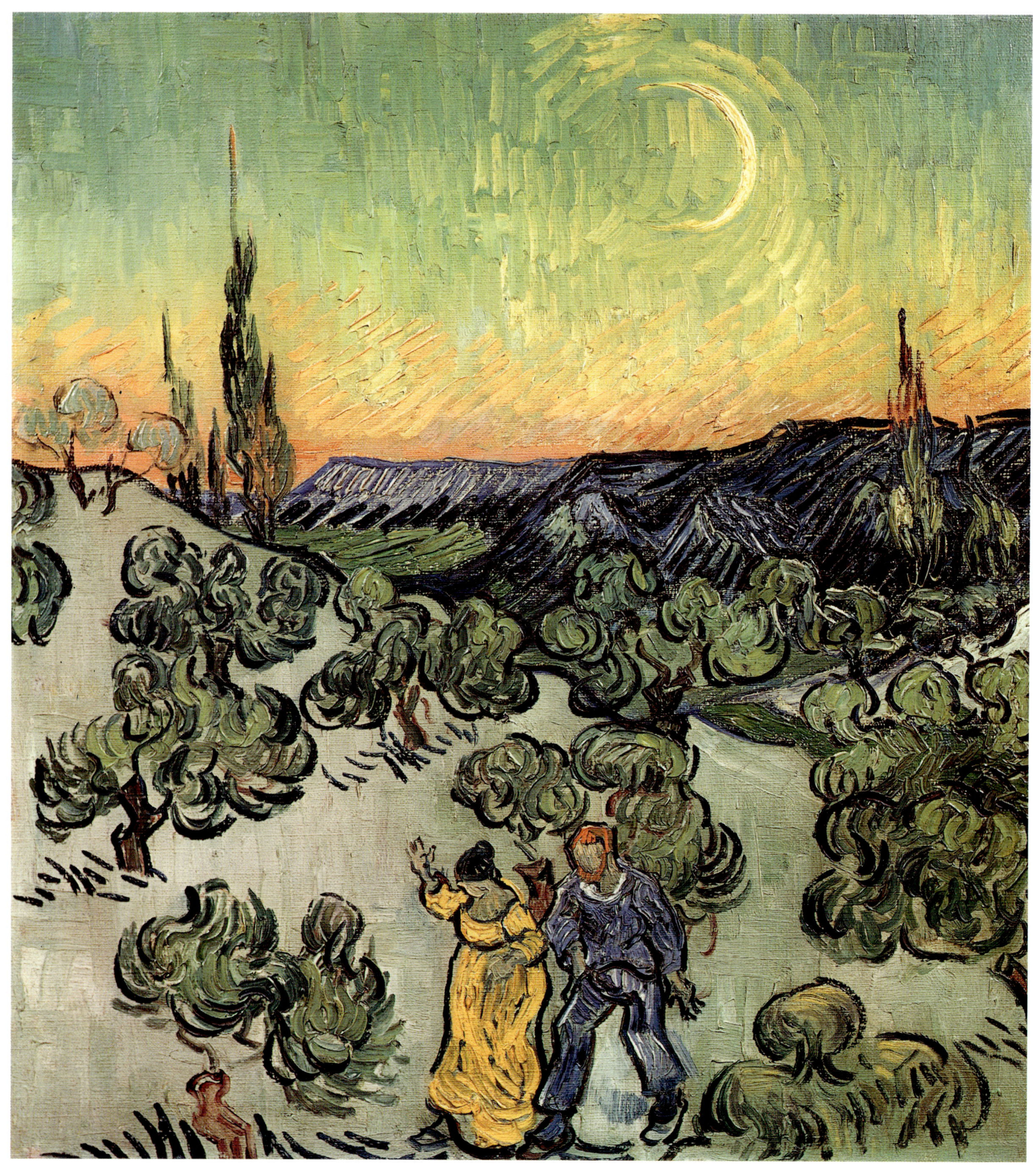

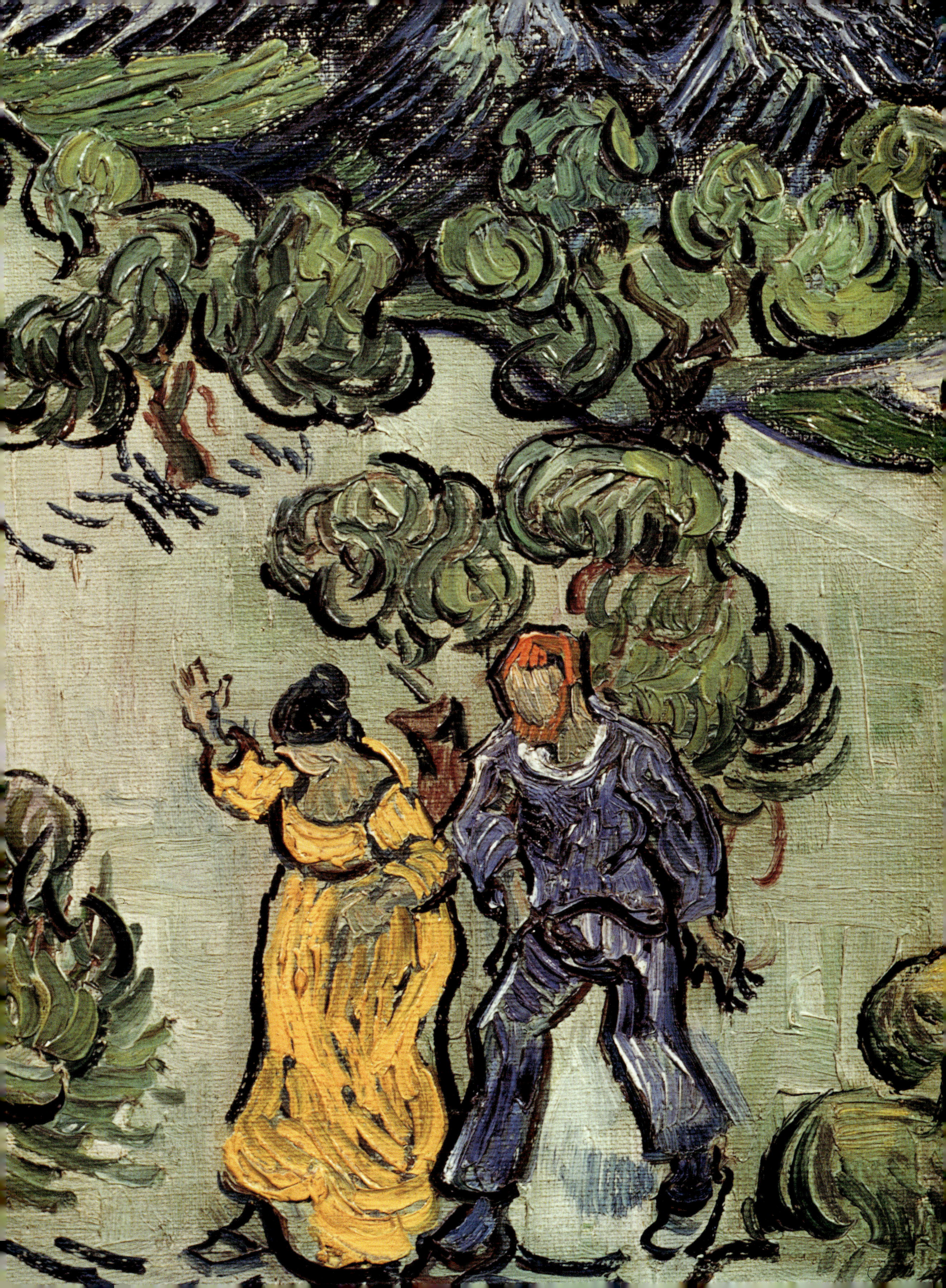

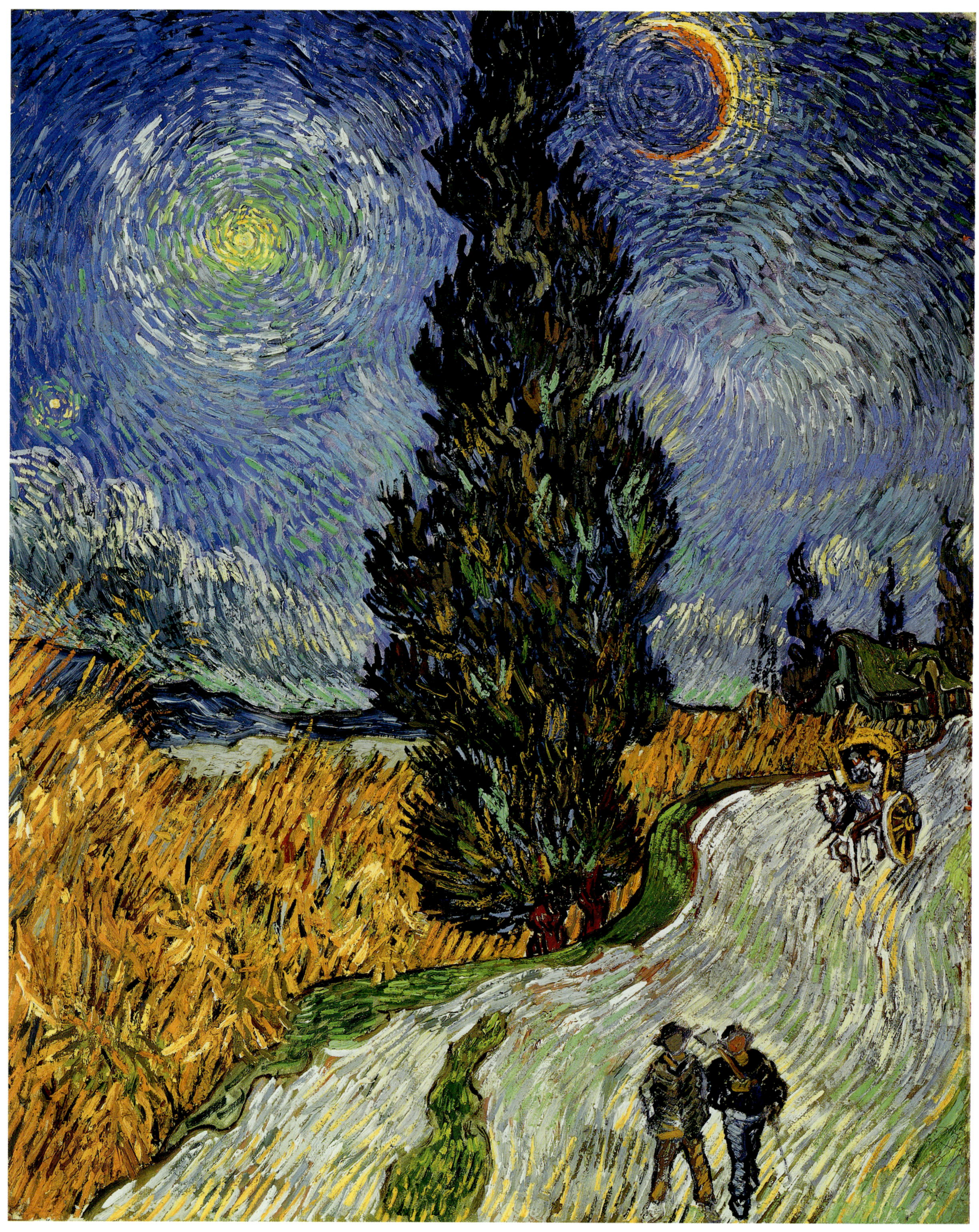

"THE CYPRESSES ARE ALWAYS OCCUPYING my thoughts, I would like to make something of them like the canvases of the sunflowers, because it astonishes me that they have not yet been done as I see them.

"It is as beautiful in line and proportion as an Egyptian obelisk. And the green has a quality of such distinction.

"It is a splash of black in a sunny landscape, but it is one of the most interesting of the black notes, and the most difficult to strike exactly, that I can imagine." *—To Theo from Saint-Rémy, June 25, 1889*

"Landscapes with cypresses. Ah, it would not be easy, Aurier [a friendly critic] feels it too, when he says that even black is a colour, and as for their appearance of flame—I think about it but don't dare to go further... You need a certain dash of inspiration, a ray from on high, that is not in ourselves, in order to do beautiful things. When I had done those sunflowers, I looked for the opposite and yet the equivalent and I said it is the cypress."

—To Theo from Saint-Rémy, February 1, 1890

"I have still from down there [Saint-Rémy] a cypress with a star, a last attempt—a night sky with a moon without radiance, the slender crescent barely emerging from the opaque shadow cast by the earth—a star with exaggerated brilliance, if you like, a soft brilliance of rose and green in the ultramarine sky across which are hurrying some clouds. Below a road bordered with tall yellow canes, behind these the blue Basses Alpes, an old inn with yellow lighted windows, and a very tall cypress, very upright, very sombre."

—To Gauguin from Auvers, May 1890

Vincent left the asylum on May 17, 1890, traveling by night train to Paris to meet Theo, Jo, and their baby, Vincent Willem. When Jo first saw Vincent, she thought he looked much stronger than her husband. He was a "sturdy, broad-shouldered man, with a healthy color, a smile on his face, and a very resolute appearance." He spent time looking at his paintings, which were on the walls and stored under the bed, behind the sofa, and in a big cupboard in the little spare room. He also visited with old friends.

Jo wrote, "Vincent soon perceived that the bustle of Paris did him no good, and he longed to set to work again. So he started on May 21 for Auvers, with an introduction to Dr. Gachet, whose faithful friendship was to become his greatest support during the short time he spent in Auvers." His new home was but an hour by train from Paris.

ROAD WITH CYPRESS AND STAR
SAINT-RÉMY, MAY 1890
OIL ON CANVAS, 36 1/4 X 28 3/4 INCHES
KRÖLLER-MÜLLER MUSEUM, OTTERLO, THE NETHERLANDS

←

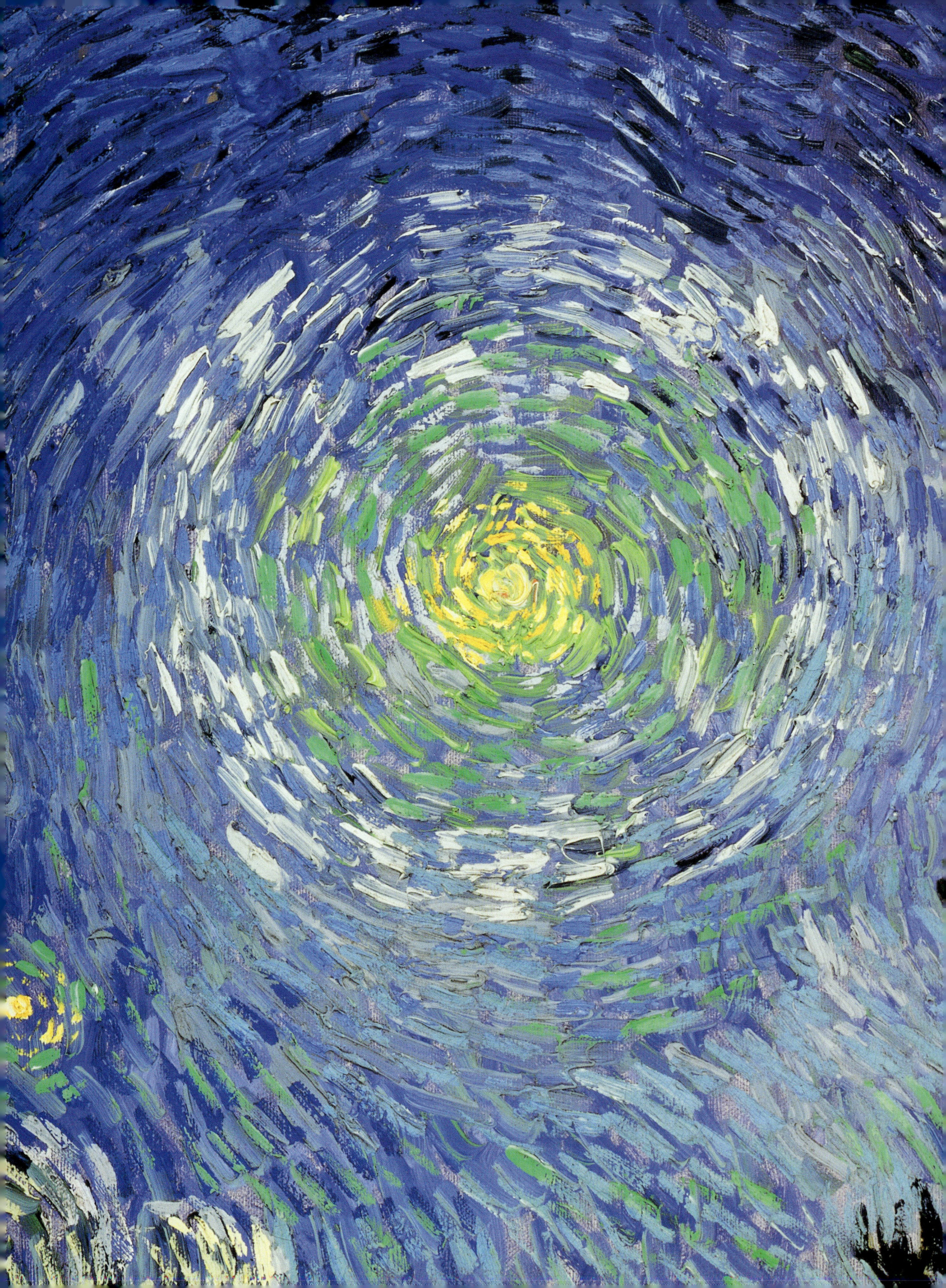

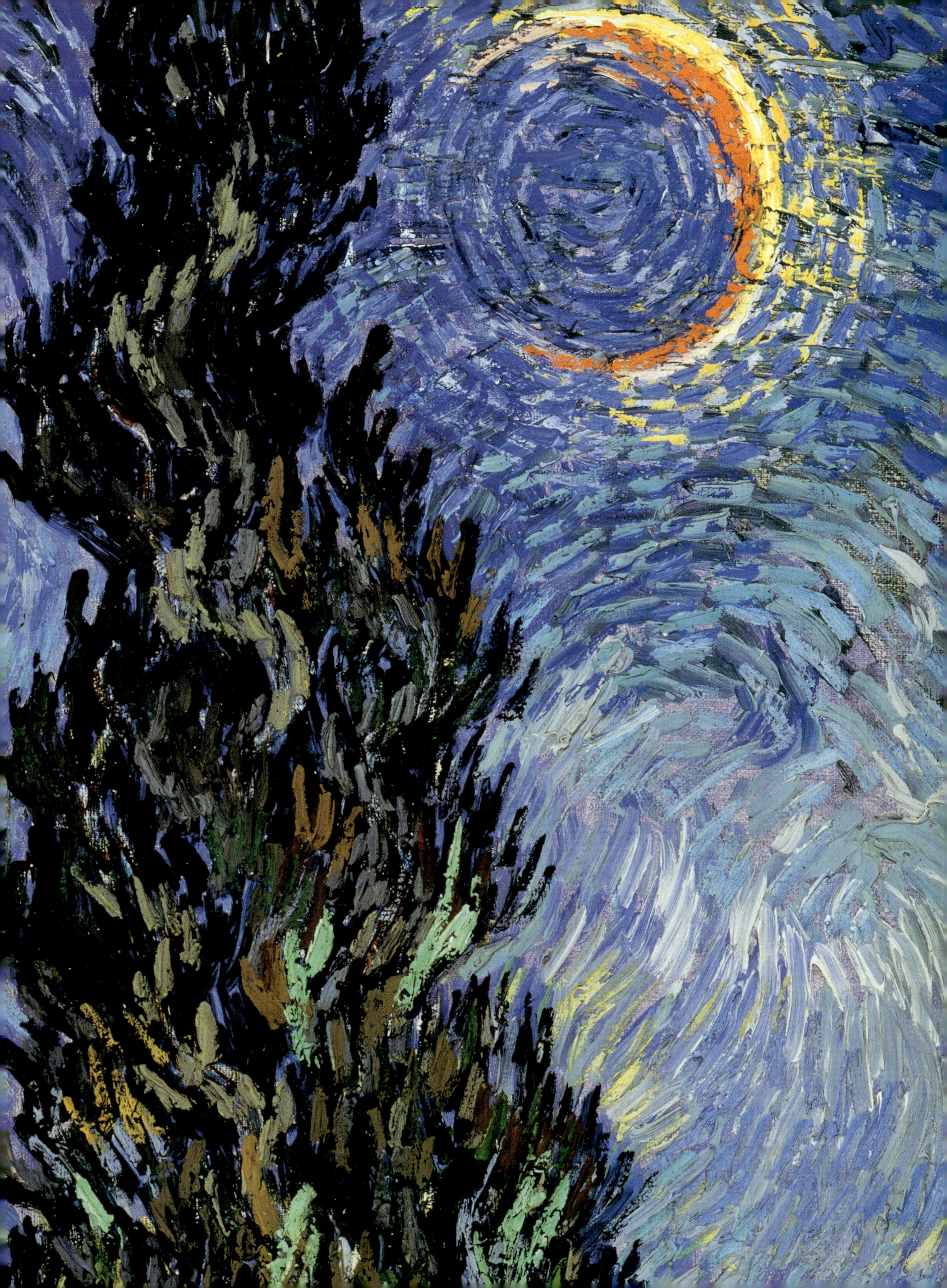

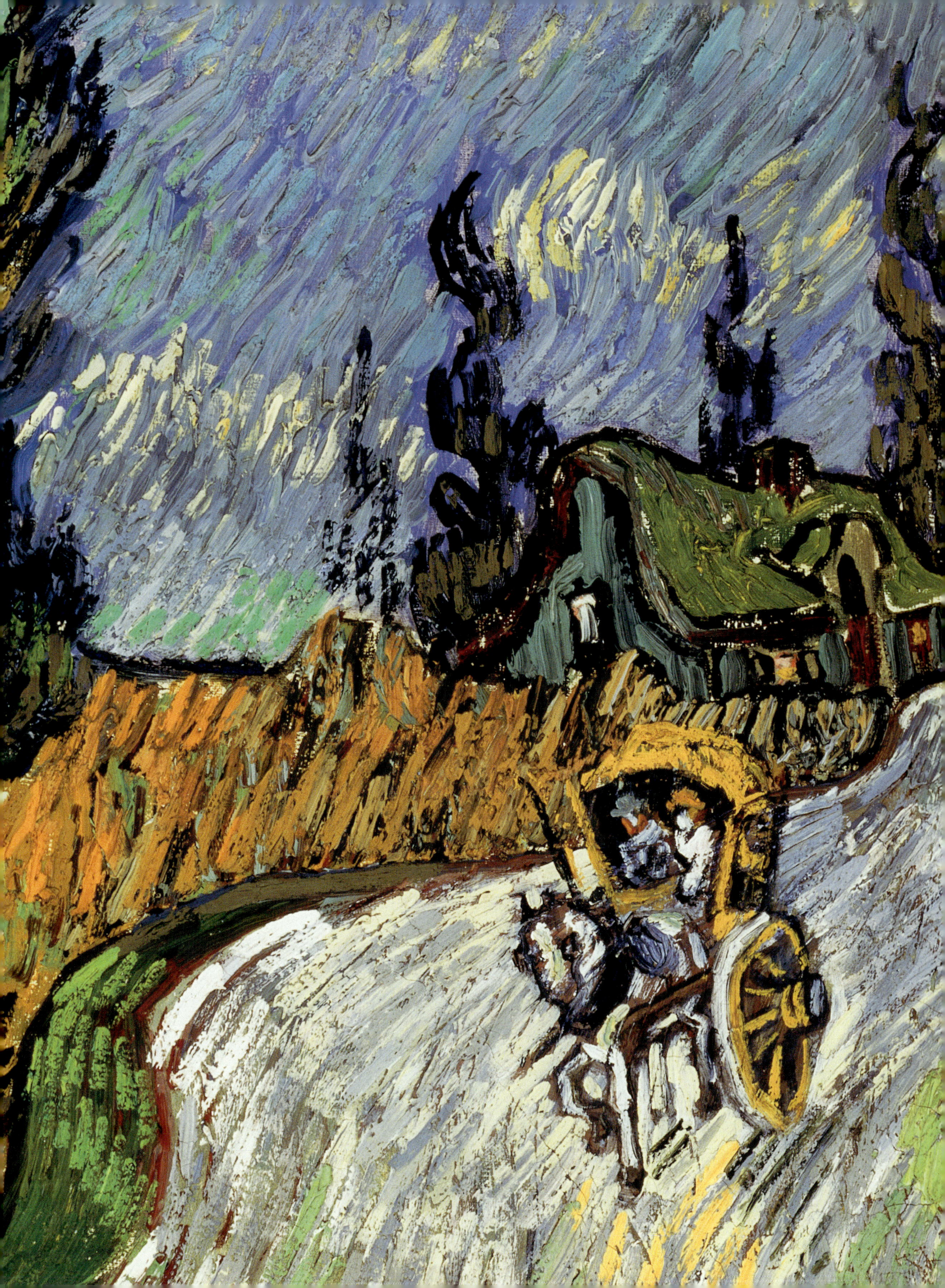

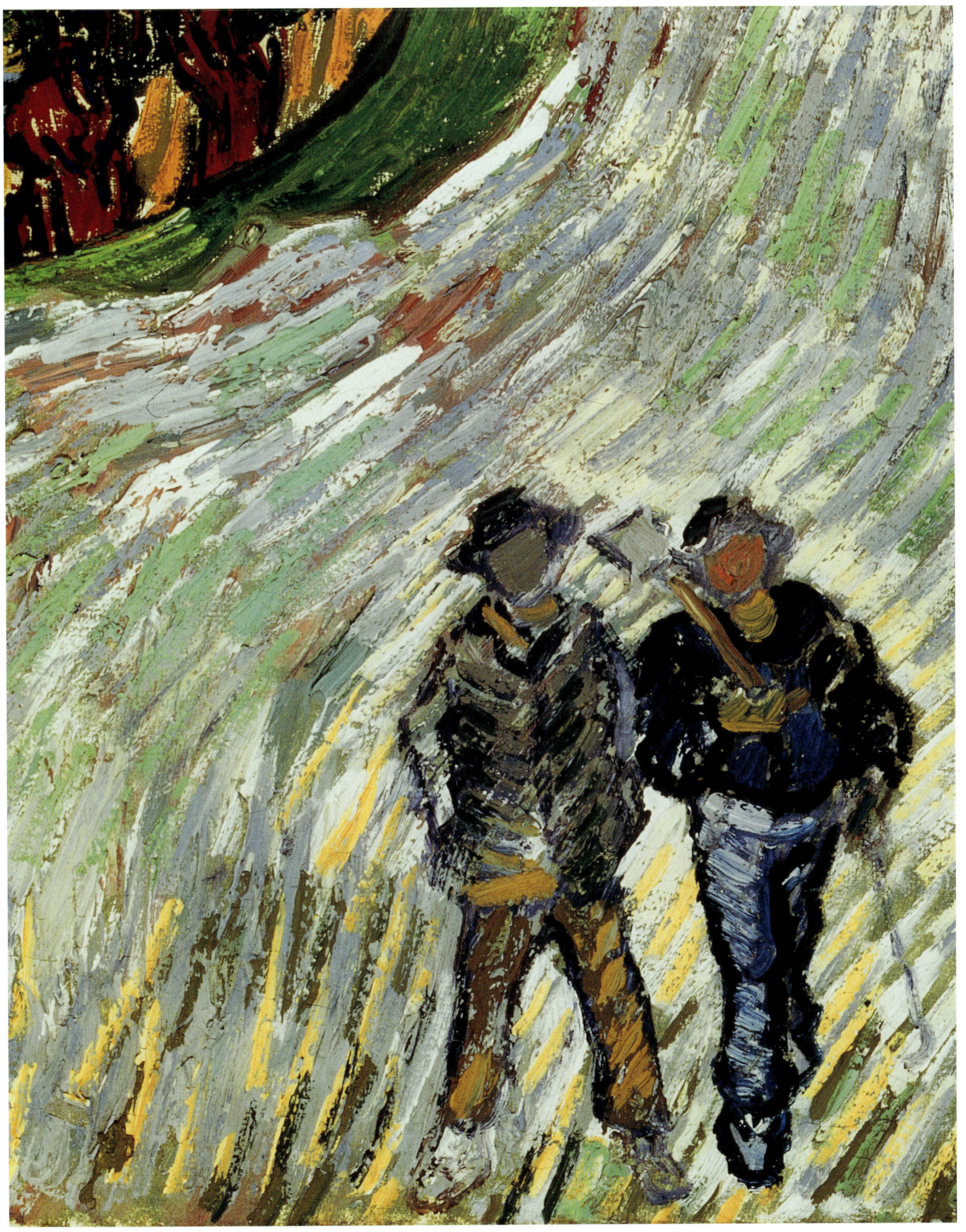

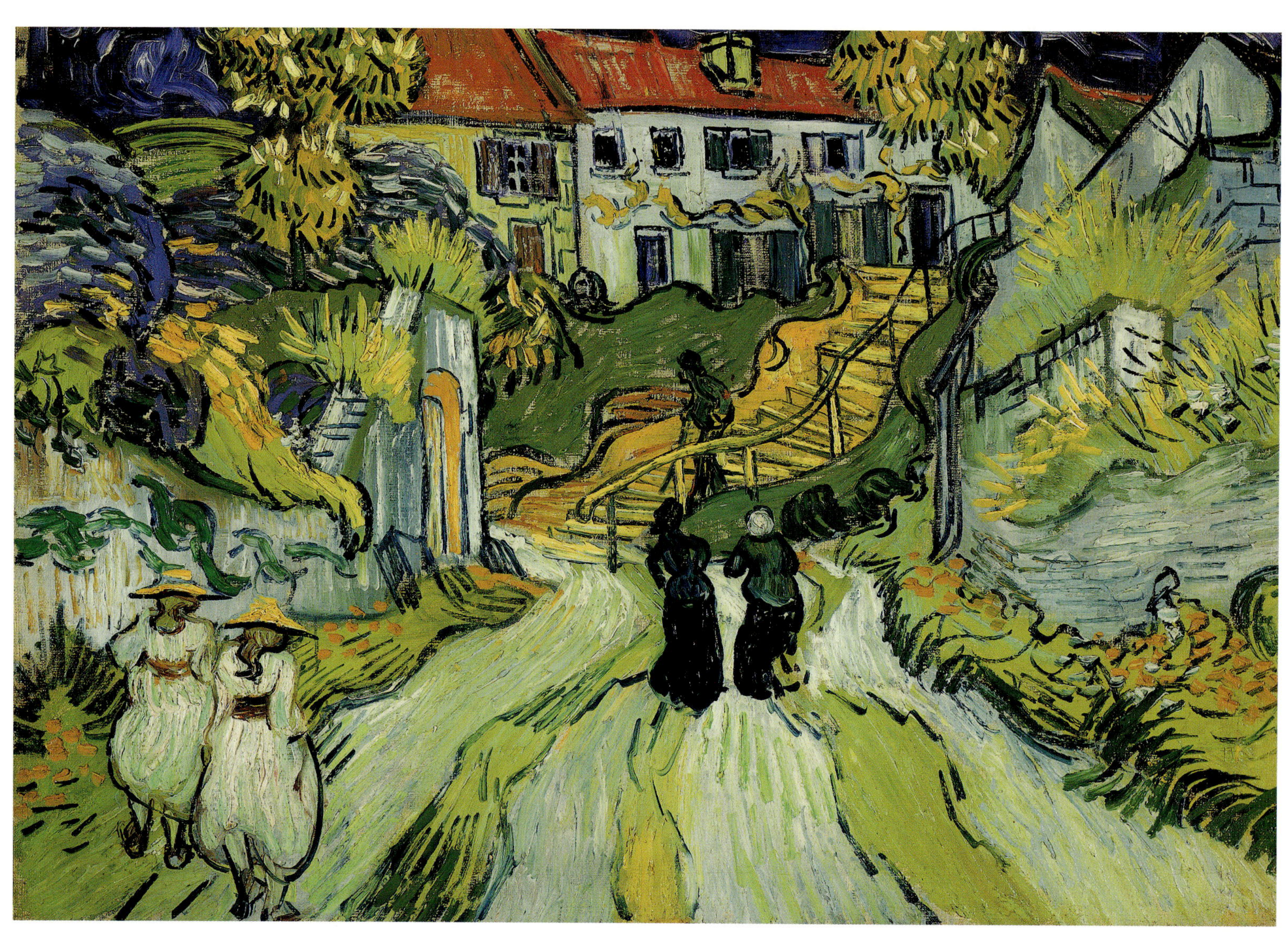

VINCENT SCURRIED THROUGH AUVERS with his paints and canvases almost like a tourist with a camera. He completed more than a painting a day during his two months there, recording the fields around the city, the church, the town hall, houses, and people. He seemed content, was free of nightmares, and was declared well again by Dr. Gachet, who did not recognize the nervous artist's sensory overload. In fact, Vincent believed that the doctor was suffering from nervous troubles as serious as his own.

Dead center in his painting of a hilly neighborhood in Auvers is the foot of a stairway. All paths lead to it and five figures are heading there, but it only marks an intersection. Nothing is there but choices to make. Should one enter the mysterious door on the left, walk around the boxy building to see what is there, go up the stairs to knock on the door straight ahead, climb the hill and scale the wall at the top of it, or just sit on the retaining wall halfway up to enjoy the view? Everything is equally emphasized. Everything is seductively bathed in sunlight. Every line is charged with nervous energy and every brush stroke with a joy of color.

Cascades of purple, blue, yellow, and green above the schoolgirls in white define no specific plants or flowers. No details are drawn. The subject is lush fecundity. In the same generalized manner, the five figures have no faces, but the colors of their costumes and the shapes and postures of their figures suggest certain ages and stations in life. Colors and impressions were Vincent's subjects as much as places and people.

VILLAGE STREET AND STEPS IN AUVERS WITH FIGURES
Auvers, June 1890
Oil on canvas, 20 x 28 inches
The Saint Louis Art Museum

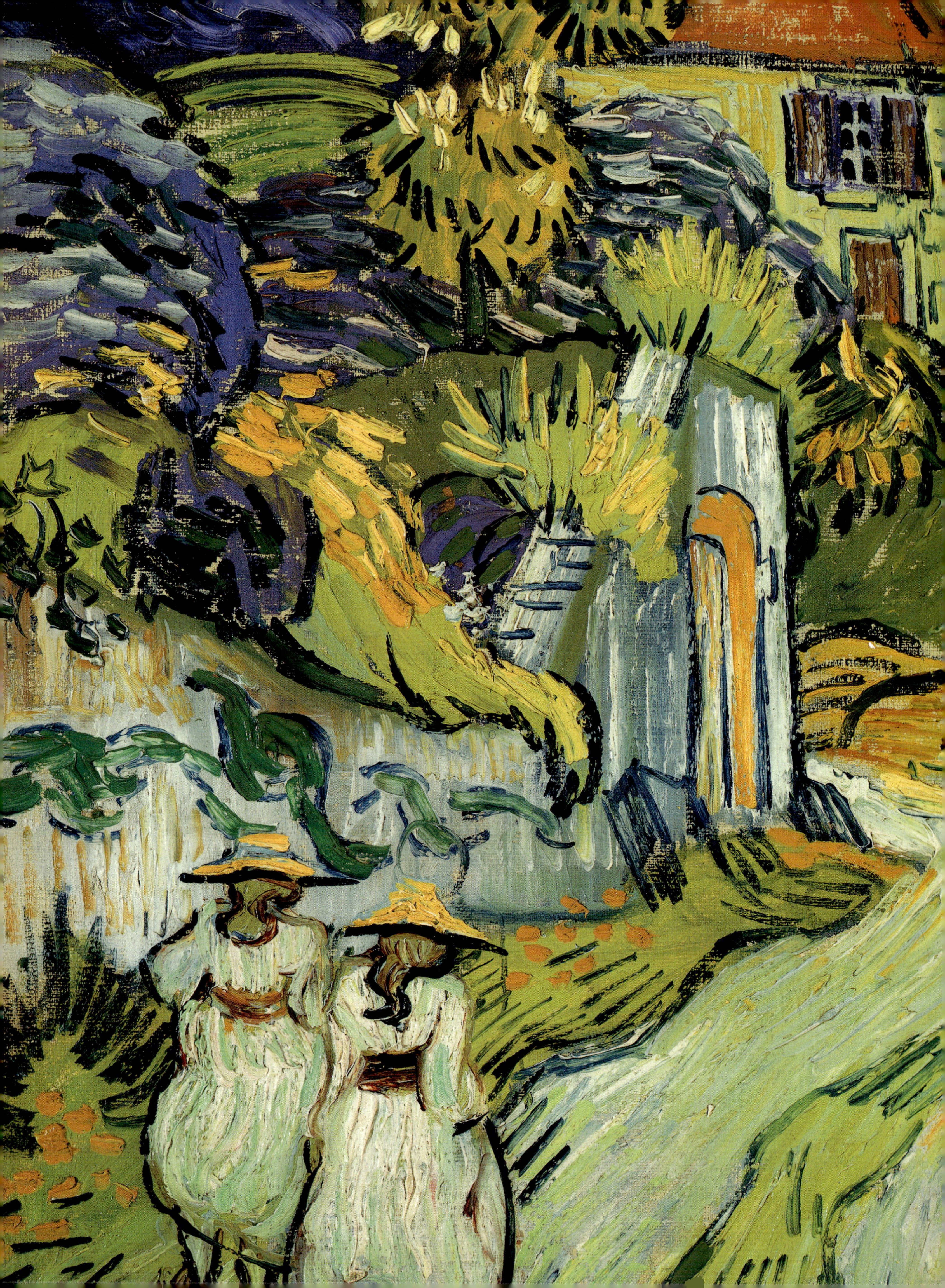

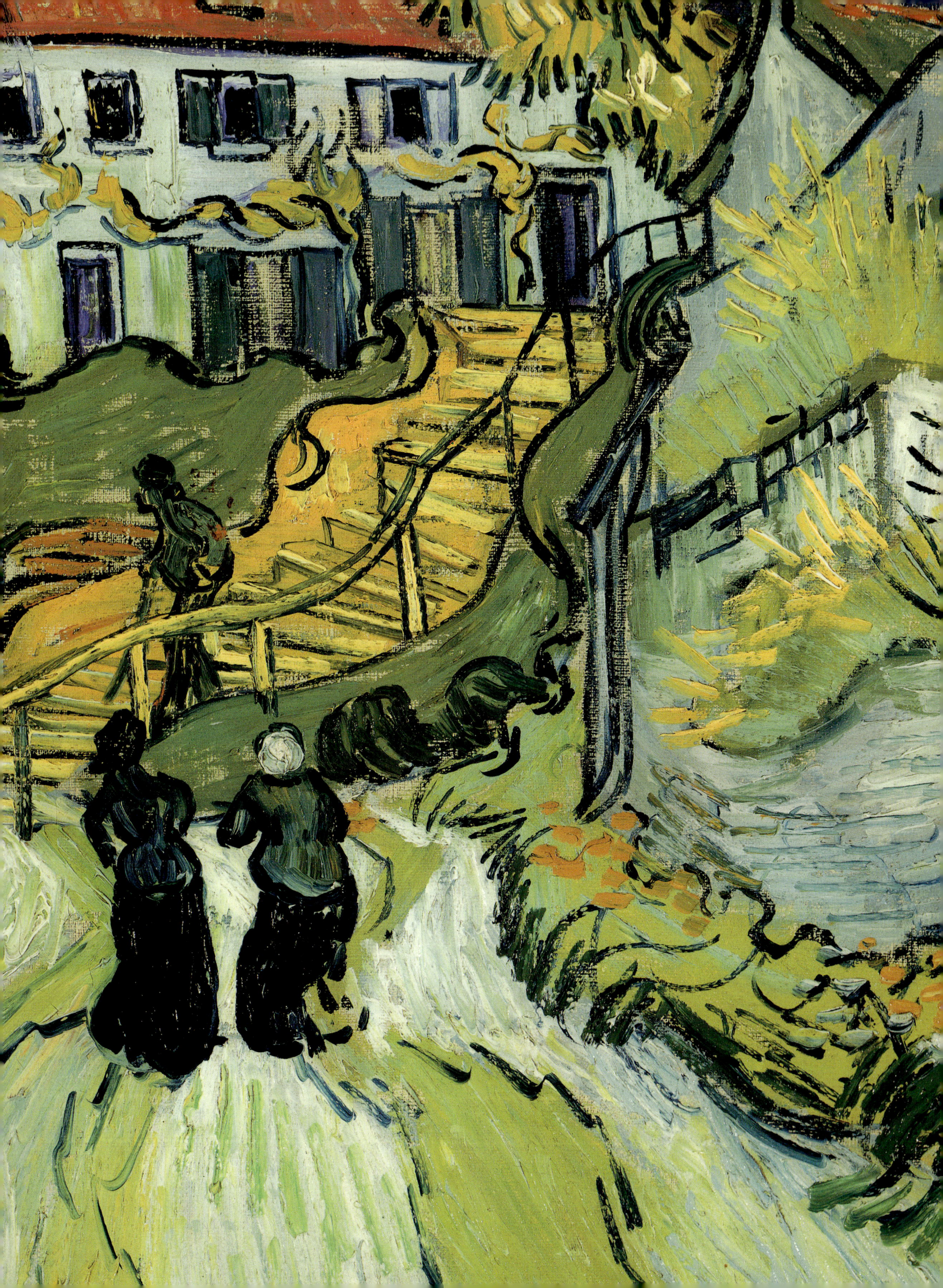

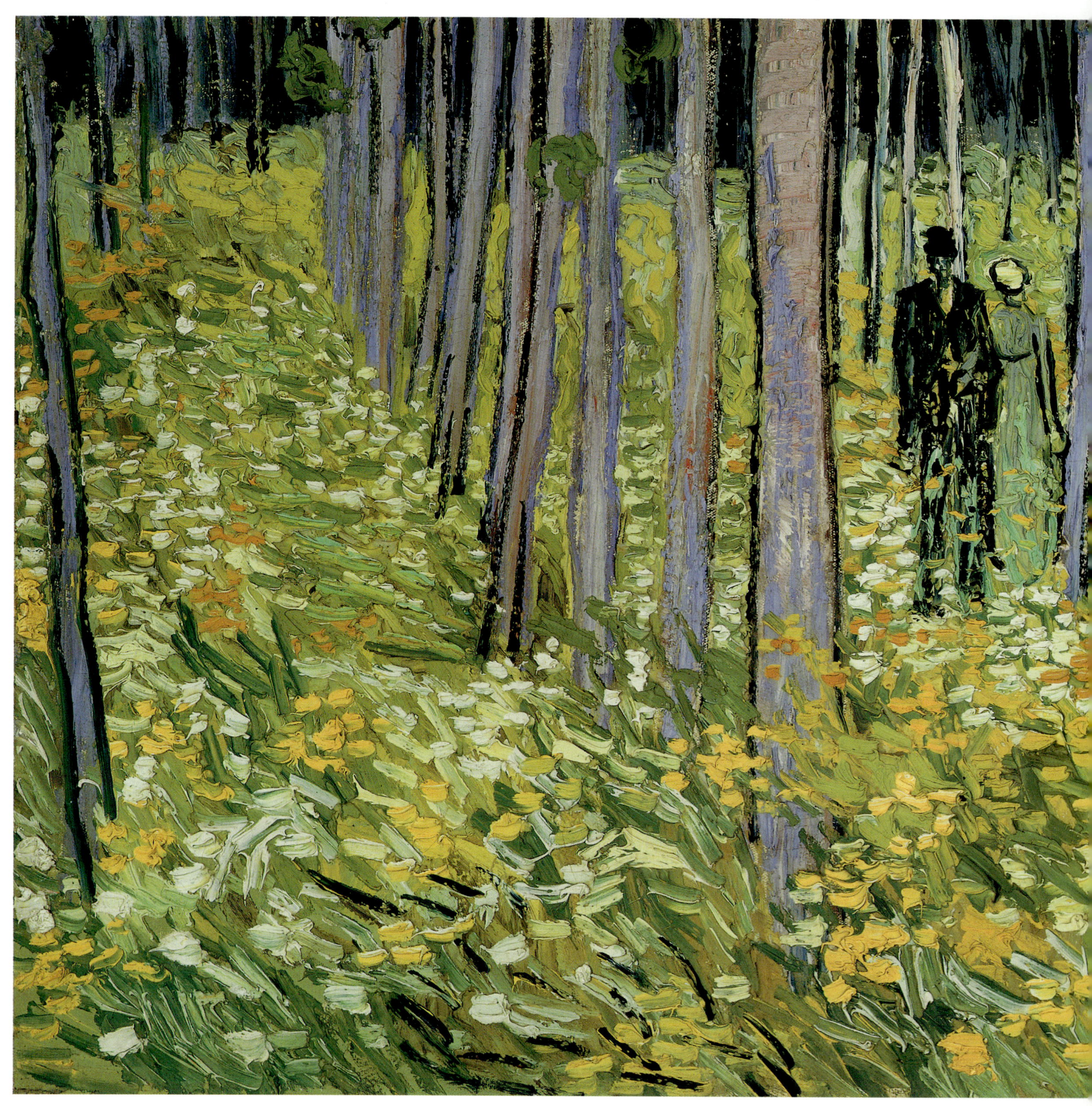

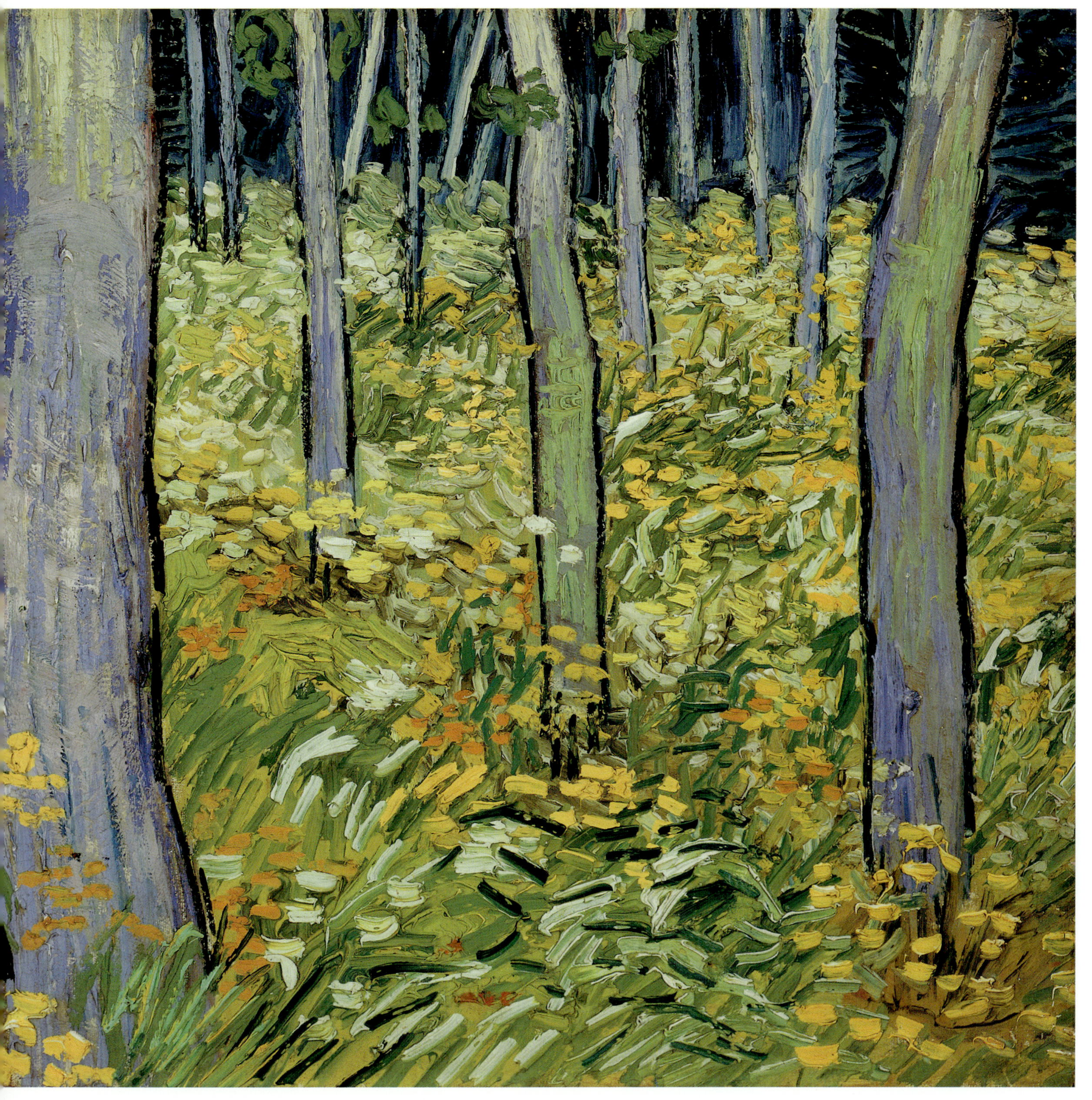

"THE UNDERGROWTH AROUND POPLARS, violet trunks running across the landscape, perpendicular like columns; the depths of the wood are blue, and at the bottom of the big trunks, the grassy ground full of flowers, pink, yellow and green, long grass turning russet, and flowers." Vincent's description omits the couple, he in top hat, she in bonnet, standing close to one another. A spray of flowers falls across their legs as though they had picked a bouquet and then dropped it. Perhaps they stand in awe of the scene they have come upon, for in front of them is the bounty of June: daffodils, jonquils, and narcissus. They have moved from the darkness of the background to this grove of luminosity.

UNDERGROWTH WITH TWO FIGURES
AUVERS-SUR-OISE, JUNE 1890
OIL ON CANVAS, 19 3/4 X 39 1/2 INCHES
CINCINNATI ART MUSEUM
BEQUEST OF MARY E. JOHNSTON (1967.1430)

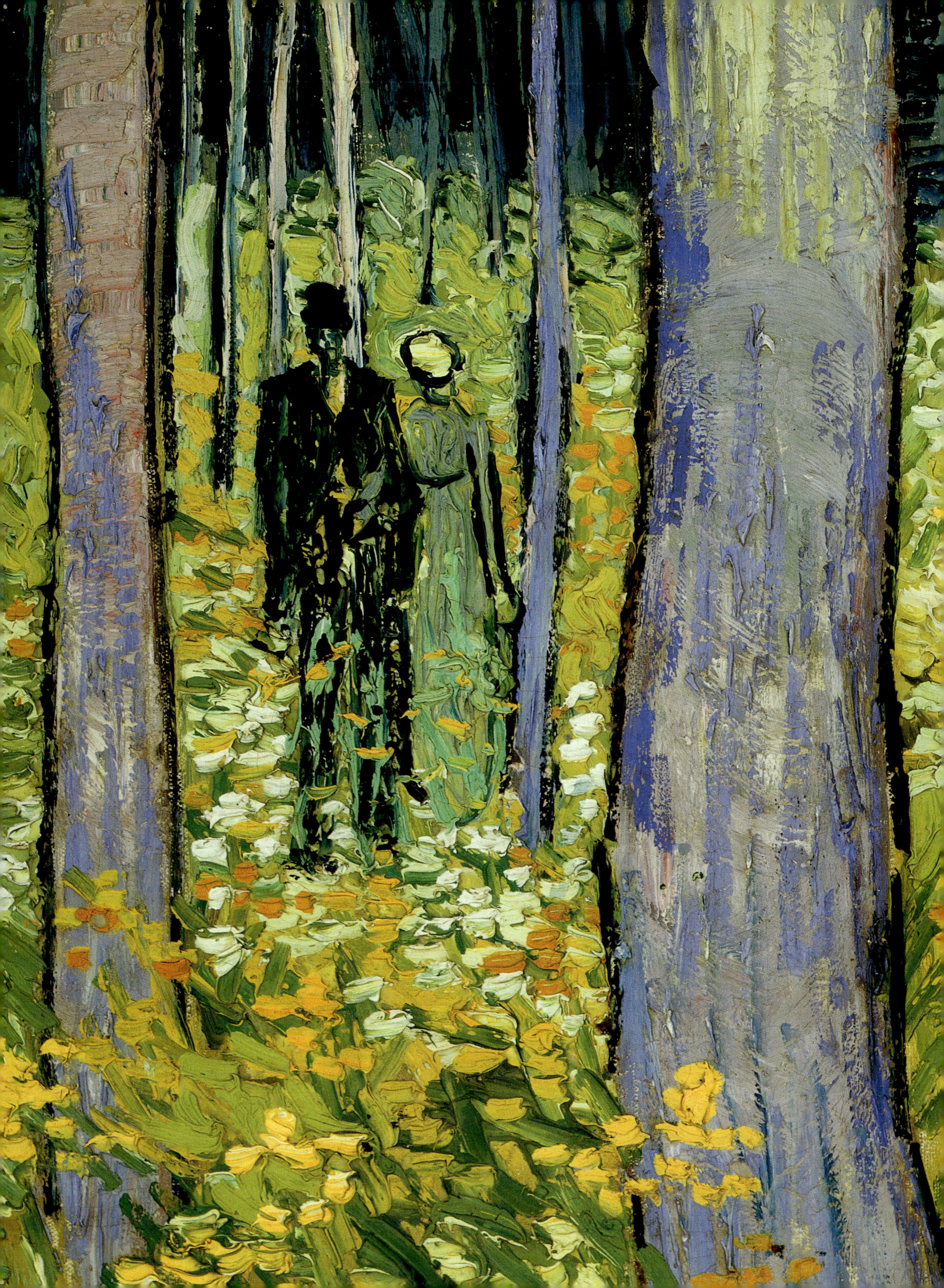

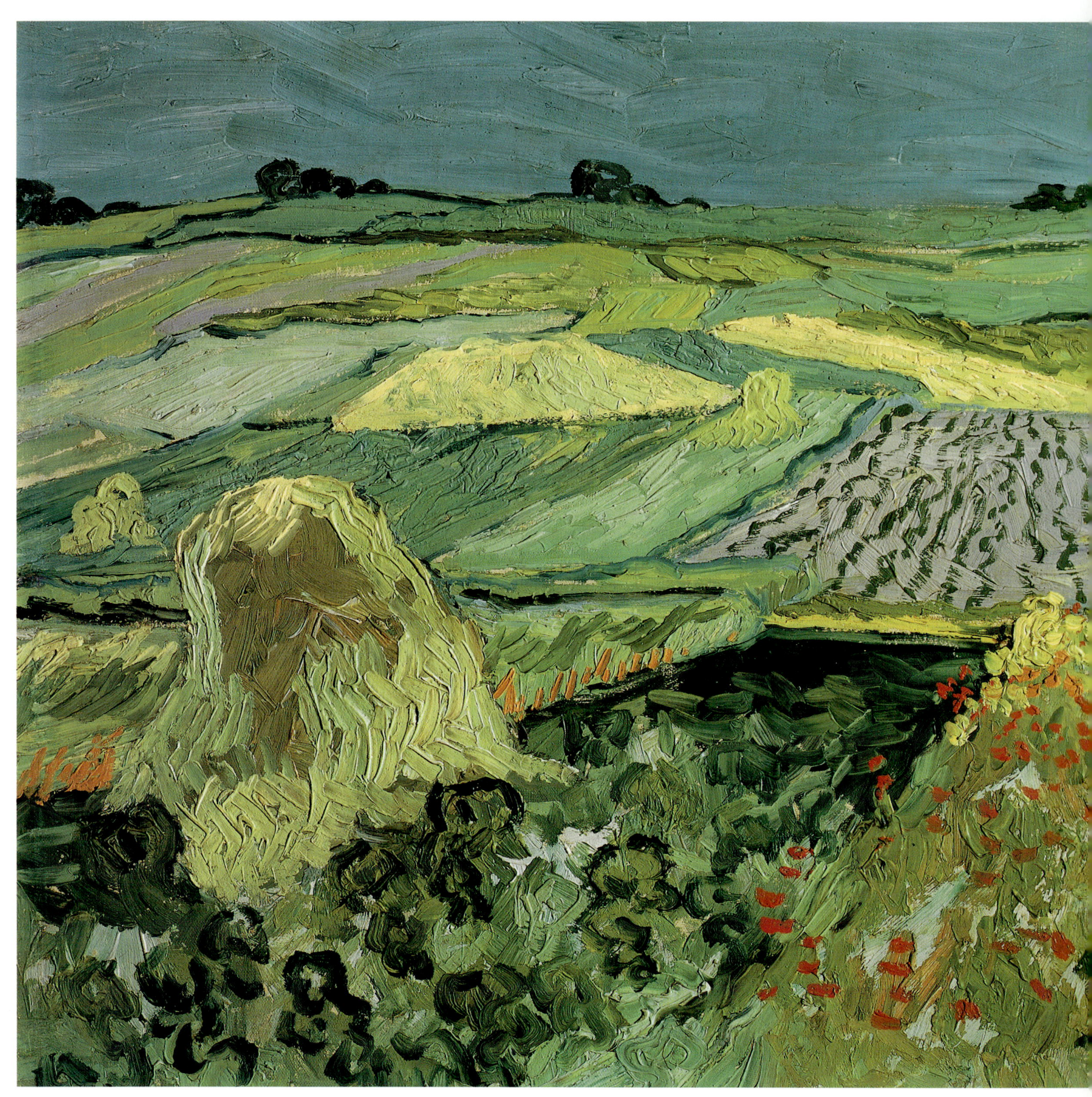

➢

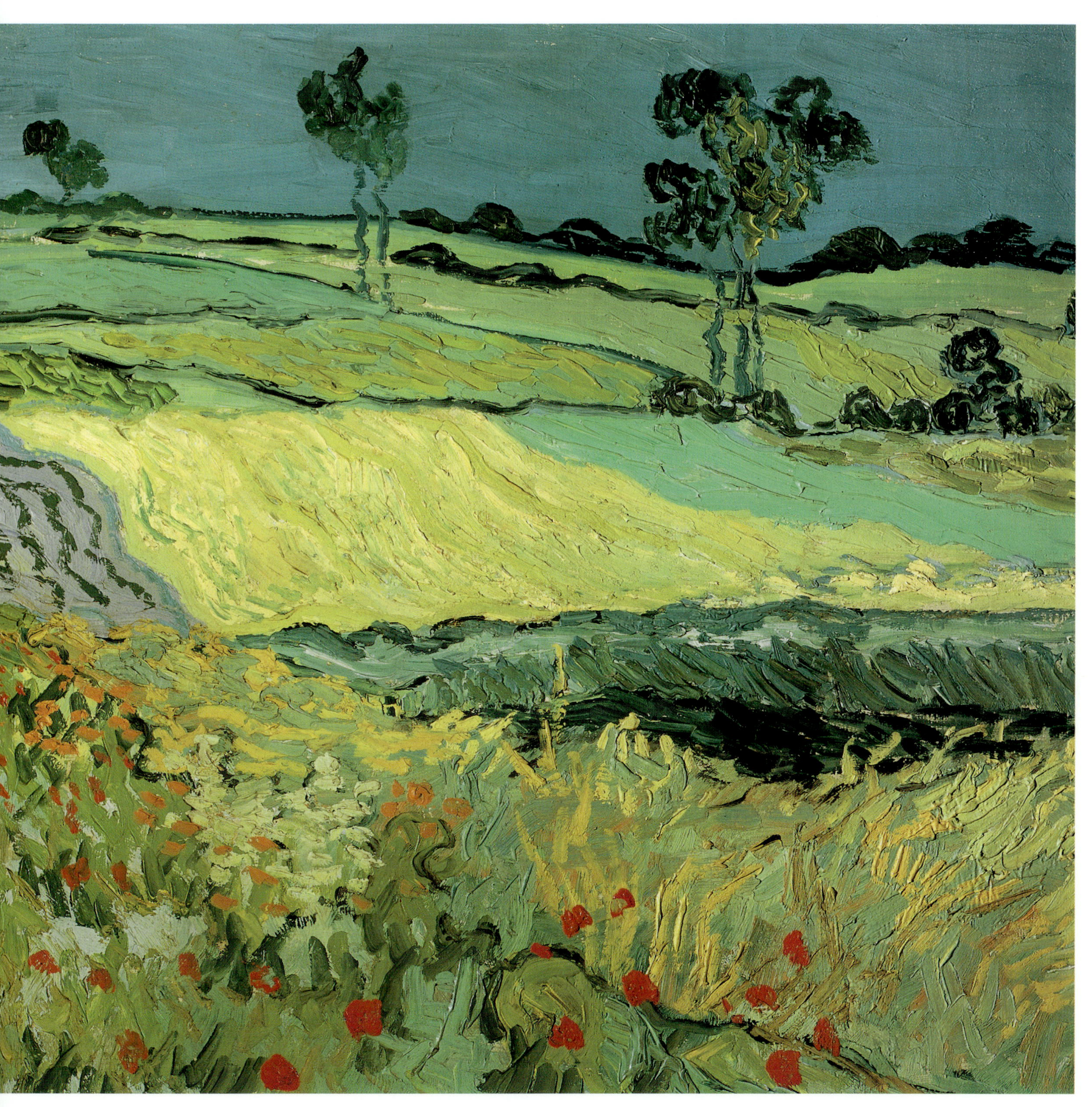

➢

VINCENT WAS STRUCK BY THE SIMILARITY of his horizontal landscape of the wheat fields near Auvers to Georges Michel's paintings. Michel was a French artist who painted broad vistas of the landscape around Paris, inspired by Dutch scenes of the seventeenth century. He died unknown in 1843. Because his works were leaden-hued, Vincent was quick to point out that his painting was "soft green, yellow, and green-blue." Thinking of Michel's works brought Vincent back to the origins of his own art in Holland.

Taking in the broad plain of Auvers in one glance would be impossible. Vincent had to look left, right, down, and straight ahead to see all the plots of land he pictured. Their diagonal edges unify them into a system of two-point perspective: there is a low vanishing point where the plot of poppies meets the field with parallel curved lines, and a second one at the horizon line. The forms in the foreground, all dependent on lavish applications of paint, are an agitated sea of flowers, wheat, and verdure that seems to move toward the quieter fields in the middle of the painting. There, a crazy quilt of green, yellow, and lavender patches heaves with the contours of the earth. The awkward geometry of the fields is broken by loosely painted trees that reach into an almost cloudless sky.

WHEAT FIELDS NEAR AUVERS
Auvers-sur-Oise, June 1890
Oil on canvas, 19 3/4 x 39 3/4 inches
Neue Galerie, Vienna, Austria/Art Resource, New York

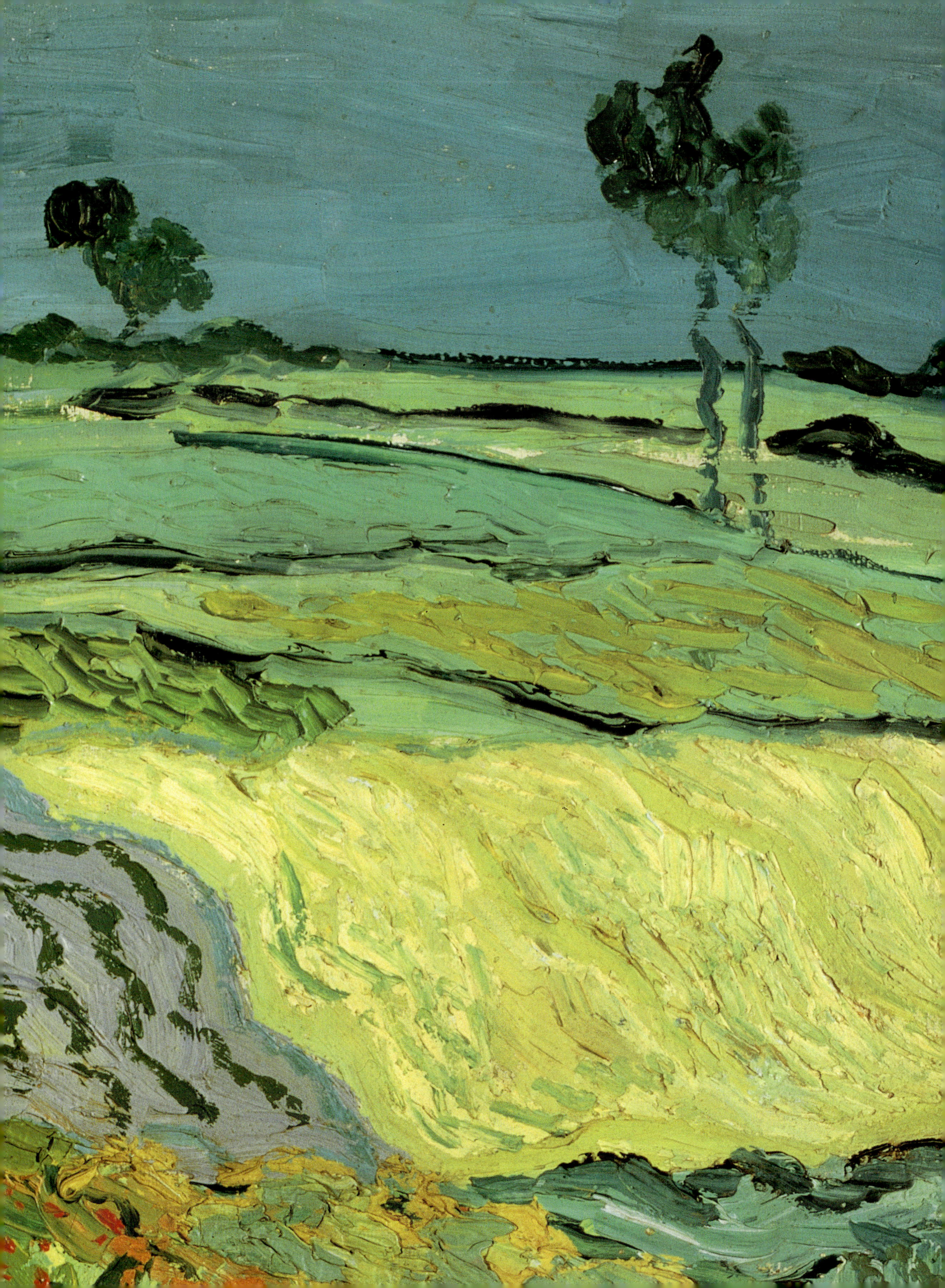

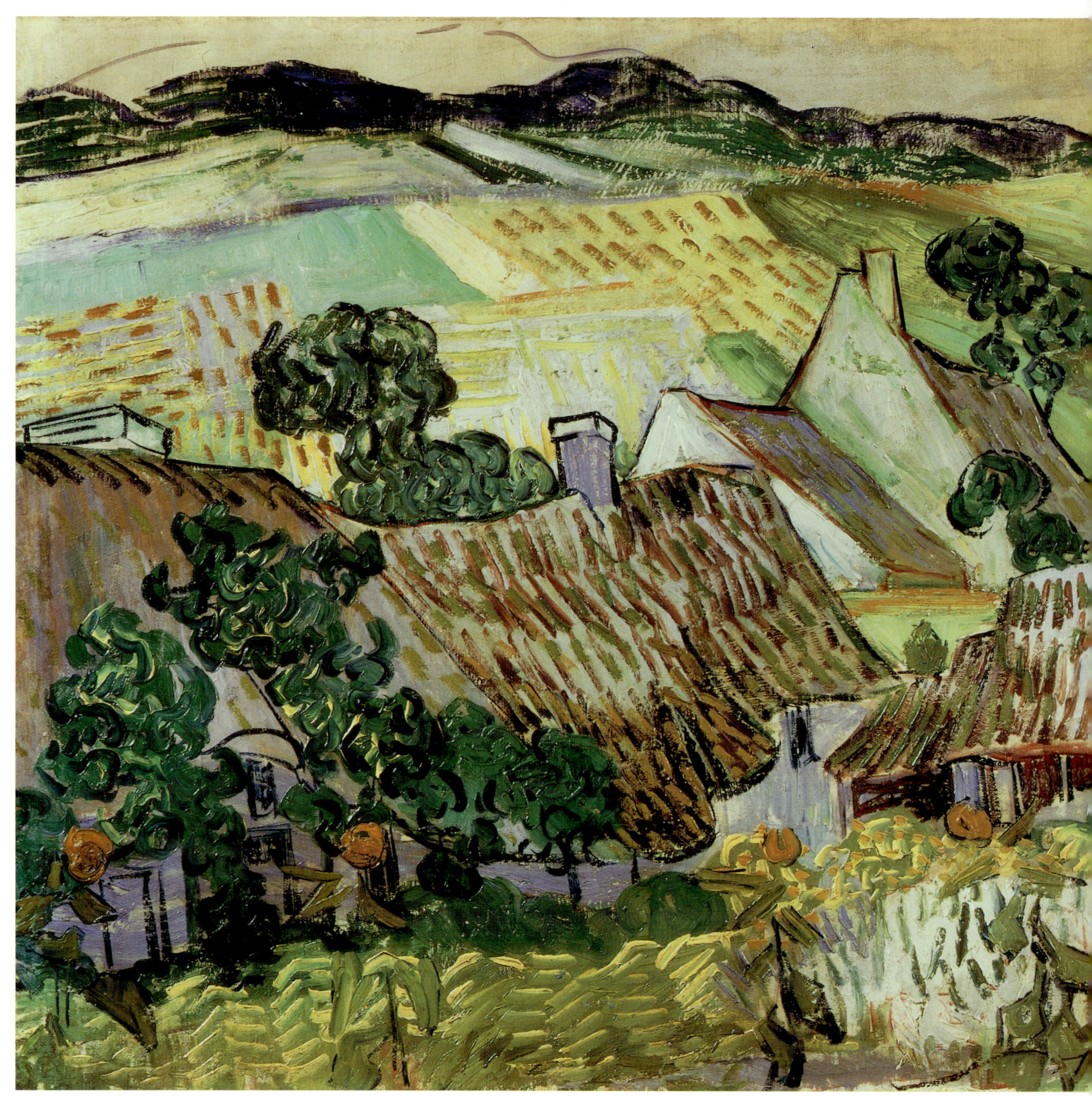

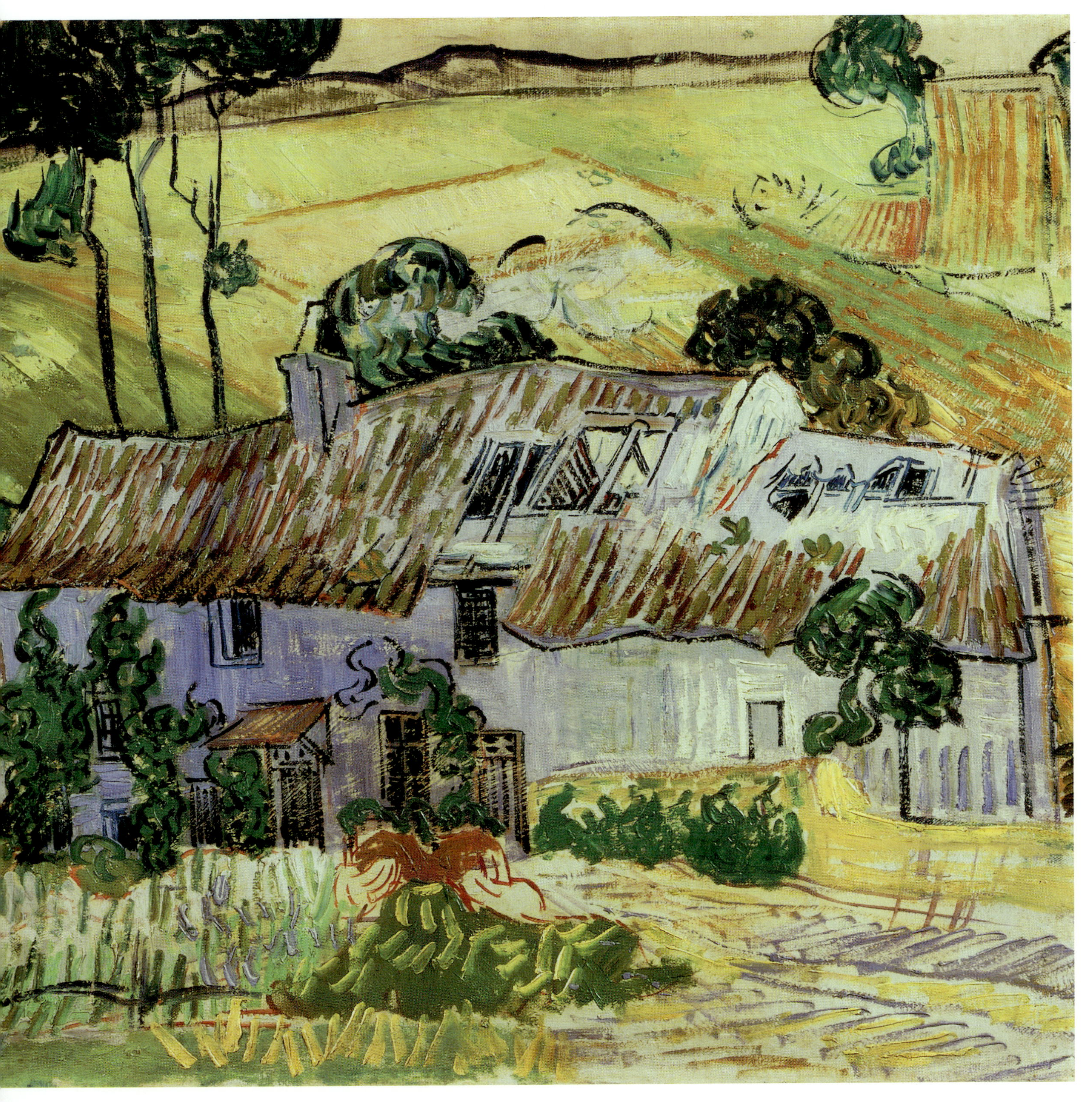

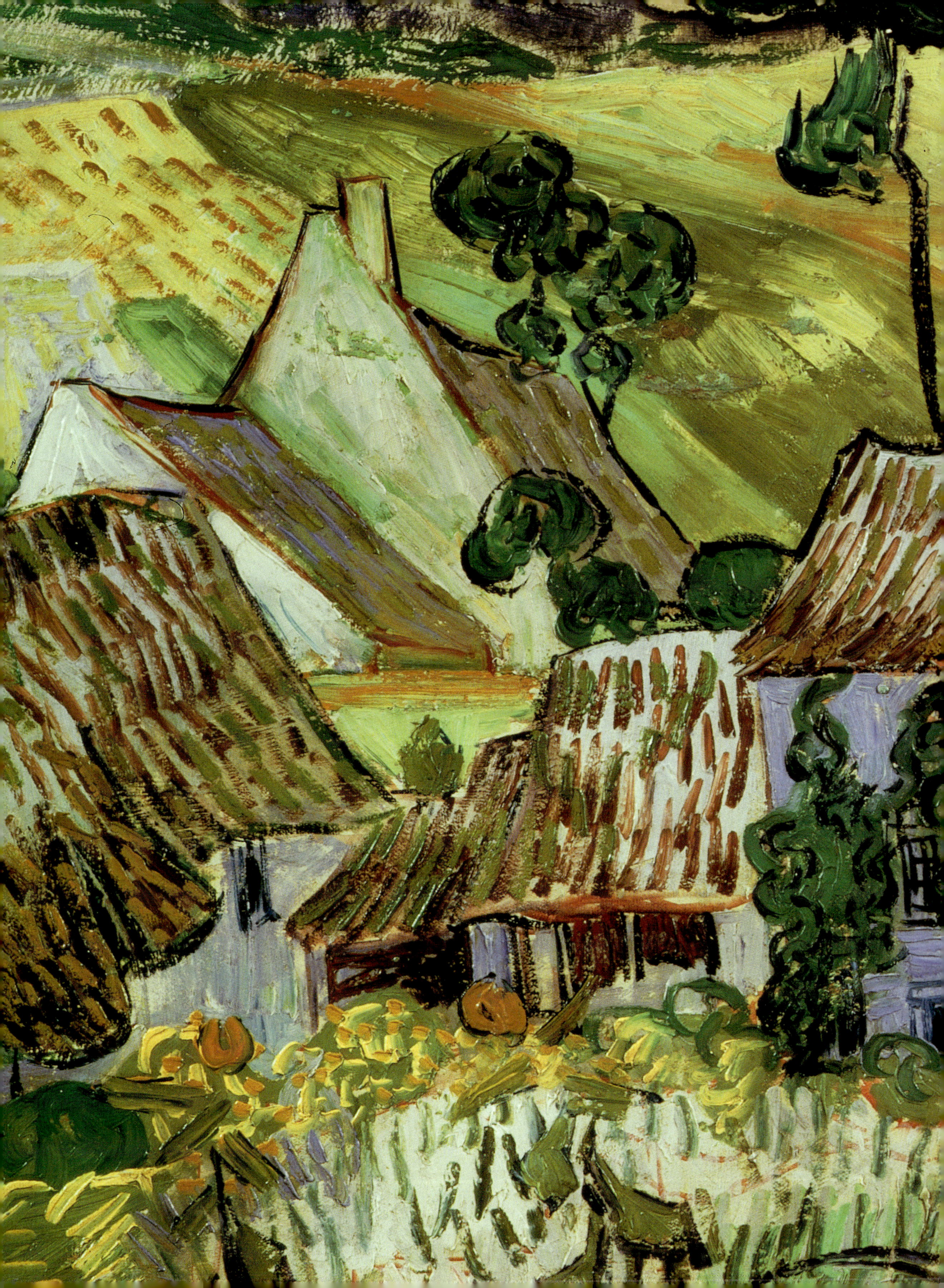

ONE OF VINCENT'S FIRST IMPRESSIONS of Auvers was that there were "a lot of old thatched roofs, which are getting rare." He hoped that by "settling down to do some canvases of this there could be a chance of recovering the expenses of my stay—for really it is profoundly beautiful, it is the real country, characteristic and picturesque".

Vincent painted about twenty different views of the thatched-roof cottages, never seeming to exhaust the possibilities of interesting angles. The roofs of this derelict neighborhood echo the sloping plots of land in the background. Vincent matched angles and patterns, visually linking the farms and the homes of the farmers. Even the vertical marks in front of the blue house that probably represent a collapsing fence repeat the slanted lines of the caved-in roof.

Vincent had hoped that a return to the north would calm him. Indeed, his paintings had lost their agitation and hallucinatory swirls. But he was living in a room above a café just as he had done when he first arrived in Arles. His art had progressed, he knew, but he had not. He worked with "the fatal conditions of vanished youth and comparative poverty," and he thought of Theo and himself as "happy possessors of disordered hearts." Even his mental disease did not prevent him "from exercising the painter's profession as if nothing were amiss."

THATCHED COTTAGES BY A HILL
AUVERS-SUR-OISE, JULY 1890
OIL ON CANVAS, 19 3/4 X 39 1/2 INCHES
TATE GALLERY, LONDON/ART RESOURCE, NEW YORK

<

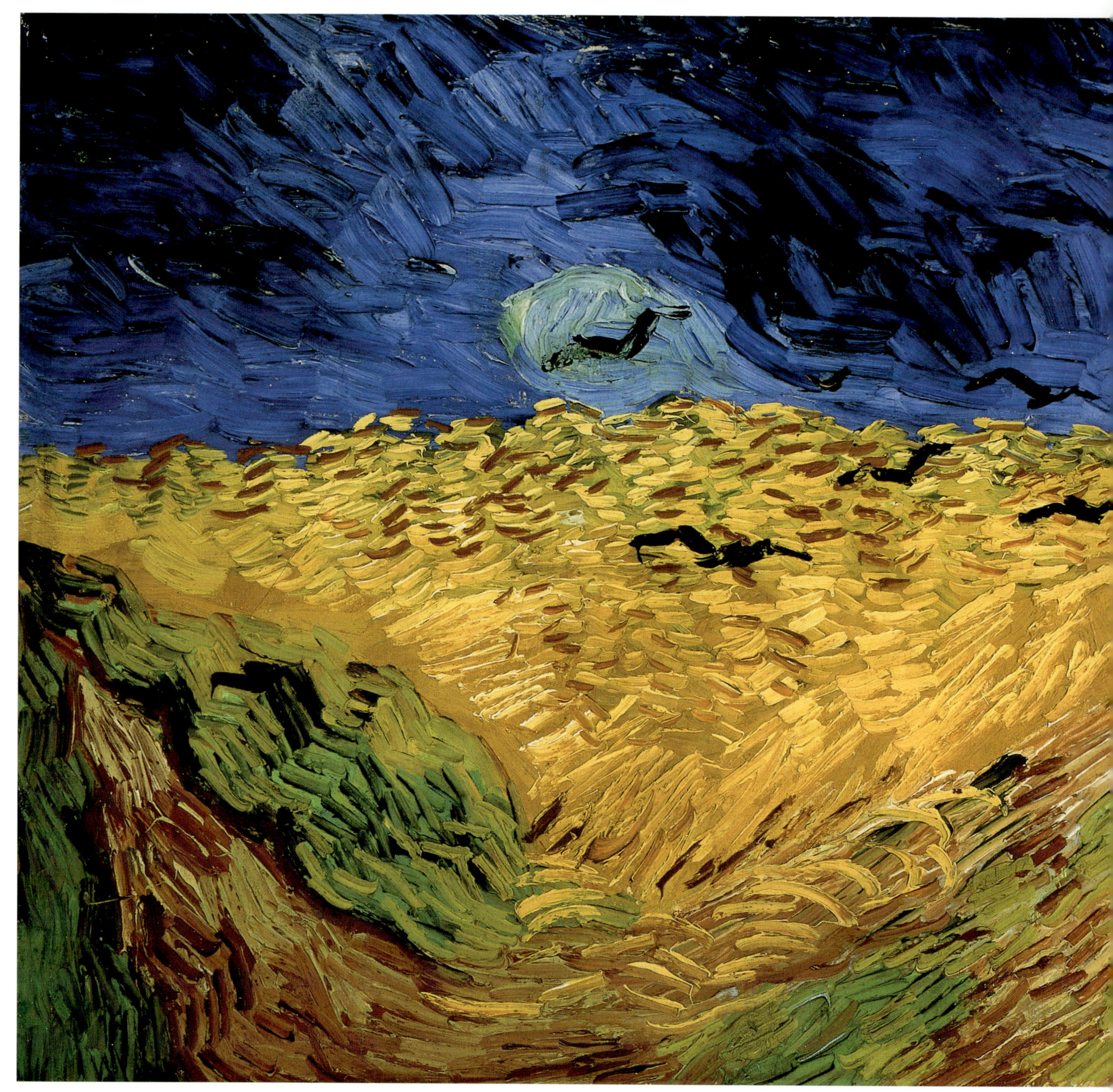

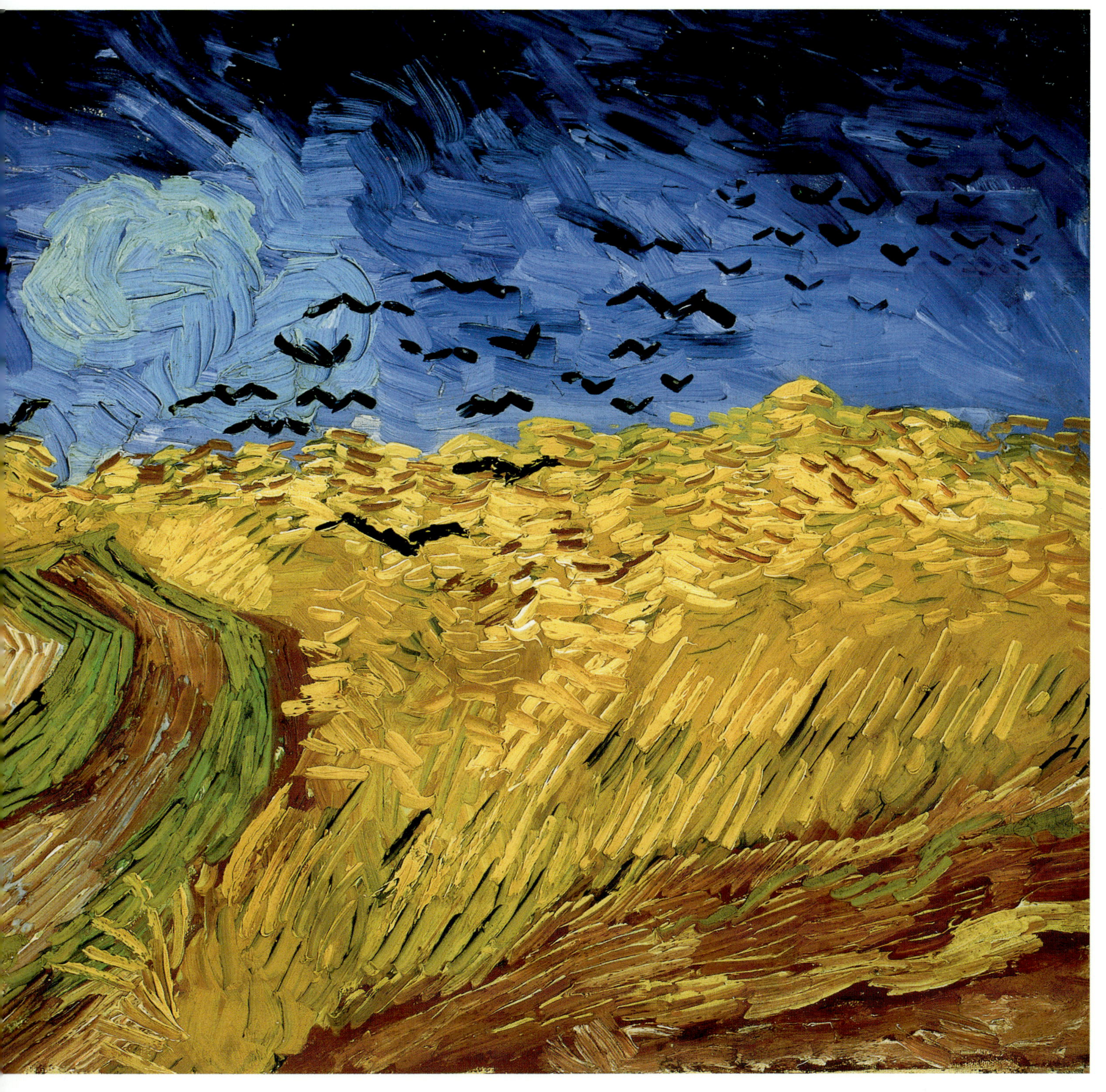

"I HAVE PAINTED THREE MORE BIG canvases...and I did not need to go out of my way to try to express sadness and extreme loneliness," Vincent wrote to Theo, referring to this painting, *Wheat Fields Near Auvers,* and a third he did not identify. "I hope you will see them soon—for I hope to bring them to you in Paris as soon as possible, since I almost think that these canvases will tell you what I cannot say in words, the health and restorative forces that I see in the country."

Wheat Field with Crows is one of Vincent's last big canvases. Because Vincent painted this panorama only weeks before his suicide, it is usually interpreted from the point of view of the bad omens it portrays. In fact, it is a straightforward painting about a coming storm. Harsh winds have darkened the sky, churned the clouds, frightened the crows, and knocked the grass and wheat to the ground. In spite of nature's wrath, Vincent has painted the distant wheat as though it were a thousand little wings ready to lift up.

The surging patterns of the foreground paths, wedged into the field, add to the drama. Vincent, it is said, had nowhere to go. The paths are dead ends, but they actually form a crossroads. There are four earthen lanes, not three. Vincent stood in the middle of them to paint the fields, turned around, and walked back to town on the road that does not show in the painting. It is comforting to imagine that he waited out the storm in his cozy room.

> *Just as we take the train to get to Tarascon or Rouen, we take death to reach a star. One thing absolutely true in this reasoning is that we cannot get to a star while we are alive, any more than we can take a train when we are dead.*
>
> Vincent van Gogh
> July 16, 1888

WHEAT FIELD WITH CROWS
AUVERS-SUR-OISE, JULY 1890
OIL ON CANVAS, 20 X 39 1/2 INCHES
VAN GOGH MUSEUM (VINCENT VAN GOGH FOUNDATION)
AMSTERDAM, THE NETHERLANDS

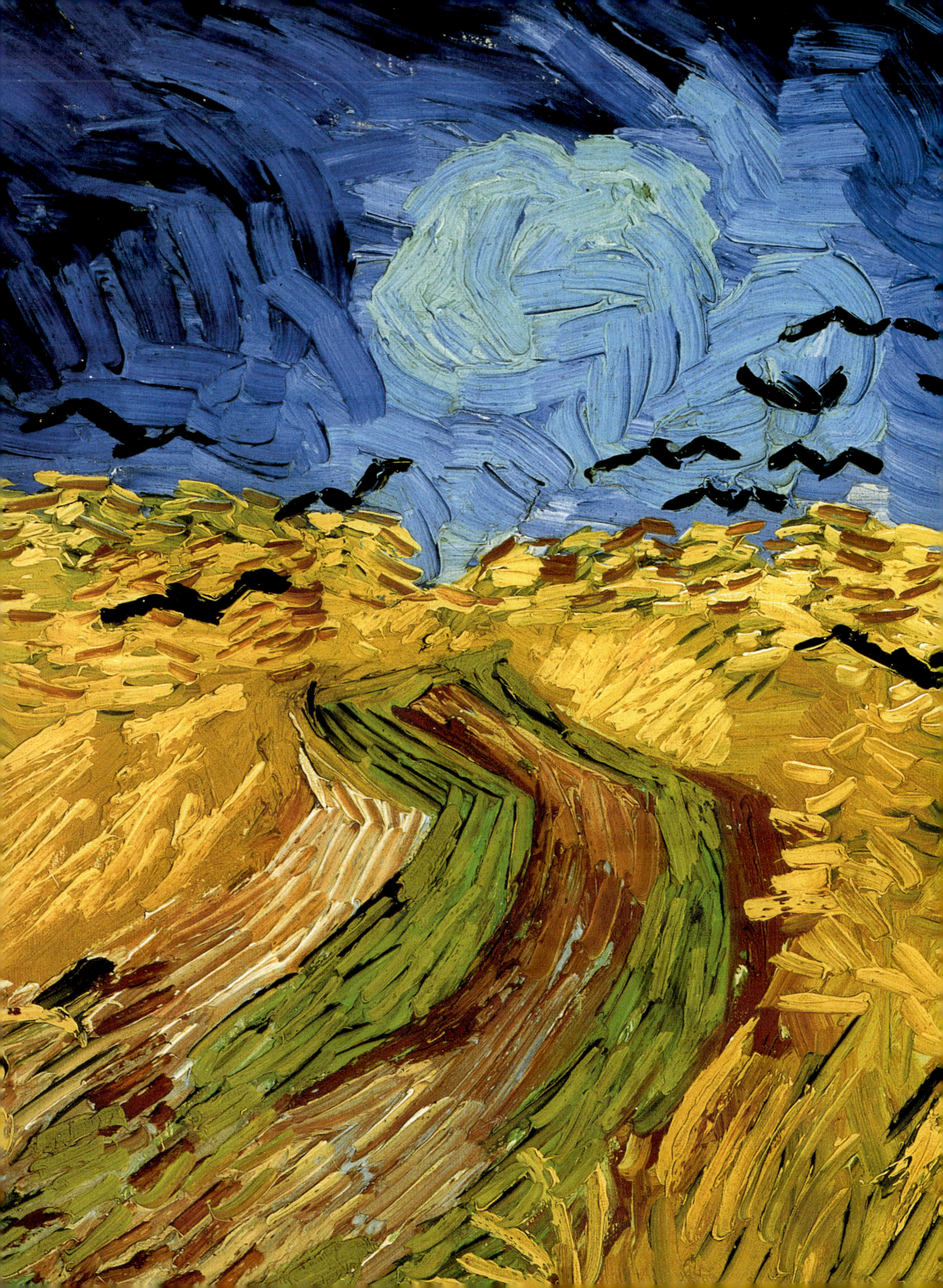

GUIDE TO QUOTATIONS

The major source for this book was *The Complete Letters of Vincent van Gogh* (3 volumes), Greenwich, Connecticut: New York Graphic Society, 1958 edition. Letters used in the introductory essay, "The Unseen Van Gogh: His Education in Art," are indexed by the first words of the text and the code of the letter: Letters to Theo, Vincent's brother, are given numerals, 1 through 652; letters to others are given an initial, to indicate the recipient's name, and a numeral, such as B 14 (Vincent's 14th letter to the artist Bernard). Letters used in picture captions are indexed under the title of the painting by the first words of the text and the letter code. Longer painting titles are abbreviated.

Van Gogh, A Self-Portrait, Letters Revealing His Life as a Painter, selected by W. H. Auden. New York: Marlowe & Company (first paperback edition), 1994 (first published by Thames & Hudson, Ltd., 1961). Quotations from this source are indicated by *Auden.*

Vincent van Gogh, the Complete Paintings, Ingo F. Walther and Rainer Metzger. Cologne: Benedickt Taschen Verlag GmbH., 1993. Quotations from this source are indicated by *Taschen.*

"The Unseen Vincent van Gogh: His Education in Art," *quiet and intimate* 9a; *always longed for* 11; *all, all, all* 340; *Go to the museum* 12; *Admire* 13; *Try to take* 13; *If you ever decide* 335; *If you hear a voice* 336; *I will take up* 136; *the land of pictures* 133; *the backbone* 224; *while eating* Auden p. 67; *makes my hand* 136; *terribly irritating* 136; *Today I made* 218; *I know* 393; *I...improvise* 221; *brought a new kind* 202; *strong and animated* 276; *are not good* 140; *very accurately* R 5; *working through* 237; *drawings which touch* 218; *It isn't there* 257; *While painting* 225; *hidden harmonies* 226; *It is a fact* 306; *The country* 171; *to progress* 444; *seize the essential* 607; *those details* 299; *Just dash* 378; *It is wrong* Auden p. 257; *You must set* Auden p. 257; *Take care* Auden p. 260; *[n]ot always* 399; *a picture in a lower key* 429; *the rapidity* Auden p. 276; *simply flowers* 459; *What I find* W 1; *If we study* 542; *frank technique* 439; *expressive force* 500; *everyone will think* 507; *a race apart* 136; *steam engine* 535; *hope by some star* 531; *I shall always* 652; *And the moral* 469 & 489.

Girl in White in the Woods: *was definitely* 182; *man added* 138; *scribble* 229. **The Potato Eaters:** *They are as reluctant* 346; *the best* W 1. **Still Life with Five Birds' Nests:** *some people* 425. **Vase with Poppies:** *acquaintances who send* Taschen p. 260. **Self-Portrait with Straw Hat:** *in default* 537; *The question* 442; *sometimes a good* 133. **The Langlois Bridge:** *I am seeing* 469. **Orchard in Blossom:** *Work* 481. **The Sower:** *only after a year* R 2; *and this* R 16; *for the most part* B 7; *torments me* 501. **Portrait of Eugène Boch:** *A face like* 505; *who dreams* 520; *infinity* 520. **The Night Café:** *[n]ight prowlers* 518; *very queer* 521; *To the great joy* 533; *I have tried* 534. **Starry Night over the Rhone:** *It is something* B 3; *a sparkling* 553b. **Vincent's Bedroom in Arles:** *empty bedroom* W 15; *nearly half dead* 553; *It's looking* 542. **Les Alyscamps:** *as fat* 559. **The Red Vineyard:** *I should be* 418. **Memory of the Garden at Etten:** *Let us suppose* W 9; **L'Arlésienne:** *That's what* 525. **Vincent's Chair:** *Van Gogh is* Auden p. 260. **Paul Gauguin's Armchair:** *I feel* Taschen p. 459; *in the absent* 626a. **Still Life: Vase with Fourteen Sunflowers:** *chrome yellows* B 15; *One could have* 514. **La Berceuse:** *absolutely identical* 574; *then the yellow* 592. **Orchards in Blossom:** *a beast* 544a. **Lilacs:** I *have tried* 585. **Irises:** *It is one* T 19. **Starry Night:** *courage* 561. **Enclosed Wheat Field:** *clods of earth* B 10; *green-blue sky* 620. **Two Poplars on a Road:** *Two yellowing poplars* 609. **Pine Trees against a Red Sky:** *tall weather-beaten* W 16; *Toward sunset* 617. **The Garden of Saint-Paul Hospital:** *a canvas* B 21. **Noon: Rest from Work:** *posed* 607. **Cottages and Cypresses:** *He perceived* Taschen p. 618. **Landscape with Couple Walking:** *To do good* B 14 [9]. **Road with Cypress and Star:** *The cypresses* 596; *Landscape with cypresses* 625; *I have still* 643; *sturdy, broad-shouldered* Introduction to Complete Letters p. L; *Vincent soon* Introduction to Complete Letters p. LI. **Undergrowth with Two Figures:** *The undergrowth* 646. **Wheat Fields near Auvers:** *soft green* 646. **Thatched Cottages:** *a lot of* 635; *the fatal conditions* 525; *happy possessors* 489; *from exercising* 605. **Wheat Field with Crows:** *I have painted* 649. *Just as we take the train* 506.